D1558219

INEQUALITY, CLASS, AND ECONOMICS

Inequality, Class, and Economics

Eric Schutz

MONTHLY REVIEW PRESS
New York

Copyright © 2022 by Eric Schutz
All Rights Reserved

Library of Congress Cataloging-in-Publication Data
available from the publisher.

ISBN 978-1-58367-941-8 paper
ISBN 978-1-58367-942-5 cloth

Typeset in Minion Pro and Bliss

MONTHLY REVIEW PRESS, NEW YORK
monthlyreview.org

5 4 3 2 1

Contents

This book is dedicated to the truth seekers and bearers.

I wish to thank Michael Yates for both his encouragement
and his critical eye in this project.

I am especially grateful to my wife Cat who supported
my work in more ways than can be counted.

1. The Crisis Underlying All Other Crises

The public conversation on economic inequality these days is seldom far from earshot, but it has not long been so. When my first work on the subject was published twenty years ago, the reality of increasing inequality was widely doubted. Even those who admitted it questioned its significance. But while rising economic inequality is now a universally acknowledged fact, its import is still widely denied. Conservatives continue to argue that inequality is a wholly necessary fact of life, the most strident of them proclaiming that in our economy, the rich should be allowed as much wealth as they wish, regardless of the rest of us. More thoughtful skeptics argue that inequality, even as great and apparently uncontrollable as ours is these days, should not be an issue as long as poverty is being addressed. But inequality, certainly the kind we are now experiencing after decades of increasingly accelerating income and wealth disparities, does matter greatly in itself. And poverty, which is closely intertwined and is still not being adequately addressed, of course matters as well. Public conversation on economic inequality is not in the least unwarranted: economic inequality is perhaps the most critical social issue of our time.

The public conversation on the issue often reflects an increasing unease and a sense of impending crisis. True, there are other more threatening issues in the background. All of humankind is facing a crisis of its very survival in the developing biophysical catastrophe of human-induced global climate change and planetary ecological breakdown. Yet the seemingly irreversible trend of rising inequality in capitalist economies worldwide may be the most significant barrier to progress on those momentous concerns.

What are the roots of rising inequality? How can we reverse it, given that it seems to portend, amid humanity's greatest crisis ever, a social life perhaps darker than in the darkest ages of feudalism?

Foreboding glimpses of that all too possible future are becoming increasingly frequent. New corporate giants, run by international oligarchs of unimaginable wealth, vie with each other for planetary dominance. They seek markets powered by an affluent consumer class with goods and services produced increasingly by armies of robots and low-wage labor in race-to-the-bottom impoverished-labor nations. Corruption, public and private, has become so blatant in the United States, reaching the highest offices in the land, unchecked by any branch of government that is not itself also corrupted. Meanwhile, greater and more frequent ecological crises caused by extreme weather or human cupidity or stupidity now occur. They elicit only failed responses from official institutional responders, devastating entire regions and populations. Alongside an obvious rise in public anger and frustration, a kind of plague of anomie and distraction had already risen well before the COVID-19 pandemic spread across the globe. Drug use and other social pathologies had arisen as well, perhaps as a kind of soma by those experiencing the economic insecurities of the middle class, as they manifest also the helplessness, frustration, fear, and despair of those less fortunate. The economic inequality we are experiencing today constitutes an increasing paralysis of the life of a once vibrant society—and at a time when we are most in need of vigorous responses to the global environmental situation in which we find ourselves.

In the media in the last few years, wealth and income inequality have become a seething political issue. The campaign rhetoric of Barack Obama, the Occupy Wall Street movement, the passage of the Affordable Care Act, and the nearly successful campaign of Bernie Sanders for the Democratic Party presidential nomination brought the issue something like the widespread attention it deserves. Indeed, the political campaigns of Hillary Clinton and then soon-to-be President Trump both responded by somewhat coopting the issue themselves..

International affairs brought the matter even more closely to Americans' attention. Uprisings in the Middle East and Europe were explicitly aimed at rising economic disparities. The Catholic Church appointed a new pope, Francis, whose pronouncements and actions often focused on economic injustice. The pope even published an encyclical that succinctly articulated the issue.[1] The British newspaper, the *Guardian,* has a permanent section on inequality. Perhaps most surprising of all, the American economics profession actually took up the subject of inequality, after decades of studied avoidance. They did so partly in response to the French economist Thomas Piketty's fine work *Capital in the Twenty-First Century.*[2] That book is now widely used in American economics classes. It is an important, albeit controversial, source of insights on the connections between capitalism and economic inequality. Most recently, the United Nations published the work of a special team investigating poverty in the United States. The U.S. government, under Donald Trump, responded by dropping out of the UN's Human Rights Council.

The topic of inequality fairly seethed beneath the simmering political conflict of Trump's one term, and the dominance of the retrogressive forces brought to worldwide expression during that time. The issue seems so far beyond the capabilities (and probably the interests) of the establishment that the opposition to his re-election nearly collapsed over the question of appropriate policies for dealing with it. Yet economic inequality is indeed getting so bad, especially in the United States, and so steadily and unremittingly, that it has been difficult for even mainstream media to avoid. We are in the midst of a pandemic that not only has stifled the world economy but also has provided rich grounds for an uninvited and unexpected political participation by millions of ordinary people. The Black Lives Matter movement reminded the world of the ongoing issue of racial oppression and economic inequality as issues of equal import in the United States.

The economic expansion just prior to the pandemic seemed to justify optimism about inequality. But Covid-19 showed just how little grounds there were for optimism. The pandemic demonstrated how poorly prepared for such a crisis a society could be that fails to provide universal, high-quality health care to a significant proportion of its population, as the case and death rates in the United States have demonstrated. That the economic downturn following the pandemic was so strong and hit middle- and lower-income people so hard was partly because of the prior lack of consumer demand by those who lost their jobs and had practically no savings from their inadequate incomes. The politics developing in this country for several decades set the groundwork for the government's failure to react appropriately to either the health or the economic crisis. What was needed was massive relief and fiscal and monetary stimulation, state investment and resource management. Such intervention was and continues to be too much for U.S. ruling elites, who greatly benefited during all this. The stock and housing markets soared and the profits of the new tech titans exploded while the rest of the economy floundered. There is now a widespread sense that all of this has signaled the end of the American experiment.

The economic inequalities are astonishing. The net worth of the 650 billionaires now in the United States increased by $1 trillion (from $3 to $4 trillion) during the nine months of the Covid-19 pandemic from March to December 2020.[3] Meanwhile, working-class unemployment kept wages and benefits at rock bottom, imperiling or erasing for a significant number of people their fragile right to quality health care as well, based as it was partly on employment (in states without Medicaid). U. S. poverty rose by the

Figure 1.1: The Wedge: U.S. Labor Productivity versus Labor Compensation since 1950

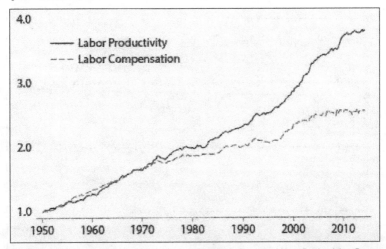

Source: B. Ravikumar and Lin Shao, "Labor Compensation and Labor Productivity: Recent Recoveries and the Long-Term Trend," *Economic Research, Federal Reserve Bank of St. Louis, Economic Synopses*, 2016 No. 16, https://research.stlouisfed.org/publications/economic-synopses/2016/08/12/labor-compensation-and-labor-productivity-recent-recoveries-and-the-long-term-trend/, using BLS Labor Productivity and Costs dataset for the nonfarm business sector.

largest rate in a single year since it began to be tracked sixty years ago, from 9.3 percent in June 2020 to 11.7 percent in November.[4]

The latest leap in inequality caused by the unpredictable vagaries of the pandemic greatly aggravated a trend that had been worsening ever since the 1970s, as illustrated in the well-known wedge diagram (Figure 1.1). At roughly that point in history, the growth in U.S. labor compensation (wages plus benefits) per hour worked began to lag relative to labor productivity or output per hour worked. The remainder from output sales after paying for labor is capital compensation, that is, profit, rent, interest, and managerial bonuses, etc. And from the mid-1970s on, capital compensation grew at a greater rate than labor compensation. As capital's share in total income began to outpace labor's share, the relative stability that had held in the distribution of income in the United States since the Second World War began to erode.

Figure 1.2: Real Income of the Bottom 50 Percent in the U.S. Income Distribution

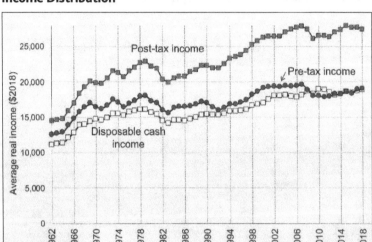

Pre-tax income is before deducting taxes or adding government transfers (sums up to national income). Post-tax income is after deducting taxes and adding all cash and in-kind transfers (including collective public expenditures such as Medicaid and Medicare, minus government deficits). Disposable cash income is pre-tax income minus taxes plus cash transfers only. Source: Thomas Piketty, Emmanuel Saez, and Gabriel Zucman, "Distributional National Accounts: Methods and Estimates for the United States," *Quarterly Journal of Economics* 133, no. 1 (2018): 553–609.

Figure 1.3. Share of the Top 1 percent and Top 0.5 percent of the U.S. Income Distribution

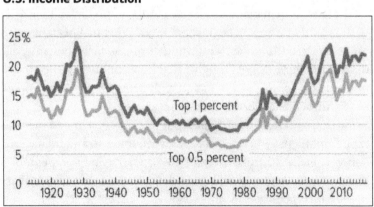

Source: "Income Concentration at the Top Has Risen Sharply Since the 1970's" Center for Budget and Policy Priorities, accessed February 13, 2021, https://www.cbpp.org/income-concentration -at-the-top-has-risen-sharply-since-the-1970s-3.

During most of that time, family and household incomes rose along with continued economic growth, but for the bottom 50 percent of the distribution of income, after-tax disposable income did not rise significantly (see Figure 1.2). Moreover, even for those in higher income brackets whose incomes did rise, much of the rise was due to women increasingly going into paid work. Average employee hourly compensation was not significantly increasing.

Meanwhile, the share in the total income of the top 10 percent, which had been more or less steady since the 1950s, began to rise as the portion consisting of the top 1 percent share took off (see Figure 1.3).

As noted, poverty in the United States increased substantially during the pandemic. There has been about a 20 percent increase in the official poverty rate. The latter rate has remained within a range of a few percentage points on either side of 12–13 percent since 1972. No lasting progress has been made in significantly reducing poverty over the long term since the War on Poverty of the 1960s—at least relative to that of other advanced industrial nations. Further progress any time soon looks doubtful.

Deep or extreme poverty in the United States (measured by, for example, the fraction of the population in households with incomes less than half the poverty line) had been increasing since 1980 until the height of the recovery from the Great Recession and the advent of the pandemic.[5] As of this writing, more than a half-million people are known to be homeless in the United States. Many are living along main streets in urban tent cities, much to the consternation of more fortunate city dwellers.[6] Deep poverty also is extensive in rural areas. There much of it is more or less hidden and probably not counted. Even suburbia is experiencing rising poverty, generally because of job scarcity, stagnant wages, and rising urban and suburban housing costs.

Some perspective on poverty in what has been the most affluent nation in history is provided by considering the aggregate poverty gap. With the rise of deep poverty, the aggregate poverty gap— the aggregate for all families of the shortfall between their actual money income and the poverty line income for their family size—has risen from about $70 or $75 billion before the Great Recession, where it had held roughly steady for decades, to $171 billion in 2016. Think of the aggregate poverty gap as the amount that could be given to the U.S. poverty population annually to lift all officially poor people in the United States out of poverty. For perspective, the U.S. Department of Defense budget (in 2016) was $600 billion. The total net worth of the *Forbes 400* that year was about $2.4 trillion. That wealth, with a return of 7 percent (modest by standards of the wealthy), would annually yield enough income to cover most of the aggregate poverty gap.

The aggregate poverty gap used to be officially published back in a more congenial and not too distant era of post–Second World War U.S. history. The point of such a calculation here is to exercise the imagination. For example, extrapolating and without even bothering with more detailed calculations, a small tax of, say, 1 percent placed on all significant wealth, such as some countries do now have, could perhaps be enough to greatly relieve if not eliminate U.S. poverty by whatever means one might prefer, be it public jobs, in-kind transfers, or simple handouts.

Speaking of wealth, inequality in the distribution of wealth has always been even more striking than income inequality. It has advanced along with the latter, most recently at increasing rates. The concentration of wealth among the top individuals and families in the United States has today reached truly oligarchic levels. The *Forbes 400*, of course, represents most famously the tip-top of the American wealth pyramid. In 1982, the least wealthy person on that list had a net worth of $210 million (in 2019 dollars), and the average person on the list had about $600 million. But in 2019, one needed *ten times* as much ($2.1 billion) to enter the club, and the average wealth of its membership was $7.4 billion.

Figure 1.4 shows what has become almost a commonplace among those who have paid attention to inequality and the twentieth-century history of U.S. wealth concentration.[7] Note that the share of the top 0.1 percent is equal to that of the bottom 90

Figure 1.4: Shares of the total wealth of the top 10 percent and the top 0.1 percent of wealth holders in the United States

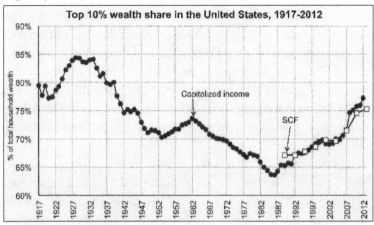

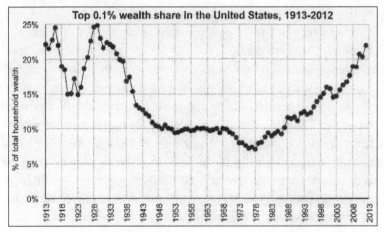

Source: Emmanuel Saez and Gabriel Zucman, "The Rise of Income and Wealth Inequality in America: Evidence from Distributional Macroeconomic Accounts," NBER *Working Paper Series*, Working Paper 27922, October 2020, https://eml.berkeley.edu/~saez/SaezZucman2020JEP(NBER).pdf.

percent. The numbers in Figure 1.4 are current only as of 2012–2013. Today, things are even worse: the share of total net worth owned by the top 10 percent is most recently estimated at 84 percent, a dramatic increase.

After all this absconding with the country's wealth by those at the top, wealth ownership at the bottom of the distribution is minimal and precarious. A broadly representative 2017 survey of 8,000 households found that 69 percent had less than $5,000 in savings, and 57 percent had less than $1,000.[8] As of 2019, the poorest 25 percent of families (by net worth) had a median net worth of about $300.[9] Given the stinginess of relief payments during the Trump presidency during a major pandemic and economic depression, the situation among the worst-off is insecure to say the least, even as many of them do the most important work of this or any other time.

It is sometimes argued that great and increasing economic disparities such as are now commonplace in the United States need not necessarily be of much concern in an economically mobile society like ours. The sting of inequality is supposedly lessened by the possibility of "moving up the ladder." Yet mobility is merely another part of the myth of American classlessness. Other nations show significantly greater mobility up the income ladder, both between generations and within one generation, than the United States. Figure 1.5 depicts the so-called "Great Gatsby" curve showing intergenerational mobility versus inequality for various countries.[10] Statistical studies today indicate that the ease of movement from one income level to another in the United States has actually declined greatly since the Second World War.[11] Not only is the length of the ladder increasing as the degree of wealth and income inequality rises; it is also getting harder to climb the ladder as upward mobility is decreasing.

BUT HAS IT NOT ALWAYS BEEN SO?

Inequality such as seen in the United States today is not all that unusual historically. Greater inequality than ours today has come and gone in societies many times, including in our own past, and for reasons well appreciated.[12] From that lofty perspective, what is happening today is just more of the same old same old, with human civilization merely returning to what would seem its

Figure 1.5. The "Great Gatsby" Curve: Comparative Mobility & Inequality—United States and Other Countries

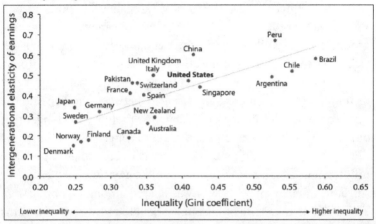

The Gini Coefficient measures income inequality. The intergenerational elasticity of earnings measures economic *immobility*. Source: Adapted from Miles Corak, "How to Slide Down the Gatsby Curve: Inequality, Life Chances, and Public Policy in the United States," December 5, 2012, https://milescorak.com/2012/01/12/here-is-the-source-for-the-great-gatsby-curve-in-the-alan-krueger-speech-at-the-center-for-american-progress/.

primary business: class hierarchy that is structured more or less rigidly for the glory of privileged elites.

Yet to have any success in dealing with the situation today, we must understand the roots of economic inequality in the capitalist system that has dominated human life worldwide in modern times. Considering broadly the thrust toward inequality that seems to have been present throughout the human experience, capitalism does not appear to constitute a significant departure from the story of class societies throughout history. But in its critical details and in its most recent incarnations, it represents a significant departure from that experience. Those differences must be comprehended if there is to be any hope of rising above our sordid past. Is capitalism actually conducive to a socially egalitarian life, as its mythology proclaims? Does it at least tend to mitigate the more stratifying tendencies that may seem to be built into the human species? Or, does it embody forces that tend to move those societies that embrace it toward even greater economic inequality regardless of their propensities otherwise?

In the United States, the relatively egalitarian post–Second World War period up to the late 1970s was one in which all income groups' living standards rose about equally. The rich did not get richer relative to the poor and the rest did not get poorer. Today that seems to have been an exception to the normal drift of our history. As the now increasing disparity between the rich and the rest progresses, it is difficult to sustain the pretense any longer that ours is a classless society. But in that more congenial time, not only did most of the world's advanced market economies experience uninterrupted high rates of growth unlike anything seen before or since, in each country, growth was shared among its population. The social democracies of Europe worked to redistribute the gains from growth away from those who would normally have monopolized them and down to the middle- and lower-income classes. In the United States, all income classes participated roughly equally in the unprecedented material bounty. This was a consequence partly of extensions of the Social Security system, of the War on Poverty and the efforts to lessen racial disparities in the 1960s, of a historically exceptional balance in American labor-management relations, and of strong economic growth itself, which helped to keep unemployment low.

Looking at the steady growth of those times, many believed capitalist economic policymaking had finally matured into a mere management science. It appeared that economics had become, as J. M. Keynes had hoped, a kind of "humble and competent" trade peopled by trusted social engineers. Considering the even distribution of the gains from growth to all groups across the income-class spectrum, many mainstream economists believed that the distribution of income in modern market economies was fixed by the market system and essentially unchangeable. Since all boats were being lifted on the rising tide, mainstream economists found little of interest in the subject of income and wealth distribution. Few seemed to care much about why some boats were so enormous while most were pretty small, why some others were barely large enough to hold their passengers, and why some others failed even to float despite the apparently benign flow of things.

Some serious thinking about the matter among mainstream American economists might have been helpful then.[13] Certainly, the gross wealth and income disparities we have today are no small matter. Yet the disparities that prevailed in the relatively egalitarian post–Second World War period of American history were themselves not at all insignificant—the rich were very rich, the poor were very poor. By the end of that period in the 1970s, the United States still had troubling economic disparities of race and sex. Its poverty level remained twice that of its competitors in Western Europe. Various measures of overall inequality in that period, even if considered moderate by today's standards, were nonetheless quite staggering.

For example, here in paraphrase is how Dutch economist Jan Pen described the situation in late 1960s America in his famous parade metaphor:[14] Imagine in those times a street parade going by as one stands on the curb. The parade will last one hour. The heights of the people marching in the parade are proportionate with their incomes, and paraders march in increasing order of their height, that is, their incomes. Suppose a six-foot-tall marcher represents the mean income level. At the ten-minute mark, marchers are still not up to the spectator's knees in height; at the thirty-minute mark, halfway through the parade, the paraders are still not yet five feet tall. The six-foot-tall parader of average height does not even pass until around forty-five minutes into the parade. (The mean income is considerably more than the median, represented by the midpoint of the parade, with half lower and half higher, since the mean is raised above the median by the very high incomes of the super-rich.) As the parade advances further and marchers' heights continue to increase, with six minutes to go, the top decile of income earners begins to march by, twenty-feet-tall and growing with dizzying rapidity from one to the next into the hundreds of feet tall. In the last few seconds, the spectator looking up can see not much further than the paraders' knees. At the end is J. Paul Getty, the Jeff Bezos of his time. As he strolls past, thousands of feet tall, spectators looking upward to get a glimpse of him can barely see beyond the soles of his shoes.

That was around 1970, during the most egalitarian period in modern United States history. Today, Pen's parade would be something else again—the height of the tallest individual passing at the end of the parade in these times would boggle even the most agile mind. In 2017, CEO Hock E. Tan of Broadcom made $103 million in income.[15] In a Pen's parade today, he would stand almost four miles tall, his knees barely visible at all, his face well past visibility. However, he would be dwarfed by any of the five United States hedge-fund managers of that year who made more than a *billion dollars* each in income, the leader among them James Simon, grossing $1.8 billion,[16] who would stand sixty-six-miles tall!

Although that is beyond outlandish, upon reflection, the extent of inequality in the modern market economy, even in what were once considered normal times, was astonishing enough. Think of J. Paul Getty: even in those relatively egalitarian times, inequality in this economy was extreme. The increasing inequality of our own time is certainly a call to action, as an army of analysts and commentators has emphasized and as this book also attests. But the inequality in our economy at any time in our history should never have been a matter for complacency.

Although it is not completely clear, the trend of rising economic inequality appears to have begun because of the same developments that led to the end of that happy era of strong economic growth after the Second World War. As the global economy gradually came into its own after the war, globalization in today's form began around that time. The competition among advanced national economies grew keener. The postwar Bretton Woods international finance system began to collapse under the gradually developing stresses of export and import competition. In combination with the consequent stagflation, these trends led to stresses also on the postwar labor-capital accord that had arisen in that period.

A kind of multinational, corporate-oriented free-market reaction had begun to develop in public governance and private business policy as an incipient response to the welfare state that had also arisen. That reaction was greatly strengthened and emboldened by the government's apparent inability to deal with the changing economy in the customary business-friendly manner.

The press of globalization on the economic condition of labor continues worldwide, of course, with plant closings, import competition, and outsourcing of production at all stages toward race-to-the-bottom low-wage countries. That, and the growth of neoliberal laissez-faire governance and the corresponding reactionary business attitude, were the historically proximate, or at least the most obvious, causes of the rise in the degree of inequality in the distribution of income and wealth in the United States today. But three additional, later developments dramatically compounded these powerful forces.

First, there was the continued progression of the technological developments that had undergirded capitalist globalization in communication and transportation, culminating most recently in the latest phase of the digital revolution in production, robotics. As the latter came on, it created for the first time unambiguously unmitigated unemployment, with all its attendant downward pressures on wages and salaries, especially those of lower-income people. Second, there was the collapse of the Soviet Union beginning in 1990. That nemesis of everything American had served as an unacknowledged check on the excesses of the post–Second World War rise of the corporate capitalist world order. Its collapse began the final unleashing of neoliberal laissez-faire both internationally and at home. The third development was the Great Recession of 2008 and its aftermath, which highlighted the enormous shortcomings of corporate laissez-faire for all to see. It also solidified many of the financial privileges garnered in public and business sector policy by those most benefiting from the previous decades of increasing disparity.

The upshot is a "One Percent" that today has been nearly

usurped by the "0.1 percent" (as in Figures 1.3 and 1.4), and what appears to be a powerful corollary movement seeking entrenchment as a kleptocratic oligarchy in government. At the same time, indicative of life on the other end of the distribution, a homelessness crisis and housing pressures even for the middle classes are now approaching a critical stage and in the context of the historical stagnation of wages threatening a long-term rise in poverty. Such heightening tensions and the rigidifications inherent in these kinds of disparities devastate the capacity for governance and the ability to respond to the increasingly pressing events of the global environmental crisis. As will be argued in this book, they indeed portend the end of the American version of democracy.

CLASS AND POWER

Until very recently, virtually no mainstream American commentators looked very closely at the real heart of inequality, the problem of class. By "class" we mean a division of society into strata defined not merely by wealth or income, but by positions of power or relative powerlessness for those occupying them. This is an aspect of inequality so widely neglected in the United States as to have been virtually taboo. Even recently, class has been mostly discussed as a phenomenon not of power, but merely of the privilege or status that comes with wealth and income in a capitalist society. Thus, an extensive *New York Times* online special series in 2005 on inequality and class mentioned neither the word nor the concept of power in the sense of individuals decisively influencing other people.[17] It portrayed the American class system as one of conspicuous privilege and status for the affluent and relative degrees of pain and anonymity for the rest. That is obviously an important enough aspect of the subject and certainly deserves elaboration. Still, neither the role of power in structuring and maintaining the classes described by the *Times*, nor the power structures and processes constituted by those class inequalities, were discussed.

Today, however, little more than a decade later, populist

uprisings both abroad and at home have given clear witness to a widespread consciousness of the power structures of class. That awareness has not entirely failed to percolate into media and political commentary. In the United States, from the Occupy Wall Street movement, the Bernie Sanders presidential campaign, and the ostensible new progressivism of part of the Democratic Party, to the Tea Party and later the Trump movements on the right, class as a *system of social influence and rule* has at least begun to move into public discussion.

Class in this sense is not a particularly pleasant subject for public discussion. The proscriptions against serious comment about it are strong, and jobs and livelihoods depend on knowing how to skirt matters that would displease direct superiors and others with power. This book maintains, however, the increasingly widespread view that the problem of rising economic inequality is not one of economics, nor of demographics or other social developments, but of class as a system of social influence and rule, and that the problem cannot be effectively dealt with except by acknowledging and dealing with that reality.

Yet, in common parlance, the association between economic inequality and class is usually reduced to a simple equivalence between class and the income differentials so graphically illustrated in Pen's parade. That is, mere monetary differentials are simply what one means by "class." Precisely how much of an income or wealth difference between people would constitute a difference of class is hard to define. Presumably, small quantitative differences, such as those usually found among people living in the same or similar neighborhoods, do not really count as class differences. But, of course, sizable income or wealth differences do indicate qualitative differences in physical and emotional comfort and in people's social presence, and these do matter greatly.

In 2019, the median household income in the United States was close to $70,000 a year. A four-person family living together on half that amount experiences a level of deprivation a little above what the federal government classifies as "poverty," given that the official threshold for such a family is a little more than $26,000. The official poverty threshold real income level, initially set in 1960, is based on a minimally adequate household food budget. That threshold is not conceived as an income on which a household could healthfully sustain itself for any significant length of time. Poverty is seen as a life situation, the stresses and hardships of which are quite serious.[18] It definitely puts one in a different class from households with a median-level income or more.

Some commentators like to argue that poverty in the United States is nothing like that found in the Global South. There, literally hundreds of millions of people make their living by begging on the street or scrounging from landfills or trying to farm on nonarable land. Yet even official government estimates are that a half-million people were homeless on any given day in 2016–17 in the United States, arguably the most affluent nation in human history at a relatively propitious point in its current affairs. Probably about two million people were homeless at some point during that year.[19] Most poor people in the United States do not live in homeless shelters, camps, or on the street. Yet most do consistently experience food insecurity, that is, insufficient food to provide a healthy life for all household members.[20] No wonder the life expectancy and infant mortality statistics, along with various measures of illness, indicate a population experiencing far more than its share of health difficulties.

On the other hand, a household living on twice the median income level, say, $130,000, has a degree of comfort and security that makes its members mostly immune to all of that. Decent health care is merely one of several factors allowing relatively affluent upper middle-class people longer and healthier lives than middle-class or lower-class people who cannot afford it. Comfortable and congenial homes; quality food; reliable transportation, including that required for vacation travel; varied and plentiful leisure, entertainment, and recreation opportunities—these are some of the things such an income can secure that provide for not only a long but also a full life. In the United States today, most people living in households with an income of $130,000 a year would refer to themselves as simply middle-class, even though that income level puts them well into the top 25 percent of households.

And naturally, those living in the higher reaches of the wealth and income scale, approaching and entering the 1 percent and higher, can take advantage of the very best of everything that is available. Toward the top of the scale, people may shop across the globe as they move multiple times a year between homes in different countries. Many can even avoid the hardships of shopping itself, with cooks, housekeepers, drivers, personal planners, attendants, lawyers, and consultants of all sorts taking care of it all for them. They can move in and out of the public view at will; they can endlessly fascinate the world if they choose. They are certainly of another class entirely.

These differences in quality of life associated with major wealth and income disparities represent enormous and profound differences in people's life prospects and abilities to fulfill their potentials and aspirations. They are dramatic enough differences to merit a strong designation such as the term "class." With economic inequality rising, with both the "length of the ladder" increasing and mobility up and down the ladder decreasing, the consequence is a steepening and hardening of what might rightly be called class boundaries, a class rigidification of great concern.

Yet this simple equating of class either with economic inequality in the merely quantitative sense or with qualitative differentials of material comfort, prestige, and status is nonetheless greatly misleading. As profoundly as these kinds of disparities among people matter, they do not get at the essence of what class means. Class is really about *power*, and the most critical connections between class and economic inequality have to do with that.

Like class, power is fraught with multiple meanings. Sometimes, it designates merely the capacity to act, to do things, to get things accomplished. In market societies, people's powers so defined are more or less equivalent to their purchasing powers. In such societies doing things usually requires buying things. Hence unequal powers mirror existing quantitative disparities of wealth and income. Such a definition has the effect of reducing class to simple quantitative purchasing power or by mere income or wealth.

However, the most critical usage of the term "power" in social contexts refers to an individual's ability to influence other individuals: to cause them to behave or to think differently from how they would otherwise. Power in that more discomforting sense is not strictly determined by an individual's wealth and income. A wealthy person may be unable to put their wealth to effective use in influencing others in certain ways, whereas a poor person may have significant social influence. Yet power as influence is definitely very strongly correlated with income and wealth. The latter enables individuals to have at their command goods or the services of others that may allow them to take actions that affect those who, lacking income and wealth, will likely not be able to reciprocate.

Power as influence is, of course, widely acknowledged in politics and business. There are frequent references to the movers and shakers involved in public issues or the wheelers and dealers effecting significant business changes or transactions. In both cases, the powerful are often recognized as not necessarily the same as those in official authority positions. The relationship between influence and wealth is generally well-appreciated. Political and business officials are often seen to be routinely overruled by sometimes less conspicuous but usually monetarily better-endowed individuals acting behind the scenes.

Yet in mainstream public discussion of economic inequality, power as influence is itself all too often understated or downplayed. The precise form of influence exerted by powerful individuals on particular events is too often left undisclosed. The influential are often only vaguely so and precisely why they are to be noted or respected may be unclear. Even when influence is noted as a function of wealth and income, the influence of the rich often is regarded as a harmless and only occasional attribute of riches. It may be worthy of note, respect, and admiration but is generally benign. It is not a consistent function of wealth, but only coincidentally associated with some notable wealthy individuals.

However, there is far more to the influence of the wealthy than is usually recognized in public discussion. That influence is true power, and while definitely worthy of note and respect, it should not be assumed to be generally benign. The influence associated with wealth is *power over people*, or again, social influence and rule. The even stronger term "domination" is often appropriate. It is not merely an occasional attribute of wealth, with some wealthy people having it while others do not. If you have considerable wealth, then you very likely have power. If you lack wealth, then you are more or less consistently subject to the power of others.

To reiterate: given that influence is strongly correlated with wealth, the social classes indeed may be more or less accurately delineated by people's wealth or income or their lack. But what defines class is its constitution of and by power, social influence, or rule. Classes are a form of social grouping that determines and is determined by people's power over other people.

Class as power in this fullest sense of the term is rarely mentioned or even alluded to in mainstream public affairs discourse. In the social sciences, at least those other than economics, it is a commonplace element in theory and analysis, empirical work and description. Power, interpersonal and social, comprises a major portion of the concerns of sociology, anthropology, political science, history, psychology, and philosophy. And class, as a particular arrangement of power, is seen as a critical aspect of most analyses of large social bodies in all of these fields. Nor do these other social sciences limit their use of the concepts of class and power to consideration of past societies. Discussions of current affairs equally incorporate these concepts as useful for comprehending present-day social reality.

In public affairs conversations outside of academia, however, it sometimes seems as if today's market capitalist society had somehow escaped the historical lineage of human societies constituted by class as a power arrangement. The idea that modern society has escaped its past in this way is understandable. Ruling elites have always most valued and advanced those ideas that shed the least light on the reality of their positions. The mythology of the modern capitalist market society is at least as effective at this obfuscation as any other in history. Moreover, the dynamism and turbulence characteristic of the capitalist system, having brought what amounts to a perennial revolution to human life, tends to distract from further inquiry with a continual succession of diversions, trends, and its own problems.

But the inattention to class and power in mainstream public conversation today also is aided and abetted by the studied avoidance of those subjects in one particular field of inquiry in which they would be expected to be of special interest: economics. The field of economics is turned to for insights on how things really work in capitalist market society perhaps more than any other social science. Unfortunately, it is also especially ideologically sensitive (see the Appendix to Chapter 2). The broad mainstream of economic thought has confined itself thoroughly and exactingly to whatever in social life may be abstracted and disjoined from considerations of power and class, and has thus significantly contributed to making those subjects taboo in public discussion.

ECONOMICS AND ALL OF THIS

Mainstream economists would probably not even become interested in the distribution of income and wealth were it not for the increasingly evident and worrying trend of rising economic inequality in the decades near the turn of the twenty-first century.[21] Now the distribution of income and wealth is a respected research agenda in mainstream economics, but little more than a decade ago it was of practically zero interest. Consequently, mainstream economists are poorly prepared to provide the analyses that will be needed to address the trend of rising inequality. Indeed, they are actually to blame for much of the misleading and obfuscating public discussion about the subject. They have been part of the problem. Yet the problem can be approached through analysis based in mainstream economic theory merely by employing concepts long and assiduously neglected by mainstream economists—class as power and social influence.

Looking squarely and objectively at the phenomenon of economic inequality, how could class and power not be suspected as significant causal factors or at least critical aspects of the subject? Presumably, whatever other import they may have, significant and enduring social power relationships would imply redistributions of economic benefit to those in power positions at the expense of those subject to their power. Avoiding such glaringly obvious suspicions requires some considerable effort. The field of economics not only has engaged in such effort, it has also been an important contributor to the greater social effort of avoidance.

Neoclassical economics, the core and foundational body of thought of mainstream economics today, bears much blame. In itself, neoclassical economic theory does not preclude analyses based on power.[22] But as it is routinely applied in the ideologically sensitive field of economics, neoclassical theory significantly discourages inquiry into power relationships, even in the face of such clearly suspicious connections as those among class, power, and economic inequality.

This is partly because neoclassical theory is based on a model of individual choice. If groups or aggregates of individuals are the objects of theorizing, as in all social sciences, then, in the neoclassical approach, behavior at the group or aggregate level must be directly derived from the behaviors of the individuals involved, with the latter assumed to be rational decision-makers. This methodology, when taken as if it were the only valid approach to social theorizing, as neoclassicism does—as if other more social or structural approaches were irrelevant to economic inquiry— unfortunately inclines many followers of economics toward a pure choice model of inequality. Those whose thinking about inequality is influenced by neoclassical economics tend to see individuals' economic fates as almost entirely determined by their personal choices. Thus, no individual's economic fate can be significantly affected by other people's choices. The distribution of income and wealth in a society is seen as no more than a simple aggregation of the individual choices made by its people.

This way of thinking has had a regrettably significant influence on public discourse. It is, however, a naive theory at best, for the pure choice model essentially precludes any discussion of the greatly varying opportunities available to people in different circumstances, especially any consideration of how opportunities are generated or where they come from. In reality, people's choices are always choices among available alternatives, and these significantly differ among groups and individuals. Disparate alternatives and the divergent opportunities they constitute are importantly shaped, often deliberately, by other people's decisions and actions, both in the present and in the near and distant past. The pure choice model precludes examining any role that power relationships, social influence, and social structures formed by past relationships of power and social influence—such as class structures—may play in shaping people's economic fates. Class, rule, social influence, domination; such realities simply are not part of the pure choice model of economic behavior.

Moreover, the pure choice model, naive and indeed absurd as it is, might have ended up with little credibility but for the particular approach taken in the neoclassical theory of markets. Nearly all students of economics are virtually smothered in this theory, as undergraduates at least, and as graduate students even more thoroughly if they proceed that far. The theory is based on a kind of benchmark concept of an economic system of well-functioning markets. According to the theory, people engage in exchanges that are entirely mutually voluntary. There are no "distortions" like monopoly or market dominance, imperfect or asymmetric information, or complications like transactions costs or externalities that might cause imbalances in people's bargaining positions. Given mutually voluntary choices and no market distortions, there are, in principle, as it is argued vociferously and logically, no occasions for power to be exerted by any individuals upon any others. The theoretical upshot is a hypothetical system of total equality of opportunity among people in pursuing their desired economic roles or occupations. Moreover, whatever income inequalities then might appear would represent nothing more than what people choose for their own economic destinies, having rationally weighed their occupation preferences against their desire for income. Economic inequalities are merely apparent and not real disparities in real economic well-being.

In economics, every application of neoclassical theory begins with this model, and all references to policy are made by comparing actual realities with this hypothetical construction. In as ideologically sensitive a field as economics, where neoclassicism remains the dominant approach, it is thus fairly easy to slide into the supposition that the purely theoretical construction is actually not far from reality, at least most of the time. Given its ideological proclivities, it is no wonder that mainstream economics shies away from questions of economic inequality generally, and especially those directly related to major inequalities of opportunity, like those involving class and power.

Nonetheless, it is both possible and reasonable to begin an analysis of power and class in the economy using neoclassical theory. Power is, among other things, a relationship between individuals. Therefore it may be theorized in the initial stages of inquiry (that is, as an entry point) in terms of the neoclassical individualist approach to understanding social behavior. And although the neoclassical theory of markets may incline economists to err by viewing markets as unambiguously benign, it may instead be used to highlight precisely how markets systematically prejudice or distort people's bargaining positions and thereby lead to immeasurable individual and social damage.

2. Economic Fantasies

In a capitalist market economy, economic inequalities seem to arise as natural market outcomes. It appears that people's income and wealth accumulation are determined in markets, which evaluate their contributions of labor, assets, or other services. But why then are the contributions of some apparently so much greater in market value than those of others? Is it because people choose to contribute differently?

No doubt people make their own choices. Yet that supposition, for all of its important consequence for human life, cannot by itself form the basis of a theory of economic inequality, though many apparently presume it does. For it ignores the obvious reality that we are able to choose only from among whatever alternatives are available to us. The specific opportunities presented to people must matter at least as much as the fact that they choose from among them. Only if the opportunities are invariably the same or equal in the scope they allow for individuals' pursuit of their aspirations can one conclude that individual choice is all that really matters in determining income and wealth disparities. Therefore, a theory of inequality that says as much must begin with a credible account of how, contrary to all appearances, the opportunities available to people are indeed equal.

It would seem then that a more credible perspective on inequality would begin by emphasizing the opposite side of the choice-opportunity duality. One observes that the opportunities available to people—for education, work, and wealth accumulation—differ greatly and in clear and systematic ways among different groups. Apparently, a market society cannot provide anything like equal opportunity for economic advancement among its citizens without government taking a major role in "leveling the playing field." Many people, for example, because of class position or race or sex discrimination, simply do not have access to as much quality education as do others. Their job opportunities are accordingly restricted, as is their ability to accumulate wealth. Their limited economic status is mainly the result of their limited opportunities and not mistaken decisions they may have made. Those blessed by good opportunities can make the worst possible choices about their lives and still achieve high economic status, whereas those with poor opportunities generally cannot achieve high status even if their decisions are unfailingly impeccable.

Considering these two different perspectives on inequality, the choice perspective versus the opportunity perspective, economists as a group have far too often and too heartily embraced the former. Yet, economics itself provides a fairly neutral vocabulary on the subject and is also quite useful for addressing it. Indeed, neoclassical economics—the core theoretical body of mainstream economics today—can help provide clarity on some of the most critical aspects of inequality.

In the constrained choice model of individual decision-making used in neoclassical economics, a person's choices are always constrained by whatever limitations pertain. The consumer goods and services among which she may choose, for example, are always constrained by income and the affordability of whatever goods and services are available. Given the prices of all the possible purchases she could make and her spendable income, the consumer decides how much of each good or service to buy based on whatever selection of quantities best satisfies her overall. But even if her income is limited, there presumably still is a whole range of possible "consumption bundles" from which to choose, since she may "trade off" some amount of each item for additional amounts of other items. Thus, in this way the constrained choice framework seems to emphasize the plenitude of available choices. But the constraints on the consumer's ability to get whatever she wants are absolute: more goods and services simply cannot be bought, nor can a greater level of satisfaction or utility be achieved, than are permitted by her total income and the affordability of the available goods.

In the neoclassical view, people are then understood to make decisions similarly about their educations, jobs, and savings, choosing from among whatever possibilities are available to them. As another particularly important example, the costs of the education required for the various occupations, along with one's income and other resources relative to those costs and the various other costs of living, place limits on the education or training one may obtain in pursuit of any particular occupation. And if one is also disadvantaged by class position or race or sex discrimination, one's available choices are more constrained than if one is not.

People can make trade-offs. For example, if a college degree in engineering is required for a particular field, with the right consumption and saving choices there may be ways of obtaining it even for someone who is otherwise disadvantaged. Still, given the differences in the trade-offs available to people in different circumstances, there may be great disparity in the scope allowed for their economic advancement, regardless of their competence in making choices. Only so much personal consumption can be given up to successfully pursue an engineering degree, and all the more so the more constrained are one's available monetary resources.

Thus, the neoclassical constrained choice theory of individual behavior would seem to clarify right from the start which of the two poles of the choice-opportunity duality is more important in determining economic inequality. As economists have focused their attention on markets, their question has been, what role do markets play in providing equal versus unequal opportunities for people making critical life decisions? This question is given even greater weight by economists' hypothetical model of perfectly well-functioning markets. There, as will be seen, a pristine world of perfect equality of opportunity is supposed, a kind of benchmark against which to compare real-world markets and toward which to aim in suggesting improvements in the real-world market system. Unfortunately, economists' attachment to and indeed enchantment with the perfect markets model have led them to be all too sanguine about equality of opportunity.

CHOICE, EQUALITY, AND INEQUALITY

Consider again people making decisions about their occupations. Such decisions can be looked at as if they were investment decisions, specifically, decisions about how much to invest in one's "human capital."[1] People consider the schooling or training required for various occupations, weighing the costs of getting the necessary skills for each kind of job against the income expected from employment in that field. There are the direct monetary costs of the schooling or training required, including those related to whatever funding may be needed (the interest and related charges). There are indirect costs as well in the form of whatever income will be lost while studying and attending classes. On the benefit side are the returns to all this investment in education in the form of the expected increase in their work income over what they might earn without the education or training.

Simplifying things somewhat, the amount of the benefits from the individual's investment in human capital may be thought of as a direct function of how much investment the individual undertakes. The more training or schooling she gets, the more knowledge, technical facility, and skill she gets in specific production activities in her chosen field. She then takes these skills to the job itself, where her "productivity" as an employee is accordingly improved. Thus, the greater her investment in her human capital, the greater is her contribution to production at work. Finally, the more productive people are at work, the more they are paid as employees. Employers are willing and able to pay more for the greater productivity attained from improved skills because their own profit is thereby greater, and because they must compete with other employers for the services of workers.[2]

What might be called the rate of return on the individual's investment in schooling or training in any particular occupation would be found by comparing the income stream from employment in that occupation with the amount of investment in schooling and training necessary to enter the occupation.[3] Suppose that in choosing their occupations, people simply seek the highest rate of return, just as they would among financial investments generally (other things equal). They would then compare rates of return among the various education-cum-occupation choices available and choose the best ones.

Equality and Choice

And here is the rub. In well-functioning markets, as people pursue their chosen occupations in that fashion, market equilibration would tend to bring people into occupations that compensate everyone equally well for their chosen investments in human capital by the incomes they earn. This occurs in the process of equalization of rates of return across occupations. For example, as people are attracted to occupations with higher rates of return, their greater demand for education and training in those fields would raise the costs of attaining schooling in those fields. At the same time their movement into work in those higher-rate occupations would increase labor supply in those fields and lower the going wages or salaries there. As schooling costs thus rise and incomes fall in higher rate-of-return occupations, those rates of return decline.

A similar process occurs in the opposite direction as people leave lower rate-of-return occupations, so higher and lower rates

of return converge as people move across occupations. When
rates are equalized—what neoclassicals call "equilibrium"—no
further incentives exist for individuals to move to other occupations than their chosen ones, for no differentials between rates of
return would exist. Since no incentives exist for people to change
occupations, one can conclude that people would all be equally
well-compensated for their investments in schooling and training.
No one would be getting more and no one less than what exactly
compensates them for what they have chosen to spend on human
capital.

Of course, when applying this logic to reality, one must question
how long such an equilibration process would take to play out.
This is a controversial matter in modern economics. In neoclassical economics, equilibration is usually assumed to take little time.
In fact, the "new classicals" (an arguably now-defunct offshoot
with unfortunately great influence in undergraduate and graduate university economics) even proposed that it would require no
time at all.[4] On the other hand, if a lot of time is required for equilibration, as other economists have argued, then since exogeneous
disequilibrating events are virtually always happening, markets are
unlikely to be anywhere near equilibrium.

And consider what the neoclassical view implies about people's incomes. Again, in equilibrium, the incomes people receive
in their occupations exactly compensate them for their total
expenditures on the educations required by their occupations.[5] If
individuals in some fields, medical doctors, for example, receive
a high income, it is merely compensation for the considerable
education and training necessary in such fields. Only such compensation can induce people to enter those fields. Competition in
the supply and demand for labor, schooling, and training—that
is, the movement of people among the various occupations and
the corrective equilibration processes thus at work in the relevant
markets—assures that doctors' incomes do not more than compensate for that necessary investment in human capital (nor do
they less than compensate them either).

Conversely, other fields, janitorial work, for example, require virtually no training. Hence there is no investment in any human capital that needs to be compensated by the wages paid in such fields to induce people to enter them. Both the doctor and the janitor are fully compensated, no more and no less, for their chosen investments in human capital. Therefore, they cannot be presumed to be anything but equally well off in real terms, regardless of how greatly their monetary incomes may differ.

This idea may easily be broadened to encompass other aspects of occupations besides the costs of human capital investment. Adam Smith first elucidated the idea in his *The Wealth of Nations* (1776) in what came to be called the theory of compensating differentials. According to this theory, occupational pay differentials exist as compensation for all sorts of negative and positive job attributes. Thus, some occupations have particular satisfactions or amenities. Teaching, for example, offers various gratifications. Teachers get to have others intently listen to them, to influence others' thinking, to organize their work time to a significant degree as they wish, and to be relatively free of physically taxing labor. Other occupations have dis-amenities instead. Garbage collection, for example, is certainly foul work, with considerable physical drudgery and even danger to health. Occupations with amenities, being more attractive at any given pay level, would tend to be paid less since, in effect, their amenities would compensate them for their lesser pay. Those with dis-amenities would be paid more to compensate for the burdens of working in such occupations.[6]

A modern extension of this logic, hedonic wage theory, adds the idea that different individuals have different attitudes about the various attributes of occupations. Some people like teaching, others do not; some may even like garbage collecting, while presumably most others do not. Similarly, only certain people are attracted to medical practice, others are not. The upshot is that the actual wages paid in the various occupations would reflect people's willingness to work in each of them. This is roughly understood as determined by the people in the labor force who consider each occupation to have overall amenities versus dis-amenities and the strength of their feelings about those job attributes.[7] As may be intuitive, this does not substantially alter the general conclusion of Smith's compensating differentials theory.

The conclusion of all this cannot be overstated. It says that people receive effectively equal compensation overall for their labor. In slightly more technical terms, it is a situation of substantive compensation equality. Wages or salaries in the various occupations (including other monetary job benefits) exactly compensate (or at least approximately compensate or tend to compensate) for people's chosen investments in human capital and their relative willingness or unwillingness to work in those particular occupations. Although monetary incomes may differ significantly, people actually are more or less equally well-off in terms of the real well-being they derive from their labor, or what is sometimes called the "psychic income" of their work.

Substantive Inequality in the Choice Model

This is a striking idea and quite unrealistic, as will be seen. Yet readers have probably heard it offered in all sincerity as an explanation for this or that group's higher or lower income. It may be its utopian appeal that has so enthralled economists. If improvements could be made in how real-world markets work, bringing them more closely in accord with the model of a well-functioning market system, presumably that would bring real progress in equity.[8] Substantive equality represents both a fair and an egalitarian distribution of labor compensation.

But the model may be less appealing when it is logically extended in some obvious directions. Accept for the moment its most critical assumption—that markets are functioning well. The model does allow one exception to equal overall compensation across occupations, namely, differences among people's aptitudes or intelligence. People who have greater ability than others in an occupation, regardless of whether their ability is innate or otherwise attained, will earn higher monetary incomes than others in that occupation. The market equilibration process will not eliminate such differences. Presumably, such people would either be able to learn the skills required in the occupation more easily, hence would need to invest less in training; or be more productive at work, hence be paid more (since others are not as highly productive, competition would not bring down the pay of the more able); or finally, be able to spend less time at work than others for a given income. In any case, people with such aptitudes or abilities will be better off monetarily than others and also substantively better off. Ordinary market movements will not equilibrate away such differences.[9]

Accounting for aptitude and intelligence differences, this basic pure choice model may be easily incorporated into a larger theory that considers not only labor income but also wealth and property income. Out of a person's total labor-plus-property income, they choose their saving or investment on the one hand, and accordingly their consumption expenditures on the other. Then, given their abilities, the amount of wealth they accumulate is determined by their income and their savings choices in conjunction with the rate of return on financial savings. Of course, individuals begin life with different wealth inheritances from their families. Hence some do indeed "start the race" ahead of others, a reality of profound importance that will be considered later. But in this account, all additional monetary wealth accumulations made during individuals' lives (that is, above and beyond their inheritances) are determined solely by their own individual choices and abilities instead of those of earlier generations in their families.

Note that now ability or aptitude plays its role not only among individuals but also among families. Some families tend to be more apt in specific fields, whether because of genetics or the passing down of family upbringing methods and enculturation over generations. If one's aptitudes are inherited from one's family, then one's total wealth accumulation, that is, one's own savings plus one's family inheritance, would vary significantly according to one's family's abilities. The specific choices of earlier generation

family members and any innate or otherwise derived "family aptitudes" would matter. In this extended version of the pure choice
model, one's monetary wealth, along with the income it generates,
is a function not only of one's own and earlier family members'
savings decisions and one's own choices on labor income but also
of one's own individual and family aptitudes.

This obviously very conservative, indeed reactionary, account
is nonetheless a logically coherent "theory" of the distribution
of income and wealth in capitalist market economies. Of course,
its naiveté about the realities of unequal opportunity and social
power are glaring, but it does acknowledge, perhaps grudgingly,
the critical role of inheritance.[10] Hearing such an account at the
family dinner table, on talk TV or radio, or from a politician (for
example, a U.S. president) or a college professor might be embar-
rassing, to say the least. Yet that theory is all too often expressed
or implicit in conservative and far-right thinking on distributive
issues. Unfortunately, economists steeped in the intellectually fascinating aspects of equilibrium in well-functioning markets, and
perhaps also enamored of the kind of feudal and dynastic picture of human affairs this theory represents, have been far more
inclined than most others to embrace it, and thereby, given their
respected social positions, also to promote it.

OPPORTUNITY MATTERS

There is a world of things wrong with this theory, and it is worth
reviewing the glaring faults that reduce it to mere mythology at
best and ideology at worst. Allow for the moment the economists'
assumption of equilibrium, according to the extended pure choice
theory. If we put aside the issue of inheritance for later consideration, then how well-off individuals are in substantive terms
would depend entirely on whatever ability or intelligence has
been bestowed upon them by their family genetics or upbringing. (Recall that if all were of equal aptitude and intelligence,
they would be substantively equal.) Fortunately, it may still be a

minority of people today who would profess belief in a theory of
economic inequality based solely on genetically endowed intelligence, although it may be a larger minority than one might think.
On the other hand, many people would espouse a theory of
inequality based on differences in family *cultural* background. Of
course, just as is true of people's monetary inheritances and their
family genetics, people do not choose but are given their families' cultural attributes. But while a cultural theory of economic
inequality therefore represents a step in the right direction, toward
acknowledging just how importantly opportunity matters, nonetheless it invites several important errors of omission.

Aptitudes and Attitudes, Culture and Material Life

Noting the distinction between innate and acquired abilities,
another relevant distinction may be made regarding people's preferences, especially those regarding such things as work life versus
leisure and saving versus consumption. Neoclassical economic
theory almost always assumes for analytical convenience that
individuals' tastes and preferences are given and unchanging, an
assumption that makes for a very narrow inquiry. The available
evidence on genetic bases of individual preferences is ambiguous.
If one wishes to move beyond the neoclassical assumption about
preferences, one would allow that instead an individual's preferences are most importantly a product of the culture within which
he or she has developed. That is, such environmental realities as
family socialization during upbringing, neighborhood and local
community social interaction, school life, the media, and so forth.
Indeed, in any theory applicable to the real world, preferences
cannot simply be taken as given, any more than aptitudes can be
taken as simply given by the genes.

Yet in thinking more broadly about both preferences and aptitudes, it is also possible to err in the opposite direction. A cultural
determinist theory would say that it is the subculture of the family,
or community background of the individual, or their racial,

ethnic, or national subculture, that most matters in the formation of these personal attributes. For example, it is often said that Black culture—the habits of thinking gained from interacting socially throughout one's upbringing in the segregated culture of African American communities—inculcates attitudes and aptitudes that tend to incline Black people toward certain choices about occupations, work, saving, and consumption. Similarly, the national cultures of immigrants are said to color their attitudes about work and are the primary determinant of the particular occupations they enter. In both cases, the cultural determinist argues that aspects of these groups' cultures are mainly responsible for failing to achieve any great economic status. That is, their culture is what underlies the great disparities in their economic well-being relative to the so-called mainstream.

The influence of culture on individuals' social and psychological development is undeniable. However, to make of that observation a full-fledged theory of why different groups pursue different occupations and achieve different levels of economic status is undoubtedly a mistake. Culture is merely one environmental influence on people's preferences and aptitudes. An adequate analysis must also include those influences that constitute the individual's material life experience. It must encompass those aspects of the person's life environment related to the family's or community's provisioning of material goods. Whether it is a farming or industrial or commercial economic environment, urban, suburban, or rural, the public and private amenities it provides, and especially the overall level of material affluence or deprivation of the material environment—such things matter greatly.

Assuming that culture does play a critical role in determining individual attributes, the question of what determines the culture of an individual's particular social surrounding must also be answered. For example, what determines the "culture of poverty" that some have said is mainly responsible for the persistence of poverty in the most affluent nation in history? Supposedly a subculture has developed that leads to certain attitudes and behavior that either incline people toward occupations that pay little (because they require little human capital investment) or else incline them toward avoiding work altogether. This is usually attributed to "government handouts" and the "dependency syndrome" that supposedly follows. Yet attributing any such culture to specific government policies should be immediately suspect. Why should not the state of poverty itself be considered the main factor here, with or without government support? Presumably, poverty's material conditions lead to precisely the same behaviors as are often attributed to a particular culture, such as ill-kept neighborhoods, underfunded schools, scarce local jobs and high involuntary unemployment among adults, especially males. Add to such features low tax revenues and thus a lack of public educational, recreational, and cultural amenities in the midst of a conspicuous but unattainable affluence in the larger society. Clearly, people's behaviors may then be seen as effects rather than causes of poverty.[11]

These crucial realities in mind, it is clear that individuals are simply *given* the cultural and material life conditions in which they grow up. To the extent that these conditions affect their aptitudes for various kinds of work and their attitudes and preferences about job occupations, they constitute critical aspects of the "opportunity sets" that determine the choices people can make. Cultural and material life conditions differ significantly among different groups. Thus, the opportunities available to them differ both quantitatively and qualitatively, inclining people toward different kinds of occupations and different investments in human capital. For example, even very bright lower-income children may be discouraged by the material realities of their lives from pursuing professional occupations for which they may actually be very well suited. They may reasonably think that they are "just not that kind of person." More affluent children observe and experience cultural and material environments that may dispose them toward more ambitious pursuits, whether they are particularly well-suited to them or not.

To reiterate, suppose that people are completely equal in their innate aptitudes, even in a hypothetical world of market equilibrium.[12] Then, if people's aptitudes and preferences are influenced by their different material and cultural life conditions, substantive inequalities in their economic well-being must exist. For economists, the critical question should be whether markets in the real world are conducive to substantive equality. One can answer that question by referring to a now widely accepted branch of economic theory that conserves the basic neoclassical viewpoint while strongly amending the choice theory of inequality: the economics of information and transaction costs.

Errors and Information

Intelligence or aptitude may be understood to involve at least partly people's ability to process information and to make the best possible choices on its basis. Even if relevant information were universally available and perfect in quality and quantity—and all people were at least potentially equally knowledgeable—some people still would be able to comprehend and act upon their knowledge more effectively than others. It is at least partly because the perfect markets model assumes perfect and equally available information that economists and others have so often concluded that aptitude differences are the sole cause of substantive inequalities in well-being. In that model, the only differences in the information people can use are in what their own intellects can handle. But in reality, there is no such thing as perfect knowledge and certainty. Major differences do abound in people's accessibility to information and the quality and quantity of the information available to them.

And these realities may totally eclipse whatever differences exist in people's capabilities of processing information. The relatively new field of the economics of information and transaction costs focuses on the various ramifications of imperfect information, that is, information that is difficult to access or totally lacking, or that is not available to all, whether unavoidably or because of the deliberate efforts of some people to mislead others.

In a world in which people cannot be perfectly knowledgeable, where uncertainty is the universal rule, people rationally decide how much information to bother acquiring. They do not attempt to gain perfect, complete information since that is impossible. Given the probability of making mistaken decisions based on inadequate information, one may decide, for example, to enter an occupation thinking that it requires less education than it does in fact, or that it has favorable amenities when in reality it is not at all suitable to one's predisposition.

In principle, if aptitude or intelligence consists at least partly of a capacity to adequately process information, then greater intelligence would lead to fewer such mistakes and to correcting whatever mistakes are made. The intelligent would better and more quickly succeed in finding and pursuing occupations appropriate to their own preferences regarding amenities and dis-amenities and their own aptitudes. They would also be better at economizing on investments in human capital and at entering higher-paying occupations. The general prevalence of "imperfect information" thus implies a greater disparity of labor incomes arising from differences in aptitude than would otherwise pertain. Therefore, it reinforces the theory of the role of aptitude in substantive economic inequality.

But on the other hand, imperfect information confounds the market equilibration process by which people's overall or "psychic" labor incomes are, in the choice model, brought into substantive equality. When all information is imperfect, attaining sufficient relevant information about the work, pay, and education and training for occupations requires time. It then takes time for the market equilibration process to remove differentials in overall labor compensation (beyond those due to differences in aptitude), as people expend resources upon accessing information and gradually correcting their various mistaken occupational choices. How much time is required depends on how difficult it is to access the information and correct mistakes. In principle, enough time may be involved that considerable differences in labor incomes may arise and endure. That is, significant substantive inequalities may persist even if there were no differences among aptitudes for processing information.

This is especially so because, most importantly, the process of human capital investment itself is one of accessing information. In education and training, people are engaged in obtaining information about the work involved in their own and related occupations. Clearly, much of the human capital investment process is time-consuming, and time is, of course, a fundamental part of the equilibration of labor markets. If market equilibration involves people in lengthy retraining, then following some exogeneous change, for example, in growth across industrial sectors, those in declining industries or regions are certainly going to suffer substantial and more or less lasting declines in their overall labor compensation. Therefore, in a dynamic economy, in which labor market equilibria are continually moving as industries and regions rise and fall, disequilibria in labor incomes may sustain indefinitely. Some people will have substantive "surpluses" of labor income while others suffer lasting losses.[13]

This is an old and controversial question in economics: how long does equilibration take, or how long is the "long run"? Is it fairly short, so that equilibrium, while perhaps elusive, is never really far off, and for all practical purposes, is "close enough"? Or is equilibrium so distant that, to paraphrase J. M. Keynes, we will all be dead before we are anywhere near it? In the latter case, major differences in real overall or psychic labor incomes—major substantive inequalities—may exist that are not at all due to aptitude or intelligence or culture. These inequalities may endure beyond the ability of those involved to make suitable corrections in their occupational choices during their lifetimes. Thus, market equilibrium itself is called into question as a useful theoretical concept.

Moreover, the information problem encompasses more than mere general imperfections. There are also significant systematic differences in the quantity, quality, and accessibility of information. And since having or lacking information confers advantages or disadvantages, regardless of differences in ability, significant and lasting substantive economic disparities may arise depending on the available information. For example, if it is difficult to access information about the long-term risks of serious disease in an occupation, people would enter it who otherwise might not. Discovering their error only later, if ever, people in that occupation would be significantly worse-off not only because of disease but also because the wage would be lower, given the excess supply of entrants. Even disregarding the effects of the disease itself, they would be substantively worse off than those in other occupations because of this lowering of their wage relative to the full-information, market equilibrium level.

Because of the advantages that are also conferred in such cases, some actors in the story have incentives to interfere with the information available to others. To pursue the example, employers of people working in hazardous occupations have an incentive to gloss over the hazards or to otherwise interfere with the availability of information about these aspects of the work, since employers' profits are increased by the lower wages required to attract employees.

Similarly, people in the professions have incentives to interfere with the information about work in their fields so that prospective entrants require more formal education or training to enter those fields than is necessary. Where they can do so (through, for example, occupational associations), they will work to strengthen their occupational entry requirements (by strengthening admission requirements into their occupational training schools) since the consequently reduced supply of potential entrants raises the in-group's wages above what they would otherwise be. To the extent that entering and passing medical school may be made more difficult than is necessary, the difference between the incomes of medical doctors and those of nonprofessional employees may include more than compensation for the costs of medical school. The incentive to restrict supply is there; so is the ability to accomplish it, via an association with great influence on medical school and certification policy, namely, the American Medical Association.

Cases such as these of asymmetric information may well cause substantial, perhaps permanent, disparities in overall labor compensation across occupations. In a world in which not only is information generally imperfect but asymmetric information relationships are widespread, labor income and hence the wealth accumulations deriving from them cannot at all be presumed to reflect individuals' (or families') aptitudes. Even intelligently made choices based on inadequate information, whether due to the deliberate manipulation of information by other individuals or merely the particulars of one's own (or one's family's) circumstances, cannot lead to optimal occupational choice outcomes. Instead, some individuals, regardless of their aptitudes, are fortunate and others unfortunate in the outcomes of their choices. There are information insiders who get ahead and outsiders who get left behind in labor market choices, regardless of their innate abilities. (There remains the critical question of what determines who is an information insider and who an outsider, a question that will be taken up later.)

This applies perhaps even more critically in investment and wealth accumulation. In a world of imperfect information, wealth is not accumulated merely by "routine saving" of labor income but instead by two other far more important routes. First, one may simply be lucky in one's investments. The returns on most investments are by no means determined solely by the decisions and actions of the investors but by a variety of external and, to some degree, unpredictable factors that are relevant but beyond individual control. Thus "some win, some lose" regardless of business acumen or financial advantage.

However, having accurate information about the relevant external factors may well enable one to take appropriate actions about things over which one does have control. Thus, assuming one has access to the funds needed for taking action, the second important route to wealth accumulation is insider information. The critical role of such information should be widely appreciated in these times of scandal and corruption in corporate governance. Since the Great Recession of 2008, it is now commonplace to suspect high-level executives in large corporations of financial manipulation and accounting irregularities in their firms. Some sizable fortunes have been made by those in corporate management and finance in the course of these escapades. (Albeit some of the wealth involved has been lost in subsequent crashes or because the perpetrators were caught or because of changes made by policymakers.) The importance of insider information in wealth accumulation simply cannot be overstated. It is a staple of "great family" biographies that family fortunes originate in the good luck of some insider information-related access to funds or investment opportunities.[14]

Thus, inequalities in access to information strongly condition the outcomes of people's choices in both labor and financial markets, and imply considerable disparities in labor income and accumulated wealth. Information issues—general information imperfection, asymmetry and access disparities, and strategic misinformation—are important. But so are other constraints on people's decision-making that are easily downplayed or ignored by a choice-oriented perspective on economic inequality. It is one thing for a person not to know what options are available for making an economic decision. It is another thing entirely when some options are unavailable, regardless of the person's awareness one way or the other. Actual impediments to labor and financial market mobility are pervasive in market systems. By blocking people into the occupations they would otherwise choose, they constitute widespread systematic disparities of opportunity and generate widespread substantive inequality.

Labor Market Impediments, Organized and Otherwise

The market equilibration process—the convergence of real overall labor incomes toward substantive equality as people move across occupations—is stymied by other kinds of transaction costs besides those involved in attaining and processing information. Transportation costs, even in the age of relatively cheap energy, make up a significant portion of most working people's budgets and constitute a barrier to equilibration in labor markets as people economize on job location and daily travel expenses.[15]

As a consequence, people fortunate enough to find themselves in areas where industries are on the rise get "surplus" substantive labor incomes that will not be equilibrated away. This is because many people whose incomes have been lowered by other industries' decline will refrain from moving because of daunting relocation costs. Wages then fail to equilibrate between rising and falling sectors. It may be argued that since people in declining sectors may choose not to relocate, the labor market is merely compensating for "relocation dis-amenities" associated with moving toward rising industry jobs. Those who stay behind choose to maximize their overall real income by remaining where they are. Yet compensation still does not occur, for those already in the industrial growth area need not make any choices about relocation but still will receive a higher wage. Outsiders who must move in to get the now higher-paying jobs must pay for relocation. As with information costs, transportation costs imply that the mere good or bad fortune of being an insider (in a rising industry or region) versus an outsider (in a declining industry or region) determines who receives the higher substantive labor income.

An important parallel asymmetry is part of the problem for those in inner cities compared to those in the suburbs. As cities expand, jobs and shopping facilities move outwards to the suburbs and exurbs. Those left behind experience a substantive income loss, especially those already impoverished, since their incomes may barely cover the cost of daily transportation to and from work and shopping facilities increasingly located in outlying areas. They may thus become locationally trapped.[16]

Transportation costs may be thought of as natural impediments to labor mobility in markets. In general, mobility costs have never been insignificant, even when transportation has been relatively inexpensive. For example, there are buying and selling costs involved in changing residences, and often legal costs, and, of course, the costs of moving internationally are considerable.

There are also organized or "artificial" interferences with labor market mobility, intentionally created to exploit the consequent differentials in incomes.[17] The AMA, as mentioned earlier, is an excellent example. Taking advantage of patients' need for medical care providers to be certified and doctors' consequent need for certification as well in order to do business, the AMA sets standards at all points in the process, from admission into medical school to grades standards in the classroom, from course requirements for medical school accreditation to internship requirements for medical degrees. Strengthening any or all of these standards constricts entry into the field, thereby raising doctors' incomes. The surplus substantive incomes of doctors cannot be equilibrated away by people moving into medicine as long as doctors' professional associations remain intact. Other similar cases abound: lawyers, accountants, professors, mechanics, chefs and hairdressers all attempt the same thing through professional associations.[18]

In all these cases, people are in effect sorted, some into and others out of the fields of their choice. Insiders are lucky; outsiders are excluded. A similarly insidious kind of exclusion occurs in what is referred to as discrimination. Some particular group is barred by another group from access to a wide variety of privileged activities or a whole set of different occupations. The in group is made substantively better off economically by the exclusion of the out group as in-group incomes are thus increased (with the restricted supply of labor to their occupations) and out-group incomes are lowered (by the increased labor supply to their occupations).

Discrimination

Discrimination is probably the most widely discussed form of interference against free labor mobility in advanced market societies today. Whether it be by race, ethnicity, gender, sexual orientation, religion, political affiliation, age, or body type, discrimination affects labor markets by relegating members of the out group to lower-paying positions regardless of their occupational aptitudes and preferences. The particulars differ in the way each kind of discrimination works, but the outcome is the same. This is not the place for an in-depth treatment (the subject will be brought up at various points in this book), but a few significant points may be made here.[19] Consider first sex discrimination, that is, against females.

Contrary to a post-feminist complacency widespread today (the #metoo movement notwithstanding), discrimination against women continues across a wide variety of settings. Women in advanced market economies still find it challenging to attain the same economic status as men. They still find themselves consigned to lower-paying and often less challenging "women's work" occupations or to home and family work. This is partly the effect of a history of legal and cultural barriers to women's rights, especially those in religious institutions. But it also continues because of a bias still manifest in the economic arena, that is, in hiring and promotion decisions, in access to education, and in credit access. To the extent this bias has nothing to do with any innate differences in economically relevant male versus female attributes, it is discrimination pure and simple.

Neoclassical economists often point out that competitive markets ought to gradually eliminate discrimination. Employers who hire qualified women, educational institutions that admit them, creditors who lend to them, should fare better in competition for employees and for customers than do those that discriminate. Since discriminators give up productivity or profitability to whatever degree they base their decisions on unrelated, extraneous factors, they should be weeded out by market competition over time. Of course, markets being imperfect, the competitive weeding-out process among firms must take time, indeed, perhaps so much time that discriminators may *never* be weeded out. Still, if one insists that markets are at least reasonably competitive, as do most neoclassical economists, then by this point in the development of the advanced industrial free market economies, one would have expected discrimination against females to be mostly a thing of the past. Even institutionally based discrimination should have shrunk before the forces of women's liberation by market processes.

But neoclassicals argue that even in the absence of discrimination, there would still be a divergence in men's and women's apparent economic status because of fundamental differences between men's and women's work aptitudes and preferences. The primary difference, of course, is that women bear and nurse children. Therefore they bring a critical interruption of their work lives into whatever non-home occupation they may choose. Knowing that their occupational work lives will yield less because they are shortened by bearing, nursing, and raising children, women would tend to choose less investment in non-home occupational human capital, that is, in education and training for paid employment. Moreover, women would tend to choose "women's occupations," for example, nursing and elementary school teaching, that are more akin to home and child-care work than other occupations since such jobs require human capital that is easier to attain.

Employers, motivated purely by profit, it is argued, even if unbiased against women, are willing to pay less for female employees than for males, in what amounts to a kind of "compensating differential" on the buyers' side of the labor market. Employers expect a significant interruption in a woman's work for each child she bears, for several months at the very least and, given that women do most of the early child-raising as well, typically several years. After bearing and raising a child, a woman will likely need some refreshing of her skills, as well as new training if her job requires new skills. Also, while she is absent, the employer will need to replace her, incurring extra expenses in hiring and training a replacement. Lower wages for women follow directly. That is, even assuming no discriminatory bias against women, their compensation is lowered by the an amount equal to the additional costs incurred by the employer because of these things. That, in turn, further reinforces women's tendency to invest less in their human capital.

Nonetheless, even though neoclassicals argue that women's pay would be less regardless, empirical evidence strongly supports the general observation that women are still significantly discriminated against.[20] If women incorporate their perceptions of discrimination into their expectations for their life prospects, they would perhaps appear to naturally prefer the course of life to which they are consigned as they make their decisions about schooling and career occupation. Yet what people would actually prefer under better circumstances cannot necessarily be inferred from what they might appear to prefer when denied opportunities. Given that actual labor-market discrimination has been well documented, women would behave the same way regardless. How much of the premium of men's over women's wages is due to these biologically based aptitude and attitude differences and how much is because of discrimination?

Nor are the different physical burdens of child-raising between the sexes wholly determined by biological differences. Women's socialization and cultural tradition, public policy, and technology can and have altered such burdens. In countries where public policy or local tradition lightens child-rearing burdens and more equitably distributes them between men and women, women's labor force participation and their occupational choices are much closer to those of men, and so too is their pay. Policies such as universal, publicly provided, high-quality childcare for working parents and paid parental leave for up to a year for both mothers and fathers, compulsory for all employers—not to mention well-enforced anti-discrimination laws—significantly broaden women's occupational opportunities (as in European and especially Scandinavian countries). Such policies show that the divergence between men's and women's economic status need not be nearly so great as it is in the United States.[21] Here then, the inability to effectuate such policies would appear to indicate, at the least, continuing discrimination in practical politics, even if more obvious and blatant forms of discrimination at the level of individual behavior might seem to be on the wane.

As in male dominance, racial or ethnic oppression is most often thought of in terms of purely individual acts of discrimination against the oppressed group. In these supposedly more enlightened times, it too seems to be waning. Yet again, substantial evidence indicates continuing discrimination against Black, Hispanic, and Asian workers, whether born in the United States or not, along with Native Americans. Both private discrimination and that which is still to be found in politics and law enforcement relegates these racial and ethnic groups to lower-paying jobs and occupations, in part through residential and cultural segregation from white society.[22] Discrimination by race or ethnicity in hiring, promotion, pay, and access to quality education, housing and residential location, credit and legal counsel constricts their opportunities relative to those available to Western European-descended whites.

Neoclassicals argue that as long as there are no legal or other institutional barriers to access to better opportunities, discrimination by individuals in the dominant group should not survive market competition over historical time. As with sex discrimination, individual discriminators must pay for their bias, as market competition punishes employers, educators, creditors, and others who discriminate on extraneous grounds such as race or ethnicity. Employers who choose their employees by race instead of by expected contributions to productivity harm their own profitability and sooner or later go under before the competition from more rational rivals.

But racial or ethnic discrimination may be protected, perhaps indefinitely, by imperfections in markets, to the extent that discriminating employers do not get punished at all by competition. And with or without market imperfections, much the same kind of sociocultural dynamic exists in racial or ethnic discrimination as in sex discrimination. African Americans, knowing that their job prospects are greatly lessened by discrimination and that their returns on investments in human capital are accordingly lessened, may find such investments simply not worth it. Therefore, many may choose not to seek higher education or training and not to apply themselves in school. School guidance counselors may be less likely to guide Black students into more promising directions, assuming Black students' education choices reflect their preferences or abilities rather than their rational expectations about the restricted options available to them.

And so too is the attractiveness of Black workers to employers similarly lessened, even to those employers who are not racially biased and seek only to employ the best contributors to productivity. Such employers may practice "statistical" discrimination (ostensibly distinct from "real" discrimination). For example, an employer with no particular biases may not even bother to interview African American or Hispanic job applicants (or women) for some jobs because their resumés appear to show that they are likely to be poorly prepared educationally (since they are so "on average"). Such realities imply that even if markets were relatively well-functioning, it could take them effectively forever to eliminate the economic impact of racial and sexual discrimination.

Discrimination, labor market impediments artificial or otherwise, information problems, all of these may be seen as hindrances to free mobility in labor markets that prevent people from attaining their best occupational fit in the sense of the ideal of the utopian story of neoclassical economics. Yet none of these limitations discussed thus far might seem to emanate from the market system itself. For mainstream economists, they are exogenous factors and since at least ideally markets could provide substantive equality in a world lacking such limitations, economists have tended to suggest, as their primary policy prescription, eliminating or mitigating such hindrances to well-functioning markets in an effort to improve upon what has seemed to them the most benign of all possible economic systems.

Yet there are still greater hindrances to free labor mobility that are inherent in market systems, or at least in capitalist market systems of the familiar kind. Certain features of even a hypothetically perfect capitalist market system would impede full occupational mobility and substantive economic equality, regardless of whether discrimination or organized or other impediments to labor mobility are present and regardless of the perennial and probably unavoidable problems of information and its accessibility. These are considered in the next chapter.

APPENDIX

I. Mainstream Economics, Power and Class

If the state is the executive committee of the great corporation and the planning system, it is partly because neoclassical economics is its instrument for neutralizing suspicion that this is so.

—J. K. GALBRAITH[23]

Economics, it may be argued, is the most politically or ideologically conservative of the social sciences in the sense that economists actually tend to look less critically on the economic system in which they live, the modern capitalist market system, than do other social scientists. Neoclassical economics, the body of theory that underlies the bulk of what is taught and practiced in the mainstream of economics, is often singled out as a major source of that conservatism. Contrary to a widespread view, neoclassical theory itself is not necessarily ideology-bound, it is merely a tool, useful for some things and harmful for others. Among those who adhere to it more or less are to be found economists leaning both right and liberal left. The analysis here, far from a conservative one, begins from a neoclassical entry point. And although neoclassical theory is indeed a major part of what underlies the conservatism of economists in comparison with other social scientists, it is more complicated than that. Suppose neoclassicism does indeed tend to incline economists toward market conservatism. In that case, the more critical question may be, why did that particular body of theory come to be selected from among a variety of possible approaches that could have been adopted for use to the exclusion of other possible approaches in the field of economics? More to the point, historically what is it about mainstream economics that inclined it toward ideological conservatism in the first place?

Discussions among historians of economic thought suggest a few things. The market system itself raises a kind of veil on those who would understand it that is difficult to penetrate beyond its fairly benign appearances.[24] People buying and selling in markets are invariably doing so voluntarily, and it appears that none are subject to anyone's power, domination, or influence as they engage in such transactions. Yet things are not at all that simple. Specializing as they do in market systems, economists should be able to peer behind that veil but they generally are just ordinary people, not necessarily adept at getting beyond the manifest phenomena of daily life. When they also find themselves subject to strongly conservative external influences, it becomes challenging, since among all the social sciences, their field is most closely involved with the concerns of finance, business, and public policies that relate to these areas of social life that indeed do tend to be conservative. Being more closely engaged with these realms than the other social sciences, economists cannot have avoided at least some of those concerns and, accordingly, some of those viewpoints. Many, perhaps most, economists' jobs lie in those areas, and academia, where most of the rest are, is strongly influenced by the concerns of representatives of those areas in academic administration and decision-making. Economics consequently is without question among the most ideologically conservative of all the disciplines.[25]

The upshot is that in providing what capitalists need from economists, the latter have more often than not failed to satisfactorily explain, indeed have frequently obfuscated, often intentionally, the harsher realities of the class system that constitutes the market economy. Neoclassical economic theory, it turns out, has served well those purposes, for reasons that have already been suggested in this chapter and will be made more evident in later chapters in this book.

The thoroughness with which issues of inequality, power, and class are avoided in economics must be striking when seen from the viewpoint of other social scientists. Every undergraduate economics textbook urges that economists, as scientists, should leave it for others to consider such "value-laden" or "ethically complex" questions as those that invariably arise with such issues—that is, distributive equity and political or social democracy. Economists, they say, should eschew "normative" thinking and stick with the strictly "positive" or "objective" concerns of simple economic efficiency. (However, mainstream economics texts do not hesitate to refer to other values when it is convenient for defending the market system against criticisms of that system's own inefficiencies or other faults.) Elsewhere in the social sciences it is commonly acknowledged that such value-laden questions cannot be avoided, and therefore must be dealt with directly and in depth if one aspires to anything like scientific objectivity, and that, if anything, it is the failure to deal openly and clearly with such questions that is actually unscientific.

Thus, although economic inequality today is seen as a legitimate inquiry in economics, and indeed has lately become one of its primary sub-fields, no more than a decade ago when it was addressed at all it was with proper nods to the difficulties of maintaining objectivity with such a fraught subject. When distributive equity or fairness was acknowledged to be a real value, it was invariably strongly qualified with reference to the so-called equity-versus-efficiency trade-off, and noted that great care had to be taken not to violate the important requisites of efficiency. Moreover, many economists, perhaps a majority, believed that the distribution of income and wealth would be mostly fair in a hypothetical system of well-functioning markets, a major theoretical error, as will be made clear in this book. That inclined them to believe also, even more egregiously, that the existing distribution in fact was mostly fair as well.[26] Elsewhere in the social sciences—in sociological, political and anthropological theory—economic inequality has been traditionally and remains an important background reality to be taken account of in all other inquiries and a major topic of inquiry itself. And inequality such as is found in the modern market system has not been widely considered "mostly fair" or "fair enough" in any social science but economics.

It is in its refusal to incorporate concerns with power per se, however, that economics has most shown its bias toward market conservatism. The concept of power is easily adapted into the foundation of the neoclassical paradigm, that is, in the constrained choice model of individual behavior, yet as a subject of both theoretical and empirical inquiry power has been simply ignored in economics.[27] In the other social sciences, the concept of power plays a role at least as critical as that played by the concept of the atom in the physical sciences. In economics, at least judging from the claims of many of the most respected economists in past years, most in the mainstream of the field have seen power as mostly irrelevant or would simply rather leave it to someone else to deal with (some have believed there is no such thing).

Up until the last decade or so, mainstream economists who did acknowledge the existence and relevance of power as a significant concern for their field mostly found it important in two places: the state and private business monopoly. The power of the state, while seen as useful for some important tasks necessary for the management of market systems, is mostly feared among economists, whose advocacy of free markets rests importantly on such markets being considered the only viable counter to the state. Monopoly power was a major concern for earlier economists, beginning with Adam Smith himself. Today, the terms "monopoly power" or "market power" may be found in economics textbooks only infrequently. Moreover, in that context the entire set of concerns relating to power, specifically the distributional consequences of monopoly, have been eschewed in favor of a narrower focus on efficiency issues.[28] Even in the "new industrial organization" and the closely related "new institutionalism"—movements which by now have achieved broad acclaim in economics while supposedly challenging the mainstream—private sector power of any form has seemed to be of little interest. For mainstream economists, including those in the "nontraditional" mainstream, only state power merits much attention. That should be no surprise for a social science discipline as subject to the influence of business and private wealth as is economics.

The concept of power, even if it relates directly to matters of concern and interest for all social scientists, also raises the specter of class. But that is a topic that modern economists are at least equally inclined to ignore. As anything more than the mere ranking of individuals by quantitative income or wealth alone, class simply does not exist for economists. And class-as-power has been of no interest to them; indeed, for them it has not even been a phenomenon of the real world of modern market systems, judging from the scant few writings of mainstream economists directly addressing the subject.[29]

All of this may appear to have changed with Thomas Piketty's *Capital in the Twenty-first Century* (2013). Yet judging from many of the criticisms of that work, it falls short of an adequate treatment of the class power relations of capital to which it clearly and rightly aspired. Piketty himself is aware of and sensitive to some of those relations, given his discussion in his book and in other work on politics, history, the media, and social change, although he appears not to have comprehended their full scope and implications, nor the breadth and depth of the class structures they involve. Thus, John Bellamy Foster and Michael D. Yates note that issues "of inequality must be seen as ubiquitous in today's capitalism, occurring at every level, the product of imperialism as well as class, race, and gender—none of which are addressed directly in Piketty's analysis."[30]

This is not the place for a thorough look at that work and Piketty's later and also influential work *Capital and Ideology*.[31] It can be said here that Piketty's economics is solidly in the tradition of mainstream neoclassical theory. *Capital in the Twenty-first Century* does not use neoclassical theory merely as an entry point from which to proceed further and then build a more concrete picture of power and class in capitalism with the help of other useful perspectives—proceeding from that point to an analysis of the past, present, and future of inequality. Instead, Piketty's economic analysis of rising inequality historically and in the future rests solely on neoclassical economic theory. From this author's perspective, that suggests a poor foundation, for mainstream neoclassical economics cannot provide a strong understanding of these things.

II. Neoclassical Marginal Productivity as a Theory of Distribution

Neoclassical economics is at least as well-known for its marginal productivity (MP) theory of production and markets as it is for its human capital theory. More popularly it is known for what may be called an MP theory of distribution. Historically it is due to J. B. Clark, and today it is defunct, although it is unfortunately all too widely extant in popular discussion of the neoclassical idea that wages are determined by marginal products. This Appendix explains both why the MP theory of distribution is invalid and why the MP theory of production and markets is also otherwise ignored here.

Human capital theory, such as is used in this book, is an account of the supply side of the labor market. In contrast, MP theory focuses on the demand side. Since the neoclassical account is one of long-run equilibrium in the labor market, in which quantities of labor supplied and demanded are equal, depending on one's purposes one may characterize the equilibrium wage just as correctly from the supply side, that is, in terms of human capital theory alone, as from the demand side, that is, in terms of MP theory alone.[32]

In MP theory, in perfectly competitive markets the firm's demand for labor is identical with its value of the marginal product of labor (which equals the money value of the output added by the last or marginal worker).[33] Since the market demand for labor is simply the sum of firm demands, the market wage in equilibrium must equal each individual firm's value of its marginal product of labor. Thus, it is said in a kind of shorthand, that the wage equals the marginal product of labor, and that therefore, also in a kind of shorthand that is unfortunately somewhat misleading, people's labor incomes are completely determined by their productivity.

But it is equally true in long-run equilibrium that their wages are determined by the costs of their schooling and training and by the dis-utilities of their jobs, for the wage equilibrates both sides of the labor market. In effect, abstracting from job dis-amenities and hedonic wage differences, since wages equal both the MP of labor and the costs of schooling and training, people invest in quantities of schooling or training up to the point at which those costs equal the value of the marginal product of labor in those occupations. As long as one is referring to long-run equilibrium, one may therefore focus on either side of the labor market and ignore the other, depending on one's purposes, as is done in those portions of this book's account that are in terms of human capital theory alone.

Note that the MP theory does not provide grounds for any suggestion that workers are paid in accord with their productivity as usually understood. In ordinary conversation, people mean by productivity what economists call workers' average product of labor, that is, output per unit of the labor used to produce it. If workers were paid the value of their average product, then none of the firm's income would be left for division among owners, creditors, landlords, etc., nor even for capital replacement. Therefore, workers simply cannot sustainably be paid their average product. Since the logic of the MP theory extends to all other factors of production and labor, every factor of production gets paid its MP. That fact, along with the firm's technical input requirements, then determines the division of the firm's total income among all its production factors.[34]

The primary reason for the failure of the MP theory as a general theory of distribution lies in its inability to account for the distribution of the ownership of production factors. Since in the MP theory each factor of production receives income in accord with its MP, it may be supposed that therefore each factor owner receives personal income in accord with the factors owned. That statement is true as far as it goes. However, a factor owner's total income depends first and foremost upon how much of each factor is owned. Although the MP theory provides an account of the factor income per unit of the factor owned, it does not explain why different individuals own different amounts of each factor. Thus, MP theory falls far short of being a theory of distribution. Unfortunately, adherents of neoclassical economics have all too often shrugged at the critical question of the distribution of ownership, saying essentially that it is determined by things beyond the economists' rightful realm of inquiry—that is, when they have bothered at all with the matter.

The MP theory of distribution was a sub-chapter in the "capital controversy" between the two Cambridges (Massachusetts and England) that roiled the field of economics in the 1950s and '60s. The Americans, including the Nobelists Paul Samuelson, Robert Solow, Franco Modigliani, and others, represented neoclassical economics as taught at MIT. Their opponents, representing Keynesian, neo-Ricardian, and Marxian views (these days many would be called "post-Keynesians") as taught at the University of Cambridge, England, included Joan Robinson, Piero Sraffa, Luigi Pasinetti, and others (none of whom got Nobel prizes).[35] Although both sides in the debates made major concessions to each other, ultimately, the Americans had to yield. However, "mainstream economics goes on as if the controversy [and the Americans' concession] had never occurred."[36]

3. Capitalism and Opportunity

A critical connotation of the term "class" is that one's given class background significantly determines one's opportunities for present and future economic well-being. This idea is easily stated in terms of the choice-constraint model of individual behavior of mainstream economics. A person's class constitutes a set of constraints on their occupational choices, or, alternatively, there are different sets of opportunities for people in different classes. People from lower classes tend to be excluded from upper-class occupations and thereby channeled into lower-class labor. In contrast, only people from upper classes tend to be admitted to upper-class occupations. Like information problems, labor market impediments, and discrimination, class in this sense thus constitutes another kind of hindrance to labor market mobility, one that is unequal for different groups of people and thereby yields enduring substantive inequalities of income and wealth.

It was noted earlier how discrimination, in effect, tends to reproduce discrimination, that is, successively from one generation to the next. Thus, discrimination is a prime example of a *class process* that generates and reproduces distinct classes of people. The capitalist market system also creates and reproduces classes. It is itself a class process, even in the absence of discrimination per se or other similar processes, even were capitalism a system of hypothetically perfectly competitive markets. This is so because of the fundamental role of finance, credit, and capital in the capitalist market system when significant disparities exist in personal wealth. This is contrary to capitalist mythology, according to which the capitalist system undermines and ultimately destroys all social class systems. It may or may not be true of the history of capitalism that it has destroyed all existing systems of social class; the matter is debatable. But if historically existing class systems are not completely destroyed by capitalism, they are substantially superseded by a system based on capitalist class institutions.[1] Consider how finance and credit work in capitalism.

CREDIT, CAPITAL, AND HUMAN CAPITAL

Credit and capital are essential elements of any full-fledged capitalist market system. In a world of significant wealth inequality, the way credit and capital markets work profoundly negates all possibility of equality of opportunity and substantive equality of income and wealth. How can credit and capital markets matter so significantly in the context of occupational choice in labor markets? They matter because of the critical connection between such markets and investment spending.

To determine whether a business investment is sufficiently lucrative to undertake, its expected return must compare favorably with the return on appropriately comparable financial instruments. If a similar financial instrument would return more than the investment in question, then assuming the firm has the funds available necessary for the investment, the investment would be forgone in favor of the financial instrument. On the other hand, if the firm lacks sufficient funds, borrowing them to make the investment will require that it similarly compare the expected return on the investment with the interest rate on the borrowed funds. (Note that the selling of equity for obtaining investment funds may be taken as merely another form of borrowing.)

This pertains as well to individuals investing in human capital. Aside from government aid or private scholarships, obtaining the education or training yielded by such investments requires expending some funds. As has been discussed, not only must the direct costs be covered, such as tuition and books, but there are indirect costs, too. Among the latter, especially critical is the income forgone by being without employment while involved in school activities. One will most likely need to pay living expenses otherwise than out of earned income.

Contrary to the theory explained at the beginning of the last chapter, for most individuals investing in human capital in the real world the critical question is not its expected return compared to that of financial instruments or other investments. It is instead, are the required funds available? Few people are wealthy enough to pay out of their own pockets all the costs of the education or training they may wish to obtain. The vast majority must get at least some of the required funds by borrowing. In fact, even after taking account of the total of higher education and training costs funded by government and private scholarships, most college students still must borrow at least a portion of the remainder of the funds they require. Thus in 2018, 71 percent of students graduating from four-year colleges in the United States had student debt. The total of all students' college debt, which has become a major political issue, now stands at nearly $1.5 trillion in total borrowed by 44 million students and former students. The average indebtedness of graduates of the class of 2017 is close to $40,000.[2]

In a purely capitalist market system, there cannot be equal access to the funds required for people to pursue their desired occupations. Were there equal access, even the poorest individual who would undertake the expensive and long-term schooling required by the medical profession, for example, could do so just as easily as anyone else. But that is not the case because, in capitalism, credit does not work that way.

Private lenders require assurance that their customers can repay their borrowed funds before they commit to lending them. Thus,

customers often must provide collateral of equivalent value to the
loan amount, that is, an asset of some sort that the lender may
take if the borrower defaults. Without such collateral, lending for
education or training is especially risky. Creditors then insist that
borrowers show strong prior indication of expected success in
repaying loans and in the education or training itself (for example,
good grades already earned) or in satisfactorily holding a job that
pays enough to repay the loan.

Clearly, the process is strongly and unavoidably biased in favor
of borrowers who already have either some wealth (for collateral)
or have demonstrated success in education and job markets. This
is to say that lending will favor people who have "prior endowments" of either financial or human capital. If lacking accumulated
human capital, the more funds one already has available, the more
likely one will obtain whatever additional financing is required to
get the human capital. Those who already have financial resources
are those most likely to get financed. Moreover, the more a person
needs to borrow relative to the total cost of schooling, the greater
is the risk of their defaulting. Thus, the cost of borrowing also will
be greater, that is, the interest and fees that must be paid, since
creditors will attach a premium for the additional risk. The prior
accumulation of financial and human capital determines both
how much additional funding one may borrow and how cheaply
loans can be gotten to acquire human capital.

INHERITANCE, FAMILY, THE "WEALTH BIAS," AND RACE

Younger people in the earlier stages of their work lives usually
have no significant prior endowments of either human or financial capital. Where do they obtain the funds required to make their
earliest choices about their future occupations and schooling?
Aside from government aid or private scholarship, young people's occupational schooling and training generally can be funded
only by their families. As they come of age, some may inherit
wealth, at which point they then may be able to finance on their

own whatever schooling they seek. Still, only a tiny percentage of young people are in such a position. And either way, the schooling and occupational choices people can make in the early stages of their working lives are most critically determined by their parents' already given economic status.

Another way of saying this is that the already unequal distribution of the wealth required for young people to get access to funding for education and training constitutes a major source of *differential immobility* in labor markets. It is an impediment to the mobility of people in pursuing their occupational choices that impacts some much more than others.[3] Enduring substantive economic inequality follows directly. Affluent families, regardless of the source of their affluence, can bestow on their offspring broader opportunity and greater labor market mobility from the start. This advantage gives them greater substantive economic well-being; less affluent families not so much. The realities of the unequal distribution of wealth in the United States, which is now extreme, are such that these disparities of occupational opportunity are great indeed.

The effect of inequality in prior wealth endowments *compounds* inequalities of opportunity that may arise from other factors and does so over successive generations. Thus, whether it be privately organized labor market impediments, information or transportation or other transaction costs, or discrimination, this "wealth bias" in occupational choice further restricts not only people's current and future incomes but also their wealth accumulation prospects and those of their offspring. The resulting inequalities in wealth endowments needed for human capital investment by later generations thereby compound the effect of whatever extra-market barriers may have already existed, further constraining those affected later.

The example of racial discrimination is indicative and especially critical in the United States today. To the extent that Black, Hispanic, Native, and immigrant Americans are paid poorly, their ability to accumulate wealth is reduced as well. They and their offspring, therefore, have that much less access to the funds necessary for accumulating further human capital. Denied the same opportunities as others, their substantive economic well-being is that much further diminished from what it would be were "simple discrimination" the only barrier to their progress.

The case of African Americans today is critical, and also illustrative. Obviously, racial discrimination has greatly diminished Blacks' opportunities in labor markets and consequently their economic well-being. But at each point in the long U.S. history of discrimination against Blacks, it has also diminished their ability to pass on endowments of wealth that later generations would require for pursuing their own human capital investment. Discrimination leads to inadequate funds for such investment, which compounds the effects of discrimination on labor income alone. And future generations are thereby even further impoverished relative to whites. This impoverishment is moreover reproduced as African Americans alter their occupational choices following their expectations of failure. When there also is discrimination in financial and asset markets, specifically in lending and housing, these effects are further compounded.[4]

Thus, the white to Black ratio of median family net wealth typically ranges between thirteen-to-one and ten-to-one in the United States.[5] It may not be too far-fetched to suppose that, were simple discrimination per se against Blacks to completely disappear (and some people even insist that it has), the wealth bias against Blacks' access to occupational choice would still be great enough by itself to fully account for the shortfall in their average income relative to whites. It might be noted here that the incidence of education debt among Blacks is the highest of any group in the country, as is their education debt repayment burden as a fraction of their income.[6]

Racial discrimination, specifically in the residential housing market, is a critical but often unappreciated factor in the history of racial wealth disparity in the United States. With their greater effective demand for housing, whites tend to leave residential areas that have increasing numbers of Blacks, as whites attempt to find areas where housing values are not "threatened." As they do so, their expectations may be self-justified as home values may become depressed. When more Black persons then move in, with their significantly lower effective demand for housing (given their lower incomes and poor wealth accumulations), home values continue deteriorating in those neighborhoods subjected this way to "white flight." Black accumulation of wealth in the form of housing—the most important kind of wealth for most people—tends to stagnate or decline with their home values. In contrast, whites' home values elsewhere continue appreciating. Discrimination in mortgage lending and in the laws relating to it, as well as by realtors and others involved, also has been and apparently continues to be a significant impediment to Black people accumulating housing wealth.[7]

DOESN'T PUBLIC SCHOOLING HELP?

Consider public schooling. In principle, publicly subsidized or provided education can alleviate or even eliminate disparities in access to occupational choice caused by wealth inequality. Thus, governments of various countries directly provide loans or underwrite private loans, provide scholarships and grants, and they directly provide education itself.

The universal availability of public schooling should mitigate the effects of unequal prior wealth endowments on people's access to occupational choice, with the children of poor and lower-income families thereby having far greater access to both general and occupationally oriented education than they would otherwise. Economists tend to focus on the efficiency aspects of public schooling, the fact that large and widespread "positive externalities" derive from an intellectually well-provided public. But the equity aspects are even more compelling. It is simply impossible to conceive equality of opportunity and substantive economic equality in an otherwise laissez-faire capitalist market economy without publicly funded education.

Yet public education nonetheless falls far short of offsetting the disparities among people's occupational choices that arise from the wealth bias and, in fact, may well compound that bias. First, children of lower- and even middle-income families in middle and high school often must work after school hours, sometimes even at full-time jobs, to supplement their families' income. Their schoolwork can only suffer as their time is cut short for study, rest, and recreation. In addition, many simply drop out of school before completion. The same applies in higher education, which is not at all universally available. Its total costs are only partly funded by government (and in the United States, the fraction covered by government is shrinking with rising tuition even in state colleges and universities).[8] Judging from the numbers of people who fail to get much further than a high-school diploma, large numbers of young people presumably are forced to cut short their schooling by the necessities of work before they can make any real occupational choices.[9] And a large number of those who do attain higher education do so while working full-time.[10]

Second, as long as private schooling is of higher quality than public school, the children of the affluent will be able to get more and better education at all levels, with a wider selection of choices.

Third, public schooling itself varies greatly in the quality of education and training offered to students. In higher education, all state university systems are multi-tiered. The lowest-tier schools—mainly community colleges—generally provide less academically rigorous, more vocationally or professionally oriented educations. They are also, not coincidentally, cheaper, for to a great extent they provide inferior quality educations, both general and vocational or professional. Per student budgets are lower, classes are larger, facilities and staff less adequate, and faculty workloads much heavier.

Similar differences abound in public kindergarten through high school that derive from fundamental inequities in our school funding system. In the United States, most such funding continues to come from local school district property tax collections. These are nearly as unequal across school districts as are the family incomes from which they are collected. The remaining financing out of state and federal government budgets is limited. It universally fails to bring total funding per student to anything near equality. Thus, the primary reason for many schools failing to "leave no child behind" continues to be the problem of inadequate resources relative to student needs.[11] To the extent that school funding per student is directly correlated with school districts' families' economic status, local property tax funding works against any mitigating effect the public school system might otherwise have upon the wealth bias in occupational opportunity.

Finally, the actual role of formal education and training in the human-capital development process also should be considered. Up to this point, school has been presumed the principal site where human capital is accumulated. But that is misleading at best. People also get much, if not most, of their marketable skill training at home, in their extended families, and in their neighborhoods and broader communities. (On-the-job training will be considered later.) When relevant learning occurs in advantageous non-school settings, those whose family backgrounds put them there are thereby favored in attaining the skills they seek from formal education. Thus, better-off families give their children human capital advantages not only through the quality of schools but also from their material environments more generally, for example, with books and other learning materials in the home. Their children are in proximity to other similarly advantaged children in neighborhoods and communities with rich recreational and cultural resources.

Moreover, not only are there other relevant sources of human capital accumulation besides school, but schools themselves arguably are not really about human capital accumulation, at least not exclusively. What do schools really do? Do they pass on productive skills to students, or something else? Indeed, students get much more than literacy, conceptual and reasoning ability, and specific intellectual and work skills. Behavioral abilities, ideas, and social attributes are certified with graduation, the relevance of which for production per se is at least arguable. The ability to sit patiently and take instruction, be prepared and punctual, be reasonably peaceful in social relations with both peers and superiors, work hard toward externally provided goals are more or less instilled in students. Similarly, a variety of ideas—some valid, some not—is passed on to students besides those strictly necessary for contributing to production in modern work settings. For example, the idea that each individual is innately better or worse at various particular things, that they are appropriately judged by designated superiors, that hard work yields a fulfilling life, that hierarchy is a necessary aspect of productive human society. Students also take with them at graduation their places in social networks of friends and acquaintances and other connections with people and institutions that directly or indirectly affect their future occupations.

Perhaps what all schools give their students are not so much productive skills and capacities as behavioral attributes and ideas that allow them to fit in socially in diverse work settings and connections that give them access to those settings. Social fit often does contribute to smoothly functioning workplaces. But in many settings, it has nothing to do with the work. Besides, other kinds of attributes can contribute just as much to productivity. People may cooperate in common work quite well without being homogeneous believers in society's ruling ideology. Although connections may be based on relevant work skills, in common usage the term refers to social networks that have nothing to do with work skills but are instead primarily based on inessentials like personality, race, sex, looks, and especially the pure luck of who knows whom.

The upshot is that the school system largely serves to place people in a social hierarchy rather than in a labor market where they make occupational choices free of major social direction and influence. Given the correlation noted earlier between school quality and the economic status of the families of students attending them, the school system reinforces the wealth bias in occupational opportunity. It works to reproduce the social hierarchy of wealth.[12]

Of course, school is not the only site in which that occurs. Unlike other sites, public schooling at least contains elements that work against social hierarchization by helping to provide a somewhat more equal playing field. Insofar as schooling provides basic literacy in language, civilization, and society and institutions, even the least effective public school provides a minimal set of the tools people need to navigate their world. Things are almost certainly better with universal public schooling than without. Still, as an institution that in principle aims to improve equality of opportunity it is in dire need of improvement.

What about other sources of social hierarchy? How significant is their effect on unequal occupational opportunity? It is a commonplace that the market system overall works against extra-market social systems of hierarchy and status, that it is a place where one might escape such invidious features of social life. But that is not so in a world of pervasive "market imperfection." As discussed earlier, even in the purely theoretical world of well-functioning markets, such markets would not necessarily mitigate racial, ethnic, sexual, religious, or other discrimination. Most critically, the capitalist market system's powerful wealth-favoring bias in occupational opportunity generates a distinct social status hierarchy of its own, one that public education is not likely to correct. Indeed, the wealth bias is significantly reinforced by unequal public education, and compounds other sources of unequal occupational opportunity, such as discrimination and other labor market misfortune. On such grounds, sociologists have expanded upon the concept of "capital" to include important aspects of economic and social life that are not usually covered by the term. They have demonstrated further grounds for doubting the supposed evenhandedness of the market system.

CAPITAL AND "CAPITAL"

Aside from an individual's financial and human capital, two aspects of social life may also be seen as "capital." The individual may, at least metaphorically, invest in, accumulate, and convert them into money: social capital and cultural capital.[13] These aspects of one's social life are closely related to and have significant bearing on occupational choice, financial and human capital, and economic status.

Social capital consists of the various "connections" in social networks of people or groups. By membership in various groups— family, friendship groups, neighborhood, school, civic groups, workplace, and one's race, ethnicity, sex, or religion—one has relationships of mutual obligation with people in those groups. From economists' viewpoint, such relationships often seem like exchange relationships. Sociologists and anthropologists emphasize that quid pro quo exchanges of support or favors between individuals related in such ways are not at all the rule. Instead, people often simply give support or favors, perhaps on the principle that, among those in one's own group, "what goes around comes around." Of course, the support from one's connections depends not only on the closeness of the connections (for example, family versus neighborhood versus larger community groups) but also on the resources one's connections offer. And because some reciprocity may be felt necessary to sustain some connections, a person's own resources for returning favors may matter as well.

This represents almost literally a kind of capital as the support and favors of connections are in a sense "convertible" into money. There also is the fact that one can sometimes "accumulate" by deliberately employing social capital in investment. The support of some connections can expand one's membership into other groups and thus attain other connections. And connections can often be used to attain economic goods or resources. Then, based on the new connections attained with the higher economic status (for example, in a new job location), more connections and economic status can be pursued.

The extent and effectiveness of an individual's social capital are directly related to the economic status of the individuals and groups that constitute their connections. Thus, the "distribution of social capital" among people may be closely related to that of financial and human capital. People's ability to give and receive support and favors is a function of their own economic resources and those of the groups to which they belong.

The importance of connections is well-known in those institutions most critical in determining people's attainable economic status, higher education and job markets. Many of the connections relevant in those contexts have no relationship whatsoever with productivity per se. But race, ethnicity, sex, religion, regional background, and civic, recreational, or other personal interests may primarily determine the connections that enable one to obtain a job, a promotion, insider information, school admission, or other economic benefits.

Cultural capital may be thought of as the "vocabulary" of social interaction. It consists of commonalities of speech, manners, personal presentation, and other interaction habits, insofar as they are shaped by associations, interests, and knowledge gained in work, civic affairs, entertainment, recreation, and other activities that people share. Closely related to social capital, it is obtained partly through activities with the individuals and groups that constitute their social capital. They may also get cultural capital elsewhere: for example, from books or cultural or recreational activities. They may develop other knowledge, interests, or social interaction habits than those of their actual associations. In doing so, they may develop other associations.

Thus, it is possible to pursue cultural capital and use it for economic gain to some degree independently of social capital. Even without specific social connections, it may be possible to join some group that can provide connections or economic resources through cultural capital. Still, there is a close correlation between cultural capital and financial, human, and social capital resources. Like social capital, the distribution of cultural capital is closely related to that of financial and human capital. Thus, someone might obtain the cultural capital required for the schooling required for a particular job independently of their financial capital or social connections. People can perhaps read books and go online. But obtaining the requisite cultural capital can only suffice if it permits access to the schooling required in the occupation one seeks and the finances required for schooling. Needless to say, the necessary books and sufficient time and money resources are not available to everyone.

Thus, cultural capital is also closely intertwined in people's pursuit of their occupational choices. Like social capital, it is only loosely related and often not at all related to people's actual or potential productivity as employees. Admissions to schools or jobs, insofar as they are based on individuals' manners of interaction, interests, and accumulated knowledge, with or without effective social connections, do not at all necessarily relate to their capacities as employees.

Everyone has social connections and culture. But people's social and cultural capital endowments vary considerably, depending on the market value of their social connections and culture, that is, their ultimate convertibility in terms of potential income. The extent to which individuals may go beyond the limits of their financial and human capital resources to pursue further education and employment aspirations through social and cultural capital accumulation is generally limited. The capacity to offer support and favors is a function of economic resources, and the groups people belong to are significantly determined by their economic status. Thus, the distribution of social and cultural capital is much like that of people's income and wealth.

In light of the analysis of social and cultural capital, the market system cannot be seen to work effectively to undermine extra-market hierarchies of social status. Instead, the wealth-favoring bias in occupational opportunity that is an essential feature of the capitalist market system is significantly reinforced by extra-market social hierarchies and reinforces them in turn. This is so with or without a public education system. Even though, in principle, public education can alleviate some disparities in opportunity, social and cultural capital accumulation occur partly in the education system itself.

STRUCTURES OF MARKET IMPERFECTION

All of what has been said in this chapter would be true even in a hypothetical world of well-functioning capitalist markets.[14] In the real world of greatly and unavoidably imperfect markets, the wealth-biasing effects of inequalities in financial, human, social and cultural capital are much magnified. To see this, consider one such perennial imperfection that profoundly affects labor markets in capitalism.

Many have noted how capitalism seems to imply bigness in industrial and financial business. Economists have stressed that capitalist reality is far from the ideal of competitive markets. They have lamented monopoly and oligopoly, market concentration and market dominance, the concentration of capital, monopoly and finance capitalism, and multinational, transnational, and global capitalism.[15] Some dyed-in-the-wool neoclassical economists may argue that most of the economy remains reasonably competitive, especially in light of the globalization of markets. Most economists, however, acknowledge that, at the very least, an important sector exists in which a small number of firms dominates its particular product or service market, and this pertains at all relevant scales. Thus, there are global market dominators and national market dominators at one end of the spectrum, and neighborhood, city, and regional market dominators at the other. In such markets, as both economic theory and empirical evidence attest, the dominating firms, more or less immune to competition, take extraordinary profit with lasting impunity. Given the realities of industries wherein such privileged positions are found, that has important implications for how labor markets work, in both the primary sector of larger or dominant firms and in the secondary sector of relatively more competitive firms in the economy.[16]

Compared with secondary sector firms, primary sector firms most often are characterized by significant economies of scale due to mass production technologies, indivisibilities (capital inputs that come in "chunks" that are not easily subdivided, for example, a nuclear power facility or airplane assembly plant), or other characteristics of production or distribution. They are typically fixed-capital intensive; that is, they use relatively more machinery, equipment, and buildings. With only a few firms in such markets, each often producing a product that is differentiated somewhat from the others, the fixed capital employed by any of them tends to be firm-specific, not easily resalable elsewhere. The result is high fixed costs of production (per unit of output) and a degree of fragility because of the relatively narrow markup on fixed costs that must be covered by revenues. Any variation in revenue can lead to relatively large fluctuations in the firm's profit rate or even significant losses.

Primary sector firms, although somewhat protected from the adversities of revenue fluctuations by their market power and high profitability, nonetheless take steps to stabilize their revenues and costs by careful and heavy marketing and cost-minimizing and cost-stabilizing managerial policies. In firms with high fixed costs, where minor disruptions can generate significant profit losses, cost management may require relatively congenial labor-management relations.[17]

This is so because, first, reducing labor-management conflict helps reduce production slowdowns caused by strikes or other labor disruptions by improving workers' morale. If work conditions are good—pay is fair or even high, the workload is appropriate or even low, benefits are generous—workers may sense that the costs of job loss would be great in the event of labor strife. They then have less incentive to confront management either individually or collectively. Second, workers may then be more productive and might be less inclined to slack off while working. And if this is so, the managerial costs of monitoring and supervising workers accordingly are lessened.

Congeniality in the workplace is accomplished by a variety of labor-management policies used by such firms. Given their high profitability, they are more likely to allow functioning labor unions with union-scale wages and benefits, especially when union officers, even despite themselves, perform some managerial functions.[18] And with or without unions, such firms may promise employees longer tenure with incentives for them to stay, for example, improved seniority pay increases. They construct internal job markets that move people out of lower-level positions or positions that become obsolete and into higher-level jobs or jobs in expanding operations in the firm. And they assure the viability of such internal job markets as a source of qualified labor by providing on-the-job training, perhaps supplemented with company-paid outside education and training. All of this has salutary effects on worker morale.

In the secondary sector, while firms benefit from improvements in their workers' human capital, they hesitate to invest much in developing it, since employees may take their human capital elsewhere by quitting and seeking another job. But the firm-specific, fixed capital of primary-sector firms implies some firm-specific human capital, which is harder for workers to sell elsewhere than within the firm itself. Primary sector firms are therefore more likely to invest in employees' human capital.

The upshot for the functioning of external labor markets is critical. Access to a major portion or an entire sector of the economy, one that is highly desirable to prospective workers, is effectively closed to many people, given the internal job markets there. The only route of entry into higher-level job positions in the primary sector is via entry-level positions, those at the bottom of their internal job market promotion ladders. Entry into secondary sector labor markets is fairly easy at all levels for qualified job applicants, but not in primary sector labor markets. Instead, getting into higher-level primary sector jobs is mainly a matter of initial good luck or misfortune in people's first forays in the labor market after leaving high school or vocational school. Some are granted access at the entry level. The rest are consigned to the less desirable secondary sector, from which entry into the primary sector is difficult, and increasingly so as a worker ages.

Given their circumstances, primary sector employers find it

both possible and profitable to select from among young prospective employees on the basis of extraneous attributes. Obviously, some promise of future productivity is relevant, but things like attitude, deportment, dress, and connections are too. Besides competence or its promise, management also needs employees who will get along, especially with management, and who will accept the job hierarchy. They also should be somewhat ambitious and should welcome encouragement to "climb the ladder" of the internal job market. Such attributes may be helpful from management's viewpoint in any workplace. But, in the primary sector, management needs to be and can be more careful in selecting people for such attributes than managers in the competitive sector.

Thus, the social and cultural capital that young job applicants have already attained count considerably more in the primary sector than in the secondary sector. And primary sector firms can practice discrimination—perhaps merely "statistical" or other subtle forms of discrimination but nonetheless effectively—based on race, ethnicity, sex, religious affiliation, age, and attractiveness not only for entry-level jobs but also for promotions and intra-firm moves in the internal job market. Given internal job-market hierarchies, relying on such extraneous attributes may also contribute to the overall peacefulness (that is, tractability, obeisance, submissiveness) of the firm's workforce by segmenting the workplace. The better jobs in the firm's organizational hierarchy are reserved for well-dressed, appropriately behaved, and congenial workers, usually of the right sex and race, just as prospective employees are selected for entry to the bottom rungs of promotion ladders on such bases as well. Notably, therefore, the firm's organizational hierarchy cannot be considered a construction for facilitating productivity and efficiency, but is at least partly mere artifice.[19]

More broadly, selectivity based on extraneous individual attributes thus becomes ensconced both within the primary sector, in the internal organization of the firms within it, and within the economy as a whole in the division of the labor force between the primary and secondary sectors. In terms of the occupational choice model, significant overall compensation differentials between jobs must be the rule rather than the exception in a world of labor markets segmented in this fashion. Correspondingly, enduring substantive economic inequalities of labor income are the rule as well. Labor markets cannot operate as in the neoclassical model to eliminate such inequalities by the equilibration process. Built-in immobilities prevail both between the primary and secondary sectors of the labor market and within the internal job markets of primary sector firms. Such structures of market imperfection therefore compound inequalities of opportunity and substantive economic disparities caused by social and cultural capital disparities, the wealth bias, discrimination, and so forth. If for no other reason than that such discrimination is well-protected by the market power of primary sector firms, it will persist.

CAPITALISM AND OPPORTUNITY: SUMMING UP

Comprehending the role of unequal opportunity as an underlying cause of economic inequality takes one a long way past naive choice-theory thinking. Not only does opportunity matter, it is, in fact, vastly more important than choice. Aptitude (both innate and culturally acquired) counts for an individual's personal fortune, assuming to begin with that there really are significant differences among people's aptitudes. Yet undoubtedly many people with little aptitude and great opportunity end up doing very well, while many others with exceptional aptitude but little opportunity are consigned to failure. The great successes among those who start with little, of which the mythology of market systems is made, are few enough that the best comparison would be with a lottery. Even those successes, when their biographies are looked at closely, sustain the point that opportunity is absolutely essential.[20]

Disparities in opportunity are not merely random across the population but instead are systematic. Modern capitalist market society aligns the opportunities available to people according to their class backgrounds, as indicated roughly by their own and

CAPITALISM AND OPPORTUNITY

their families' accumulated financial, human, social, and cultural capital. From the individual's viewpoint, access to the occupation of one's choice—via the financial, human, social, and cultural capital resources necessary to get education or training—is impeded by being on the short end of the class hierarchy. Or, it is advanced by one's being closer to the high end. A person must then either accept jobs on the low end of the occupational hierarchy, that is, lower-class jobs with lower incomes, or perhaps be grateful for having started further up in the class hierarchy.

Looking at the labor market as a whole and the various impediments to labor mobility that have been considered, the pattern is clear. Incomes in higher-class occupations are raised, while the incomes of lower-class occupations are reduced by constraints on entry into the former occupations and the consequent excess supply of entrants into the latter occupations. The class system is thus reproduced, as those higher and lower incomes then get passed into higher and lower wealth endowments for the families of each successive generation of job market entrants.

Where does the class structure of the capitalist market system come from, or more precisely, what determines its structure? The simplest answer might be that it is reproduced and structured in this fashion over the generations in ordinary processes of occupational choice in capitalist labor markets, subject to the wealth-favoring bias of capitalist financial markets. In effect, social class in the capitalist market system is not purely social at all in the sense of being an extra-market phenomenon, something of society that has nothing to do with the market system itself. Instead, social class exists precisely as an artifact of the ordinary working of the capitalist market system.[21]

4. Power and Class in Capitalism

The story of economic inequality and social class often ends with an account of how people's life opportunities are organized by class systems, understood as social hierarchies structured by economic disparity, with capitalism being foremost among such systems. That leaves the most critical aspect of the subject to be considered, however, the question of power. Class generally is defined by power, or at least it should be, even if this most fundamental aspect is studiously avoided all too often.

At the most basic level, the connections between economic inequality and class as a social power structure are straightforward. In any monetary society, money gives its possessor capabilities. These are, in effect, the very opportunities with which this book has thus far been concerned. Capability is, of course, also synonymous with power, at least in one connotation. Expanding human capabilities ought to be a goal of governmental and nongovernmental social programs. That terminological equivalence, however, should alert us that insofar as individuals are capable of doing things, they may be capable of influencing other people, or of exerting power over them.[1] And, of course, money may confer power in this sense as well. More precisely, significant disparities in possession of money enable some to attain access to power or influence over others. Those possessing or having access to more money may gain influence or power over those on the shorter end of a significantly unequal distribution of income and wealth. In effect, having enough money enables people to buy positions in a class hierarchy, giving them power over those lacking sufficient money.

Contrary to what one might suppose from perusing most of the literature in economics on inequality and class, no account of these can be complete without reference to social power. To comprehend the role of power, we might reflect on the patterns or contours of constraint and opportunity that determine different individuals' and groups' economic prospects. Where do these patterns or contours of constraint come from? What precisely does power have to do with the differential opportunity that seems to be the essence of inequality?

It is often convenient to consider the determination of structures of constraint and opportunity in terms of social decisions. People decide how to order the broader features of their world, given what is materially possible as determined by nature and their historical past. The specific constraints faced by or opportunities offered to each individual in the society are essentially the outcome of such decisions. People are then seen as deciding individually how best to order their individual lives and socially how to organize the broader structures of constraint and opportunity within which each carries on as an individual.

However, social decisions are enormously complex in the myriad of interactions and interrelations of individuals and groups in the intricacies of human affairs in historical time. Making sense of social decisions about structures of constraint and opportunity is greatly simplified by the concept of social power. Whatever the various processes might be that are involved in social decisions, different individuals can exert unequal amounts or degrees of influence in those processes. That is, some can bring more power to bear than others. Thus, a society may make choices about the structures of opportunity within which its people live, but different individuals and groups count differently in making those choices. The voices of some matter more than those of others.

Elsewhere in the social sciences, the concept of power is as commonplace a theoretical tool as the concept of the molecule in chemistry. Yet the field of economics has, to its own detriment, largely neglected it. Arguably, social power should be a fundamental element in any theory that gives an important place to individuals making choices. If people are seen as making choices in which they react to and make the best of the constraints and opportunities given them, they should also be seen as having an effect on the constraints and opportunities to which others must react and make the best of. Power consists precisely in people having such an impact on the things that condition others' choices. A theory that treats individuals as choosing yet having no impact on others' choices is one in which humans are totally nonsocial creatures, mere reactive digits, not active agents. As a critical element of social decision-making processes, social power is a profoundly important aspect of the lives of actual human beings in the real world.

Although neglected in economics, the concept of power is nearly universally acknowledged as an essential tool for comprehending every aspect of society. As it pervades all social life, most people probably understand it intuitively more or less well, at least well enough to know one of the most basic principles of the economics of power.[2] Power usually brings material benefit. Those who have it generally profit from it; those who don't have it or have less of it usually are materially worse off. Thus, it is always at least potentially implicated in any inquiry on economic inequality.

This fact highlights what is perhaps the most critical and problematic kind of social power. The ability to influence people's behavior by altering their circumstances or directly or indirectly commanding them when they cannot reciprocate is commonly referred to as power over people. Power in this sense may present particular analytical challenges in the social sciences. But most people intuitively comprehend the idea because most have likely experienced it in their lives.

Nonetheless, most mainstream economists have studiously evaded the subject of social power. To see just how important that omission has been, consider the example of racial income and wealth disparity. Most people who have gotten past naïve choice-theory thinking about racial disparity attribute it primarily to discrimination. Empirical study strongly validates that theory, to which most economists probably adhere. Yet accepting the obvious reality of discrimination, a critical question still remains.

Presumably, in any case of group discrimination, each of the two groups involved is equally capable of actually discriminating against the other in a great variety of ways. When one group is discriminated against by the other, the latter usually reciprocates in whatever ways may be available. But if that is so, then, in the case of racial discrimination against African Americans, why is the outcome of such reciprocal discrimination mainly one-directional, that is, to the economic detriment of Blacks? If discrimination is presumably reciprocal, should not the economic impacts of the two groups discriminating against each other more or less cancel out? Why is whites' discrimination against Blacks apparently so much more effective than Blacks' putative discrimination against whites?

Obviously, a theory of racial economic disparity cannot be complete without answering that question. The answer is that there is far more involved than simply discrimination. Social power is involved. In general, one group has greater influence and power than the other in whatever social decision processes have determined the two groups' economic status. Thus, in particular, the oppressions of segregation, exclusion, social and cultural demoralization and outright abuse.

Domination organized on such lines—racial or ethnic oppression—represents a structure of social power. Male domination or patriarchy, which underlies male-female economic disparities, is another such structure. Each such power structure yields power to individuals in certain groups. Racial or ethnic power structures yield power to individuals in the advantaged racial or ethnic group over those in the oppressed group, along with associated benefits. Patriarchal power structures similarly grant males power over females, with associated benefits. Class is similarly a power structure: higher class standing generally yields an individual power over others, and material benefits follow.

If racial power structures are defined along the lines of race, and patriarchal structures are defined along the lines of sex, how are class power structures defined? Examining class in the diversity of human societies historically, the most common and probably useful definition of class is along the lines of a given society's organization of its main economic activity or productive labor. Class as a power structure refers to the power that operates in the working lives of people. The particular class to which an individual belongs is whatever position they occupy in that structure. Thus, in the most basic and paradigmatic account, one may be a boss or a worker.

As might be suspected, class historically has been more or less closely intertwined with the other two power structures just cited. In both male domination and racial and ethnic oppression, the oppressed group has generally been consigned to a lower social class. In many historical cases, the class structure was totally defined along the lines of sex or race and ethnicity. In the modern capitalist market system as well, these three power structures are at least closely associated. However, it remains useful to distinguish among them.[3] Class is undoubtedly the one most distinctively associated with the economic inequalities characteristic of developed capitalist market-based societies, given that the main determinant of people's economic well-being in such societies is the selling of their productive labor time in markets.

Our consideration of class in capitalism begins with the simple model of social class used by the earliest theorists on the subject. The classical theorists' basic model divided society into two groups, an upper and a lower class.[4] Reality in their times, just as today, was more complex, of course. When it came to particulars, earlier theorists moved quite far from the simple two-class model. Still, as is true of most of the theoretical models in economics and political economy, the simplicity of a model like this helps focus on certain aspects of reality, even as realism requires beefing up the model in other important ways.

EMPLOYERS AND EMPLOYEES

The essential heart of a relationship of power over people is the power dyad: one individual is superior and the other is subordinate in a relationship of command, direction, and exploitation. The two-class model is built directly from that essential relationship. The upper class is a group of people, each of whom, as an individual, has power over other individuals in the lower class. In principle, each of the two classes might act as a class, that is, as a group of individuals cooperating in concert toward their groups' aims. For present purposes, there is no reason to suppose that they necessarily do so. Except where other behaviors need to be considered, it will be supposed that individual members of a class act purely in their own individual self-interest. Similarly, class consciousness need not be assumed either.[5]

Exactly what might define such upper and lower classes in a modern capitalist market society? Most people would acknowledge that although democracy at least ostensibly prevails in political affairs in most industrially advanced societies, the economy is not even nominally democratic. The private business firm, the heart of the capitalist market system, is essentially a power hierarchy. We can simplify by looking at two basic groups in that hierarchy, business owners and their employees. The owners, of course, own the firm and all its assets, that is, its buildings, machinery and equipment, land and other structures, and all input and product inventories, as well as its financial assets. The employees own virtually none of this.[6]

All social decision-making in the firm is fundamentally defined by this essential feature of its private ownership. What one owns one may do with mostly as one wishes; what one does not own implies that one must do with mostly as the owners wish. When employees come to work, they enter someone else's private property. If property ownership gives a person power to do things, then it also may give power over those allowed to use or occupy it, at least as long as they are involved in doing so. Thus, can the capitalists command their employees while they are on or using his or her property, subject only to whatever legal restrictions may pertain to business property in general, for example, against its use for crime against persons. Their private ownership of businesses then is the essence of capitalist power. However, it is a necessary but not sufficient condition for that power.

A few points should be noted about this simple, two-class model before proceeding further with it. First, the firm's owner may be referred to as an individual capitalist for brevity's sake. Individual ownership is accurate enough for the majority (or at least a large minority) of business firms. However, a very large proportion of business assets belongs to large corporations owned by groups of individuals, those largest stockholders who have a controlling interest in each firm.[7] Even in those cases there often is a single individual, partnership, or family with real controlling interest, that is, dominance within the group holding the majority or controlling interest portion of the stock. Moreover, stockholders may act vis-à-vis their firm and its employees as a single homogeneous group. Thus, even group ownership does not essentially alter the account.

Second, another distinct group besides owners and employees does warrant at least a mention, even at this early stage in the explication. Managers are special employees who in effect translate the wishes of the owners into specific commands that they then convey to the firms' other employees. How and how well managers perform that critical task is a major subject of study in itself. This distinct and most important middle class will be closely examined later on. For the moment, managers may be supposed to be merely part of the working class.

If capitalists' ownership of their firms underlies their power over those they allow to work in them, what do they do with their power? Businesses are strongly inclined by competition in markets to pursue their own profit. That is, to pursue their owners' maximum income, for any business that behaves otherwise is likely not to be around long. Thus, business owners find themselves in a situation where they must behave as if motivated solely or mainly by the pursuit of their own monetary self-interest. What they do with the power they have over employees is what anyone motivated by monetary self-interest and in a power position would be expected to do. They try to get benefit in the form of profit for themselves from their employees.

Business owners extract benefit by getting employees to work for them, commanding and directing workers to produce the business's salable good or service, then keeping a portion of the net sales proceeds (after paying for non-labor expenses, such as materials, depreciation, and rent) for themselves rather than giving it all to those who produced the good. Whatever fraction of the total net proceeds of employees' work that business owners can take for themselves, they will take, pleading their right to pursue their monetary self-interest with their private property while insisting that they are not paying employees anything less than market wages. Thus, given the wages the owner pays them, employees produce, say, a day's worth of product or services, the net sales of which do not go solely to them. The portion above and beyond what the owner gives them as their wages is kept by the owner as profit. In effect, the employees work only a portion of the day for themselves; they work for the owner the rest of the day. To put it bluntly, the business owner is exploiting them. A business owner who tries to do otherwise will more or less quickly be put out of business by other firms willing to exploit their workers. Those who exploit the most will be most successful in competition in the long run.[8]

Still, although capitalists may be inclined by their positions of ownership to do all this, it is not clear that they are actually able to. Do business owners actually have this kind of power? If so, what exactly are its bases? Mere legal ownership of the business seems a flimsy guarantee that the owner can prevent employees from more or less avoiding commands, for example, by shirking and perhaps even taking de facto command of parts of the firm and of its net sales proceeds. In principle at least, the employees could have the decisive voice in all of the firm's decisions as well as its profits. The capitalist's legal property ownership and voice in running the firm might be merely figurehead powers, like those of the anachronistic monarchies still extant in many formally democratic nations today.[9] Although most people would acknowledge that real-world business owners are not mere figureheads, their power over employees should be considered more closely. What are the real sources of capitalists' power if not simply their property ownership?

EMPLOYER POWER

In principle, if the power relationship were otherwise structured, employees could indeed control the overall direction of the firm and take all of the firm's net sales proceeds for themselves in the form of higher wages plus perhaps some variable bonus income. That they cannot do so depends fundamentally upon two realities of their situation. First, they are on the short end of a distribution of wealth or property (financial and real or physical assets) in a highly unequal economy. Second, they generally find themselves in a labor market that is perennially beset by an excess labor supply, that is, unemployment.

In a monetary society, where there is a significant disparity in wealth distribution, those with enough wealth can, in effect, buy their way out of having to work for a living. Not only can they avoid work by living off the returns on their financial or real assets (dividends or profit, interest or rent), thus avoiding having to be employees in someone else's business. They also can buy their own firm or participate in the ownership of one or several firms.

Capitalist business owners may also work, but people on the short end of the distribution *must* work for a living. Lacking sufficient financial or real capital, they cannot live from interest or rental income, nor can they afford to invest in a business and become someone else's boss since they lack sufficient access to the necessary funds. Their own wealth (plus whatever additional they may borrow using their wealth as collateral) is insufficient to make the required investment. To subsist, low-wealth people must become wage employees in wealthy people's firms. Sufficient disparity in the distribution of wealth is thus the sine qua non of exploitable labor.

Still, cannot employees accumulate enough wealth of their own by saving and then become capitalist employers themselves? Some employees do just that, but the number who can is extremely small. Moreover, among those few who do succeed, the vast majority, judging by the numbers of small business failures, end up falling back into wage-employment status.[10] Can the employees pool their resources and cooperatively buy the firm from the capitalist? There are cases of employee buy-outs, but those with any degree of success are extremely rare. According to those who have studied these cases, the primary reason for this is insufficient investable funds.[11]

Capitalist business employees are not there simply because they prefer to be taking commands and being exploited but because they *must* be there, even though they do indeed generally "give their consent." The question remains, what is it exactly that prevents their accumulating sufficient capital to successfully escape? Moreover, even if those on the short end of the distribution of wealth must become employees in someone else's firm, does that mean they necessarily have to take the owner's commands and direction? Why must they do so? What is it that makes them "consent" to do so? In principle, the owner could be merely a figurehead commander of the firm's employees. What is it exactly that makes the capitalist more than that?

The market system has built-in mechanisms to assure both that employees' total compensation does not get out of hand (from capitalists' viewpoint) and allow employees to escape by moving up or buying out, and that employees will dutifully take the command and direction of their bosses at work. The critical thing here is unemployment in the labor market: an excess supply of labor or people looking for jobs who cannot find them.

First, unemployment is the key to wages never increasing to a point that capitalists might consider excessive. A supply of applicants who are in effect waiting outside the door and willing to accept jobs at lower than prevailing wages enables the capitalist to refuse whatever wage increases his employees may wish, and even to lower his employees' wages, ostensibly to stay in line with market rates. The threat that they may lose their jobs and be replaced by others eager for work sustains employees' willingness to take direction from their bosses and do the firm's work conscientiously and diligently, with the commitment required to produce the firm's product or service in sufficient quantity and quality for the owner to make the requisite profit. Unemployment similarly enables business owners to prevent or at least keep some control over their employees' propensities to use the countervailing power of unionization and thereby secure wage increases and an easier time at work.[12]

That the system naturally tends to full employment has long been an important element in the mythology of free markets. The myth is sustained by many in the mainstream economics profession, committed as they are to the idea of well-functioning markets. Nonetheless, there is always significant unemployment in the aggregate. As often as not, considerable unemployment is localized regionally, by industrial and occupational sector, and by race, ethnicity, or gender. Mainstream economists have supposed a "natural unemployment rate" to be around 3 percent. The actual annual rate has been at that level or below only once since the Second World War, in 1953, when the U.S. rate was 2.6 percent. Black unemployment is generally about twice the national level; for young Blacks, it is usually twice that, and young Black male unemployment is significantly higher yet.[13] Some Native American unemployment rates have been more than 50 percent in recent times.[14] How can it be that unemployment is ever with us when supposedly the natural direction of markets is to eliminate disparities between supply and demand, in this case in the job market?

PERENNIAL UNEMPLOYMENT

Aside from the simple empirical fact of perennial unemployment throughout capitalist history, strong grounds exist for expecting unemployment to have been the normal state of affairs in this system. Consider first the nature of capitalist technological change. As firms adopt new production processes or offer new products for sale, successful ones tend to provide labor-saving, or more precisely, labor-productivity improving, ways of fulfilling customers' wants and needs. This is an essential feature of capitalism as a historically ascendant system—it satisfies human material wants using progressively less human labor.[15] Such technical changes, however, release labor, that is, they cause people to be dis-employed in the affected industries.

In the mainstream neoclassical economic theory, those who are thus dis-employed should find employment elsewhere, since in the very act of releasing labor, technical changes reduce product prices, thereby increasing consumer purchasing power and providing increased demand for labor in other industries. But how soon the technologically dis-employed find new jobs depends critically upon how well the system re-equilibrates, that is, upon workers' mobility from one industrial sector to another. That depends critically on the amount and cost of the retraining and relocation that are required. Obviously, for some technical changes, little may be needed. For others, enough may be needed that re-equilibration cannot effectively occur before the next significant technical change throws the system off equilibration possibly even further.

Moreover, there is also the critical problem of selling the expanded output produced by a given labor force after a technical change that improves labor productivity. If it cannot all be sold, then production cutbacks will have to occur, generating even more dis-employment than the original technical change per se. Falling prices due to a technical change do not themselves guarantee that all the additional output can be sold when unemployment has increased because purchasing power also has declined. Only if enough of the dis-employed can retrain and relocate to jobs that pay sufficiently well compared to the ones they lost, and can do so quickly enough, will purchasing power improve. Moreover, given such barriers to quick re-equilibration, the new jobs must pay sufficiently more than the old to re-establish the former level of purchasing power after covering the retraining and relocation costs.

However, as has seemed all too common in recent decades, and contrary to the widespread mythology, if technical change is de-skilling, there is no reason to expect the dis-employed to find jobs that pay better than those they left behind.[16] If this is so, since the dis-employed then take pay cuts in their new jobs, there is no reason to expect that purchasing power will be sufficiently improved, even with the expected price declines, so that all the additional output can be sold. Barring a boost in aggregate demand from government, some lasting long-term unemployment is a likely consequence of technological changes.[17]

Besides the more or less steady stream of competition-induced technological unemployment, what may be called the business-cycle dynamics of the system also work to sustain perennial unemployment. To see this, consider the consequences if there were no unemployment for some significant duration of time. The employer-employee relationship would begin to unravel, from the boss's viewpoint, just as from that of the employee, things would begin to look up for a change. Seeing that the threat of dismissal is a hollow one, individual workers would begin to work differently at their jobs. Some would slack off, socialize more with co-workers, take more breaks, arrive late and leave early, take excessive sick leave, and so on. Emboldened by the prospect of the company's having no access to replacement workers, individual employees would press with increasing success for better compensation. Groups of employees would begin to successfully organize informal and formal labor unions, similarly pressing for and increasingly succeeding in getting better wages and benefits. Managerial control and discipline fall; labor compensation rises. The consequence for the typical business's profit rate is pretty straightforward.

At this point, in what might be called the normal course of affairs, the economic system may be expected to right things more or less automatically in the deteriorating balance of power in the workplace. For low profit rates due to "high" labor costs invariably lead to either capital flight or a capital strike. That is, business investment spending naturally either moves somewhere else geographically (where profit rates are more suitable) or else it simply shrinks, seeking higher returns elsewhere than in productive assets. Or it simply waits for returns to improve, and either way the consequent decline in aggregate spending induces a recession or depression. Voilà, unemployment naturally rises again to a level sufficient to undergird the power that business owners need to keep their employees working well and hard and not asking for too much.

Yet there is no particular reason to expect the recession or depression thus induced to automatically self-correct; that is a completely different issue. The capital that has flown or gone on strike may well remain out of commission, leaving the economy in the doldrums, until, to quote J. M. Keynes, "in the long run, we are all dead."[18] Since the Great Depression of the 1930s, this approach to sustaining the balance of power in the workplace and letting the economy right itself has not worked in the United States and other advanced capitalist economies.

Instead, when the balance in favor of employers deteriorates as workers get out of line, it may be a wage-price spiral or the threat of one that leads to a resolution of employers' dilemma. In this case, as labor costs and firms' product prices rise, if the monetary authorities accommodate the increased demand for money, economy-wide inflation will certainly ensue, as standard mainstream economics textbooks state.[19] The reason is that employers do not simply sit by and watch their profit margins decline as labor costs rise. They attempt to maintain their profits, by passing on their cost increases in higher product prices. Employees then insist on compensation increases sufficient to cover their rising costs of living. This inflation continues as long as monetary policy accommodates and gradually then becomes built into the economy as a routine expectation and a serious problem in its own right.

But the more fundamental matter is that as long as unemployment remains zero or negligible, the upset in the balance of power in the workplace cannot be resolved in owners' interest. It will be sustained in employees' favor if there is a significant duration of anything like full employment. Something has to give. In principle, only a couple of possibilities would seem to exist for a satisfactory resolution. An appropriately major technological change could generate enough dis-employment to bring things back to normal. This is a possibility but not a necessity. An intercession of some sort in the larger environment of socioeconomic and political realities that undergird the employer-employee power relationship may be undertaken. This might take the form of political and legal attacks on labor unions and workers' rights, either broadly or in localized cases that impact workers' ability to use their otherwise strengthened bargaining position. Cuts in the "social wage," for example, pensions, unemployment insurance, may also contribute here. Perhaps the simplest intercession would be a tightening up by the monetary authorities, invariably using inflation as the excuse. This would induce a recession and immediately re-establish the requisite level of unemployment, as was used to dramatic effect to stifle the stagflation of the 1970s. All of these things have occurred at various times in capitalist history.

CAPITALISTS PROFIT—IT'S THE SYSTEM!

This is a self-sustaining or self-reproducing system. Inequality in the ownership of property or wealth forms part of the foundation of class power. Those on the short end of the distribution of wealth must hire themselves out to subsist, while those on the long end hire them. The exercise of class power, that is, command over and exploitation of labor, then reproduces the already given economic inequality, as employers sustain their wealth with profit income extracted from the net proceeds of selling the product of employees' work while squeezing employees' income and ability to accumulate wealth of their own. The consequent perennial and episodic unemployment is the other part of the foundation of class power. Unemployment acts as a regulator (along with obliging action by government and monetary authorities) in the ebb and flow of the conflictual relationship between the two classes in the workplace, assuring wages sufficiently low and profits sufficiently high that enough economic inequality is generated to sustain and reproduce the class system.

This simple model brings into stark relief the essential features of the class system of the modern market society. The normal functioning of the market economy itself, with help from the authorities, generates and sustains the structure of power relationships necessary to a social class system. A number of major complications are yet to be explored, including the many ways in which things other than purely economic conditions undergird and sustain the class system. But the basic model itself nonetheless clarifies certain important concerns about the economics of inequality in the real-world market system, most importantly, the nature of profit as a form of personal income.

Employees are exploited in capitalist firms. Capitalists' profit certainly includes the proceeds of a taking from their employees. This does not square with the standardized perception of profit income, according to which capitalists make several important economic contributions for which their profit is typically asserted to be an appropriate and generally equivalent recompense. These supposed contributions have been proffered as rationales for capitalism since the dawn of this system. They have never stood up to critical reflection, however, as the following brief (albeit somewhat technically involved) point-counter-point suggests.

—Profit is often argued to be an indirect return to labor itself, insofar as most people who receive it do so by having put aside a portion of their labor income that then accumulates into the savings that they then invest in one way or another.

However, it is simply not true that most business investment comes from accumulations of personal savings out of labor income. Only a small fraction originates this way; all the rest, the preponderance of total private business investment, comes from business retained earnings.[20] More critically, if savings are accumulated from labor income over some portion of a working life, then although those savings themselves do represent a deferred part of one's earned labor income, the additional income from whatever assets those savings are put into (for example, as interest) is not a return to labor but to property. It is income above and beyond what has been earned by one's labor.

The key point about profit is that it is a form of property income. As such, it accrues to whoever owns the business assets involved, regardless of how they attained those assets and is thus the reward to ownership itself and nothing more. The same holds for all forms of income-earning property, whether the property is accumulated by saving or otherwise. Thus, interest received from savings accounts or financial assets and rent income or other returns on real-estate assets are similarly rewards to ownership and nothing more. Still, perhaps more strongly than with interest and rent income, those who receive profits may appear to have done something for their particular kind of income. Is profit actually a reward for some such contribution after all? Consider the most critical kinds of services said to be legitimate grounds for profit as a return on capitalists' supposed productive contributions.

—Business owners (as well as landowners, lenders, and other investors) receive property income for the very specific service they perform of managing resources, obviously a critically necessary productive activity.

Resources need to be managed, and managing them is surely a kind of productive labor. But owners hire managers to do that and pay them for it. Owners' profit income is the net of the salaries they pay their managers and other labor costs. In the case of smaller capitalists who actually do some management themselves, only a portion of their total income is strictly attributable to their contribution of managerial labor. All their income above and beyond that portion comes from merely owning the property involved, in this case, a business.[21]

—*Capitalists' profit income, like interest income, is essentially received in return for their refraining from spending their income on personal consumption, thus making it available for business investment instead.*

In neoclassical economic theory, in competitive capitalism, normal profit rates are determined by the interest rate on investments. The latter is determined by investors' supply of saving in conjunction with the demand for investible funds. The supply of savings is determined by people's propensity to refrain from spending on consumption goods. Capitalist profit, therefore, at least normal profit, like interest income, is thus said to be the reward for the service of saving, obviously another critically necessary function for social production, since saving must occur in order for investment in capital goods to be undertaken.

But for one thing, neoclassical economics by no means has a monopoly on credible theories of the rates of interest and normal profit. In Keynesian theory, widely upheld even within the mainstream of academic economics, interest rates are determined by the conjunction of liquidity preferences and monetary policy, not by people's propensity to save out of their incomes but by their demand for and the availability of money. People's saving is determined mainly by their income, not by their willingness to postpone consumption in exchange for a return of interest income. As for normal profit rates, if they are determined by interest rates in the long-run; in the short- and intermediate-run, they are determined by the states of aggregate demand and investment opportunity given the current stock of productive capital goods.

Aside from these abstract theoretical points, the neoclassical account is mainly wrong about the sources and motivations of saving. The richest capitalists, whose personal savings are the vast majority of total personal savings, cannot be supposed to be refraining from consumption when they invest in financial assets instead of spending their income on consumption goods. Their personal incomes are so great that neither they nor their families can spend even a major fraction of them on consumption. It is beyond their capacity to consume so much, so the excess must be either invested (in personal financial or business assets) or simply given away. As for that portion of their income that remains in their businesses as retained earnings rather than being withdrawn as personal income, its use is either motivated mainly by the compulsions of business competition (firms that do not invest in growth end up dying) or else is unavailable for withdrawal by owners in firms in which it is top managers who have control instead.[22] In these senses, owners' income cannot be understood as recompense for a service performed by capitalist owners, since either it would otherwise be performed anyway or else it is not even performed by them.

Finally, the majority of people who can save are indeed postponing the gratifications of consumption insofar as they are providing for their retirement by seeking the best arrangement of their lifetime disposable income (albeit that which is then accrued above and beyond their labor income per se is accrued property income, as explained above). But again, in light of the above comments, money saved by such motivations constitutes a small fraction of the total going to business investment.[23]

Next, consider the supposed justification based on risk-bearing.

—*As business owners, like other property owners, have taken risks with their capital by having it invested, the income they thus receive is the return to risk-bearing, another important productive activity when seen from the viewpoint of the larger society.*

First, although there are risk premiums built into many kinds of business profits, they are not necessarily explained by risks associated with production or with productive investment. Much risk instead arises solely from market speculation and manipulation. In such cases, any return received cannot be for a productive contribution. Indeed, as Keynes took pains to show, such activities are actually counterproductive to real investment activity. The stock market, for example, has been called the world's biggest and most wasteful casino.

Second, since government-issued assets, and especially U.S. government assets, are generally risk-free, only that portion of a private-issue asset's rate of return that is above the government-issue rate (that is, above the rate on an equivalent payoff and term-length government-issue asset) can be construed as corresponding to a return for investors' bearing risk. This is so since government and private issue assets that are otherwise equivalent are substitutable from an investor's viewpoint except for their risk premiums. Thus, a substantial portion of the total return on any private asset cannot be construed as a risk premium even by standard financial interpretations.

Third, the actual returns to risky business and financial investments are not returns to risk-bearing but to the actual success of the business or financial asset. This is easily seen insofar as owners of those investments that end up performing poorly enough to yield no return or a negative return receive no such compensation for having taken risks. If bearing risk is supposed to yield a return in compensation, why do those whose investments yield no return or a negative return not get such compensation for it?

Finally, entrepreneurship is usually thought of as consisting of the last three of the above supposed contributions, plus inventive or innovative activity that brings new technology or organization into production or provides consumers with new kinds of goods or services.

— *Profit is the reward for inventive or innovative activity, which is, of course, clearly productive.*

Partly this is an issue of semantics. If by "profit" one means the above-normal or what is called economic profit arising from successful innovation, then while that profit is often attributable to contributions of innovation, normal profit is not. Normal profit is best construed as the quantitative equivalent of interest, as noted above.

When economic profit comes from actual contributions of invention and innovation, the latter are more often made by other people than the capitalists who actually receive the profit accruing from them. Today most inventive and innovative activity in private businesses is done by hired technical, managerial, or marketing people. Moreover, looking at scientific research and development as a whole, most of it is done via government financing, that is, in public universities, in government entities, or in private entities responding to government contracts. In such cases, most people responsible for innovative successes are rewarded with higher salaries and promotions, not private profit. Historically, much of what the most famous capitalist inventors contributed was accomplished by employees whose work their bosses took credit for and also reaped the profit. Thomas Edison, for example, had a staff of employees. This is not to deny that there are real innovators who have profited only from their own efforts. But again, profit goes to the owner of the productive assets committed to the enterprise, be it an enterprise producing an ordinary commodity or service or one engaged in research and development leading to invention and innovation.

PROPERTY AND "THE SYSTEM"

Although perhaps not conclusive for some readers, these counterpoints should cast doubt on the notion that capitalist profit is a return for productive services rendered of the same kind that employees render for which their wages and salaries are compensation.[24] Looking at profit as just one form of property income, alongside interest and rent, sheds additional light on the role of the private property legal system in all of this.

In a nutshell, all property income is the reward solely of ownership and not of any personal contribution made toward the requisites of social production.[25] In effect, property incomes amount to no more than a return for granting others permission to use an owner's property. The business owner allows employees to use the firm's productive materials and capital resources and receives profit. Financial investors allow borrowers to use their funds and receive interest income. Landowners allow tenants to use their land or buildings and receive rent. All receive their "due" income, but in no case does it have anything to do with performing productive activity.

We may think of this reality as simply the way the system works and blame this or that negative feature on the system and not on any individuals involved in it. In the view of many, it is the very same system that provides the individual liberty so cherished by all people. Whatever the ill consequences, we can thus perhaps live with them. There seems to be no individual responsibility. People engaged in exchange or otherwise lawfully making use of their property are merely doing what they can with what they have and cannot be condemned for it. The culprit is the system itself.

This view of the property system highlights the sense that it seems an objectively given structure that is beyond any individual's ability to avoid, much less to alter or influence. There is certainly truth in that. But it is also a human creation, the product of choices made by countless people in history, the outcome of a process of social decision-making that is continual. It is always changing, in ways that we, its subjects, decide in all those contexts where the laws, rules, institutions, and norms of our daily social lives are created, altered, and enforced.

The system thus both embodies and is a product of social power. People in the specific positions and roles defined by the property system are responsible for the various exercises of power that it structures and permits and for the system itself.

It is not true that all of us are equally complicit in this system; some are far more complicit than others. The private property system is not merely a neutral structure of social order but the essential supporting structure of social class. Individuals occupying the positions of power that it confers have an interest in this system. Presumably, they use their positions, more or less consciously and intentionally, to command and exploit the rest of the population and maintain, strengthen, and expand the system that enables them to do so. The system is the artifact of countless power exercises in making, sustaining, and modifying its rules of social behavior over historical time. It is an accretion of laws, institutions, and norms whose enforcement manifests the ultimate power, that of the state. The creation and enforcement of those rules represents the acts of individuals using power positions at least equally as much in the private sector as well, as we will see below. Rules are a means of rule. Because the private property system represents the collection of rules that constitute the market capitalist society, that system should be thought of as the primary instrument of class in that society.

5. Realities of Class Today

The basic two-class model of social class outlined in the preceding chapter provides a solid groundwork for understanding social class as a power relationship. It certainly helps clarify the nature of capitalist profit income and the property system. Yet looking at class in the modern capitalist market system, one is struck by what seems a great complexity of rankings and statuses in industries and occupations, within which there is associated a range of levels of wealth and income and social privilege. How can one begin to make sense of all this with such a simplified model?

Of course, having economic status, privilege or social rank is not the same thing as having power over people. A great complexity of privileges, ranks, and levels of economic status may be consistent with a given basic power structure. To that extent, sorting out that structure in the real world may actually be simpler than it might appear. Nonetheless, the basic two-class model is too simple for much further inquiry into the realities of social class today in two important ways. First, there are other important power structures involved in today's class system besides that encompassed in the model of employer power. An adequate account of class in the modern capitalist market society should consider these other related systems of power. For example, in the political power system, purportedly democratic mechanisms structure class power in social rule-making processes. In the cultural power system, speech and other expressions in the media, education, and elsewhere influence how people think and live in a class milieu.

These other power structures do not share the stage on an equal footing with employer power in governing the capitalist market society's economic activity. What makes this a capitalist market society is the fact that although other power structures exist in forms long familiar in other kinds of societies, employer power is the key to the command of economic and many other activities. By contrast, for example, in traditional, that is, tribal or village-based societies, patriarchal or matriarchal kinship power dominated economic activity. In statist societies in recent times like the former Soviet Union, the state's power dominated economic activity. Still, power structures other than employer power are critical to the modern capitalist class system. They cannot be omitted from any account of social and economic reality today.

Second, there are other important and delineable social classes besides business owners and employees whose connections and roles in all of these social power structures should be examined. Even within the structure of employer power itself, that is, within the system of business firms and their labor markets, one other class grouping is essential for a clear understanding of employer power: managers are critical for everything about capitalist business firms. And other occupations and statuses would appear to constitute distinct classes in business and other realms.

THE REAL WORLD OF SOCIAL CLASS

Surveying the groupings of people most often delineated as distinct classes usually begins at the top of the social hierarchy, with those in the most superior positions of status or power. In the basic model, these are the owning classes, those who own businesses and wealth in general.

Capitalists and Rentiers

The very top may consists of those listed in *Forbes* magazine's annual "400 wealthiest" individuals and families in the United States, whose personal wealth collectively amounts to what is owned by the bottom 64 percent of households. Their wealth exceeds the GDP of Britain.[1] Contrary to popular mythology, a large majority of them arrived at this position because of financial and other advantages conferred by their families.[2] Some heirs have kept their ownership positions in the firms handed to them by their parents. Others have sold their inherited ownership positions for financial wealth. Others inherited wealth from the sale of original business ownership positions by parents or earlier family members. Thus, many in this top group do not actually occupy business ownership positions but are instead *rentiers*, people wealthy enough to live comfortably on the income from their wealth alone without having significant business ownership positions per se. The rentier class extends downward to a level considerably below the bottom of *Forbes*'s top group, perhaps as far down as the top 5 percent or more of the population. However, much further down than that, people do not have sufficient wealth to live upon comfortably without additional employment.[3]

At this historical moment, it appears that those at the topmost tiers of the owner and rentier classes are ready to assume overt command not only of industry and finance in but also of government itself. Thus, during President Trump's administration an attempt seemed to have been made at dominance by the owner and rentier classes within capitalist government. Although a new era in U.S. politics may seem to have begun, government in the United States always has been significantly peopled from the topmost of this class, beginning with the country's first presidents and congressmen. Capitalist power and politics will be examined more closely later.

Most rentiers lack immediate employer power and sufficient wealth to become owners of businesses of any great size while still avoiding having to work. But the closer to the top of the class of rentiers one is, the greater is the ability to use one's wealth to purchase sustainable and effective business ownership positions. At the top are many business owners, some of whom arrived at the top themselves as their businesses thrived. Others inherited or purchased their business ownership positions. Some may own several distinct business firms ("ownership" here defined as having controlling interest); others own mainly a single business (for example, Amazon's Jeff Bezos and Microsoft's Bill Gates). Certainly, most business owners, especially those of any size, have diversified their personal holdings beyond ownership of their main business firms. Hence, they are themselves partly rentiers.

There are altogether some 25 to 35 million private businesses in the United States today—corporations, partnerships, and pro-prietorships in all sectors including agriculture, plus a substantial informal sector. Many are quite small.[4] At the bottom of the owning classes are those who own and operate their own businesses with-out hiring employees. Many of these are "kiosk capitalists" at best, for example, sidewalk snack-stand operators or independent lawn-service providers. Many of these are not counted in the number of firms just mentioned, since they operate as often as not "off the books." Like rentiers, these lack employer power; they are not really capitalists. Unlike rentiers, however, they cannot even buy positions of employer power. Since they must themselves manage their own firms and do all the work of production as well, they are actually working-class people.[5]

A notch above them in the business hierarchy are small-business owners who can hire employees, even though they must do all or some significant portion of the managerial work themselves. They include those who employ family members, for example, many independent restaurant operators. It may be useful to define a true capitalist as a business owner who can hire one or more man-agers, such that the employer can totally avoid both production and managerial work. On that basis, the larger the firm, the more likely one would expect to find it owned by a true capitalist. By another definition, Michael Zweig, studying data on occupations, supposed that firms that employed twenty people or more were probably big enough to permit their owners to be true capitalists. Zweig found that about 2 percent of the total U.S. population of able-bodied, working-age adults were capitalists.[6]

Managers and Other Professionals

The groups at the bottom of the owning classes, that is, people who own businesses but still have to work in them to a significant extent, are what was once called the middle class. In the twentieth century, the historical decline of small business, the concomitant increase in the size of typical successful businesses, and the consequently increasing need for all sorts of organizational and technical expertise, the middle class came to include a growing number (in both relative and absolute terms) of two other important groups: managers and other professionals.

If "profession" means occupations that require full higher education (at least a bachelor's degree), including additional training, instruction, and certification, then the professions include medicine, law, accounting, teaching, engineering, architecture, counseling, scientific research. Today, business management itself fits this definition as well, albeit perhaps true that more can practice it without full certification or education in management than in other professions. Management here refers to the task of overseeing production processes involving groups of people working. Wage employees oversee the equipment they use in assembly work; their manager or supervisor oversees them and their work. Because other non-managerial professionals such as doctors and lawyers frequently are not wage or salaried employees but independent operators of their own businesses, and because many of these businesses employ non-professional staff or similar workers, such non-managerial professionals often do some managerial work in addition to their professional work. Alternatively, like other business owners, they may hire managers to oversee their workers.

These groups—small independent business owners, salaried managers, and many or most professionals—are middle class in that they stand between the true capitalists and true wage employees. (The latter are those who do not own businesses, are not in positions of command, and cannot live from the proceeds of business or other personal wealth.) Of these middle groups, managers are of particular interest because of their critical role in capitalist businesses, the defining institution of this economic system. In the typical firm of any size, they take the commands issued to them by their business's owners, usually expressed only in general terms, and then translate or refine them into more specific directives, which they issue to their subordinates. The latter may also be managers who take the commands from above and translate and refine them into even more specific directives to others below them in the hierarchy. At the bottom of the command hierarchy, production workers carry out all the various specific production activities required. This command hierarchy is both a site and an instrument of employer power.

At the top of the business managerial hierarchy, among chief executive, financial, and operating officers, especially of larger firms, managers have enough income and accumulated wealth to consider becoming full-fledged capitalists themselves. For many whose economic status is not sufficient, their positions in the business organization and in the broader business hierarchy may give them de facto capitalist ownership nonetheless. On the other hand, the lowest-level managers, such as floor supervisors, may not be much removed from the true working class, even though they have power over workers. Sometimes their titles belie a reality even harsher than that of their working-class subordinates, for example, in the length and intensity of their workday. Moreover, given their limited income, their inability to accumulate wealth also assures their exclusion from the higher reaches of the class system.

The typical large business may employ many other non-managerial professionals in various tasks: accountants, personnel or human resources specialists, finance officers, marketing and

advertising specialists, laboratory researchers, engineers, information technologists, lawyers, public relations specialists, and
lobbyists. Many of these are in supervisory positions over lower-
level professionals such as clerks in the accounting and finance
departments and lab technicians in R&D departments. Many
lower-level professionals are certified and have baccalaureate
degrees, but most lack supervisory power. Although they do have
powers that working-class people lack, they are nonetheless in
working-class positions in the business hierarchy. Many of the
professionals supervising them, on the other hand, do have the
ability to consider going into business for themselves, for example, in independent accounting, advertising, public relations, law,
medicine, engineering, or research firms of their own.

The Working Class

The true working class then consists of those without positions of
power. They are subject to superiors' power but lack power of their
own over those below them and also lack the means to obtain it.
Zweig estimated some 60 percent of the able-bodied, working-age
U.S. population to be in the working class so defined. However,
obviously, there are shades of meaning here, and counting those in
lower-level professional or managerial or kiosk capitalist occupations might increase that estimate significantly.[7] The working-class
occupational range includes taxi drivers, delivery truck drivers, hospital orderlies, physician's assistants, nurses, short-order
cooks, bartenders, police officers, jail guards, janitors, maids, bar-
bers, manicurists, cashiers, bricklayers, carpenters, electricians,
construction equipment operators, assemblers of machines and
electronics, butchers, bakers, textile machine operators, phone
solicitors, poll-takers, data processors, and computer support
specialists. Many working-class occupations require considerable
skill and often highly specialized training and certification, and
significant job experience. Other occupations require little or no
particular skill beyond a brief exposure to the work itself.

Some of the variation in the pay of working and professional class occupations is probably in accord with the human capital and compensating differentials model described earlier. Yet major disparities exist in the availability of occupational choice. There are, therefore, major wage and salary differentials among working and professional class people that must be attributed solely to unequal opportunity. And, to the extent that the class of wage employees, including many professionals, is subject to employer power, other major distortions in pay differentials exist simply because constructing such differentials is profitable or convenient to employers.

Many people in working-class occupations are independent contractors, for example, in long-distance trucking since that industry was deregulated, in gig work such as food delivery and ride-share drivers, and in household cleaning and repair. These are kiosk capitalists, in effect. Despite such jazzy terms as the "gig economy" and "subcontracting," the vast majority remain de facto wage employees of the firms with which they do business. Whether they actually work on their own or not, they are subject to great economic insecurity. They lack union-contracted grievance rights at work, pension and health insurance, and other benefits. The few who happen to make "high" incomes experience great income instability. Although they might not be subject to a boss's direct command, they are certainly subject to the vagaries of highly competitive and unstable markets or to the command of those larger businesses to which they are attached, either contractually or in other ways. In either case, their lack of accumulated wealth, whether financial or human capital, makes them particularly vulnerable.

Similar vulnerabilities have been on the increase among people in the "true" working class. Independent contracting is merely one kind of contingent labor. As part of a strategy to strengthen their power by assuring more compliant labor, employers have been striving in recent times to convert as much of the workforce as possible to insecure and ill-paid work. Part-time or temporary employees or outsourced employees (either independent contractors or employees of subcontracted small businesses) are invariably less well-paid and more insecure than those fortunate enough to hold traditional jobs in larger, established firms. This important current trend toward the use of contingent labor will be discussed further in a later chapter when we consider the subject of increasing economic inequality.

Even narrowly defined, the working class encompasses a considerable range of economic status and privilege. It comprises those few with well-paid, virtual lifetime positions in large firms in stable industries (fewer and fewer these days); as well as those paid sub-poverty wages in part-time or temporary, seasonal or migratory jobs with no security whatsoever, nor any compensation benefits such as health insurance or pensions. The primary labor market, as traditionally understood, is definitely shrinking these days. Working people everywhere are increasingly threatened with the prospect of marginality in the sense of losing the kind of stable connections with the larger society that depend upon a minimum of economic security and comfort.

Poverty

It is the threat of marginality that enables employers to exploit wage employees. That is the source of working people's insecurity, worrying their luck may fail or they may not be paying enough attention to the strenuous requisites of getting and keeping decent work. The essence of that threat is the frightening prospect of poverty. The previous chapter discussed the critical role of unemployment as part of the underpinning of employer power. Poverty is what the experience of chronic, frequent, or even merely occasional unemployment means.

About a third of the officially counted working-age poverty population are, however, employed. Such low-wage and marginal work is not at all merely the province of young jobholders.[8] Instead, as the visible face of unemployment and misfortune in the job market, poverty is part and parcel of the set of social structures that underpin class as a form of power. The physical, emotional, and social stresses that go with it are the lot of the unfortunate. Their employers may have downsized, outsourced or moved, for example, with their industries' decline or the globalization of their markets. Or their families were of the wrong race or ethnicity, or resided in the wrong part of the city to get quality schooling and decent jobs or college admission and financial aid. Or their parents suffered an illness or other catastrophe that prevented them from moving to a better job or paying for schooling. Perhaps they "made wrong decisions" in planning families, dropping out of school, and taking early jobs, slacking off at work, or confronting an obnoxious boss.

If so-called wars on poverty seem to have failed, even in this most affluent of societies in human history, it is an indication of the critically important role played by the visible existence of poor people in the social processes of work in a capitalist market system. Essentially, poverty is the threat required to sustain employers' power over their lowest-paid employees. Job termination cannot constitute a serious threat unless it implies a significant contraction in the employee's livelihood; hence for employees in the lowest-paying jobs, the required contraction necessitates the existence of an economic status even lower yet to make credible the boss's implicit or explicit threat of job termination. Eliminating poverty, in the absence of other major changes in the social processes of work, would undermine the very foundation of this economic system. Despite an occasional flurry of political rhetoric and hand-wringing, a real war on poverty is probably not possible in this system.[9]

These days the poverty population also includes large numbers of the globally dislocated, whose languages and cultural backgrounds cut them off from sources of social and cultural capital. The legal status of many of them—in the United States, they are referred to as the "undocumented" or "illegal"—shuts them out of even the most basic public services and protections. Immigrants are perhaps the most vulnerable of all to the harshest forms of employer power. It is upon them that practices of outright slavery in modern times have most often occurred.[10] Given the critical role of poverty in the class system, the regulation of immigration is an important matter. Too many immigrants who are too vulnerable (for example, the undocumented) tax the system of social protections. Too few, however, may tax the even more basic system of employer power.

FIVE STRUCTURES OF POWER

Reflecting upon the astonishing array of status positions—from the wealthiest of the super-wealthy, the few multibillionaires, to the tens of millions in the poorest and most vulnerable groups— what can one make of the simple two-class model of social power? Even employer power per se is more complicated than suggested by that simple model. Capitalists are not a homogeneous group, and their firms are of several different major kinds, not all of which are purely capitalist in form. Managers are critical in the employer-worker relationship but constitute a separate class. Besides managers, other groups are in-between owners and workers. And poverty as a social phenomenon, among both the unemployed and people with jobs, plays an important role in underpinning employer power.

All these and other considerations need to be accommodated in understanding class in modern market societies. So too do other important power structures besides employer power. In fact, analyses of social class as power invariably must go far beyond society's strictly economic realm because power works that way. Social power, certainly in modern times, is invariably built on multiple power structures undergirding and reinforcing each other. One helpful approach to thinking about the various kinds of power constituting the capitalist class system today is in terms of five distinct power structures that are effective in the strictly economic realm. Employer power remains foremost and is the heart of the system. However, four other major power structures are closely intertwined with it as constitutive of the class system: professional power, that of individuals in the professional class; business power, that of individual businesses in markets; political power, or voice in the making of public policy; and cultural power, wielded in the culture industries, especially the media and education.

PROCESSES OF EMPLOYER POWER

Employer power rests mainly upon two basic realities of the capitalist market system: economic inequality and unemployment. But the actual power that employers have over their employees is more complicated. First, employer power is also bolstered or augmented by the internal organization of businesses and workplaces. There, employer power is leveraged by organizing the workplace in ways that allow employers maximum control over their workers.

Using their power to limit workers' ability to exercise discretion over the organization of the workplace, employers can structure the workplace more in their own interests to gain even more power for more profit. Among the various alternative workplace structures that firms have tried and adopted, those that augment employer power have tended to survive in use since firms adopting them have been more likely to succeed and advance against their rivals in competitive markets. Several organizational features of the typical capitalist firm are easily seen to belong to this category. They have arisen historically because they have worked well in augmenting rather than detracting from employer power.

Perhaps primary among these is the expansion of management as a specialized segment of the firm. The increase in the fraction of the capitalist workforce engaged in management is partly caused by the expanding need to organize production in ever larger and more complex firms. But it also reflects the salutary effects on employers' control of their workers from improvements in monitoring and directing workers. This can be seen in the growing numbers of supervisors, overseers, checkers of various sorts, and associated staff and technologies.[11] Workers getting out of control, running things as they wish, may be taken as a direct function of how much the balance of power in the capitalist firm tilts in workers' favor. The expansion of management is about tilting that balance the other way.

A second organizational feature of the capitalist firm is the minute stratification and specialization of workplaces and tasks. This, too, is easily observed in business history. Some of it may be attributable simply to the well-known efficiency improvements gained from increased specialization. Yet increasing stratification and specialization within the workplace also make it more difficult for employees to organize themselves either for productive work or to resist employer demands. In effect, minute stratification and specialization serve to divide and conquer the firm's workforce. Workers find it more difficult to coordinate and organize with each other on their own initiative when they are in greatly different ranks and positions with different statuses and privileges. And employers then find it easier to play off different groups of employees against each other: white-collar versus blue-collar versus pink-collar, permanent versus temporary or contingent employees, non-managerial professionals (for example, engineers, researchers) versus similarly well-educated managerial professionals. Workers are thus prevented from organizing their work lives and their workplaces in their own interests and especially from resisting or struggling against the owners' interests, for example, by forming unions, going on strikes, sit-downs, or less formal actions.[12]

A third aspect of capitalist business organization that has served to augment employer power, at least in larger firms, is bureaucracy, the careful and extensive codification of a finely delineated departmental and command structure and the insistence on compliance with that code. In part, bureaucratization reinforces the effects of stratification and specialization just noted. Equally important, it also serves to deflect employees' attention from the discretionary powers of their bosses. Commands and directives, though issued by individual managers, appear instead to be impersonal or merely by the book or according to the rules. Managers and supervisors can say to their inferiors, "we must accomplish such-and-such" instead of "you must accomplish such-and-such," since managers now appear to be just as subject to the rule book as those beneath them. This deflection of command responsibility from managers and owners thus helps reduce disobedience and recalcitrance by lending legitimacy or at least impersonality to the directives of owners and managers.[13]

Employer power is also critically bolstered and strengthened by power structures and other realities external to the workplace and labor markets. One broad set of such realities determines the cost of job loss for employees who are terminated. Dis-employment is an effective threat that gets employees to obey their bosses' commands and stifles their "excessive" expectations about work and compensation. It is effective because it imposes serious costs on those who lose their jobs. Terminated employees experience major declines in their income and material security. The greater the decline expected by employees, the greater the threat wielded by employers. The amount of such costs the typical unemployed worker must bear partly depends on the extent and ease of acquiring unemployment insurance and other social welfare benefits, such as housing subsidies and health care.[14]

The availability of these things is determined politically, that is, as the outcome of public decisions that involve the exercise of power in another realm than that of employer power: state policy. As a generalization, employers have important and dominant power in politics, even if they do not always speak as employers per se. (Much of their political power comes simply from being wealthy.) Their power in politics bolsters the power they have as employers and conversely, their employer power garners the wealth they bring to bear in influencing politics. Of course, it is not a foregone conclusion that employers always win in the political realm, but what happens there matters greatly for the state of employer power in the firm itself, for it directly affects the cost of employee job loss.

Note that at the same time, given the income one may receive on job termination, the cost of job loss is also a function of the compensation employees receive at work. All other things being equal, the higher the compensation at work, the greater the cost of job loss, and the more serious the threat of job termination. Not only may employers set up finely delineated pay scales based on merit, seniority, and job classification to stratify their workforces; they may also use the overall level of workers' pay itself as a variable that affects employee incentives to work assiduously. Pay them a little more than one might otherwise be inclined, and they will feel more seriously the threat involved in possibly losing their jobs.[15]

Labor-management relations constitute another important and closely related set of external realities affecting employer power, and which also are determined in politics. The extensive regulations regarding employment, worker and management rights and responsibilities, and labor unions are critical in this regard. These include laws on minimum wages, overtime, health care benefits, retirement and pensions, accidental injury insurance, job safety and health, job termination, free speech, and assembly at work. They may be seen as integral in determining the full costs of job loss. They profoundly affect all working people, union and nonunion alike.

The laws on labor unions are especially important. To the extent that government-recognized unions thrive, even nonunion workers' incomes and job conditions are improved. At work, employers respond to the threat of their employees unionizing by buying good labor relations (that is, good nonunion labor relations) with wage and benefit increases. In politics, labor union strength translates into stronger social welfare and employment state policies and laws on such things as unemployment insurance, retirement, health care insurance, and the minimum wage. Such public policies serve both union and nonunion workers' interests by improving all workers' bargaining positions in the labor market and strengthening workers' ability to organize generally and to create unions in particular. Similarly, various laws, such as those on child labor, retirement, and immigration, affect the availability of a pool of relatively cheap, unemployed or semi-employed workers to which employers love to turn when seeking greater control over their employees. Thus, the political activities of labor unions have been critically responsible for whatever benefit these laws have given to working people in general.[16]

Obviously, the laws directly affecting unions are a key variable in determining their strength and prospects. Regulations on the formation of unions—how the certification voting must be done, how the employer may and may not behave as workers vote—are critical for the viability and strength of unions. So too are laws on how employers may relate to existing unions and their leadership, such as the arbitrary firing of union leaders, hiring strike replacement workers, worker grievance procedures, contract negotiation and mediation or arbitration, and legal and illegal strikes. All of these issues affect how well unions promote members' and non-members' wages and benefits, attract new members, and exert influence on relevant political issues.[17]

The amount and duration of unemployment in the economy, overall and regionally, and by occupation, is another important determinant of employers' ability to credibly threaten workers with job termination and is itself significantly determined in critical social power structures. Although the market system may regulate the level of unemployment more or less well, by no means is it completely effective in automatically producing the desired result from the employers' perspective. Sometimes it goes so far in generating unemployment that the demand for output shrivels. (As labor income falls, consumer demand falls with it.) As it does, business profits shrink as well. Other times, the market system fails to generate sufficient unemployment, allowing employees to attain higher wages and benefits from some of the income from production that employers consider rightfully theirs. Attempting a proper balance is one of the great tasks of the central bank in its role at the apex of the system of financial power. Fiscal policy is also involved, hence the determination of economic policy in the legislative and executive branches of government.

Finally, the larger informational and cultural environment figures importantly into the equation of employer power insofar as it affects working people's perceptions and attitudes about work and the labor market, labor unions, politics, what can be accomplished and what cannot. These have a critical bearing on the relative strength of employer power vis-à-vis workers. If employees do not believe in labor unions, for example, as seems widely to be the case these days, they will not even consider organizing them. The systems of cultural power in the larger society matter greatly in their role of sustaining the structure of employer power in the firm.

PROFESSIONAL POWER

In an important sense, modern society is run by professionals, that class of people with the trained expertise required for many of the kinds of tasks and activities characteristic of human life today. Knowledge and technology in many branches of practical human activity have advanced so far in the direction of in-depth specialization that extensive formal training is routinely required for practitioners in those fields. In contrast, whole sets of new, even more highly specialized occupations have arisen both within and alongside them. Business, government, and other organizations have become hugely complex affairs requiring trained expertise, not only in specific technologies and fields of knowledge but in that particular branch of knowledge having to do with organization itself. That latter branch has evolved a whole variety of important specialized sub-branches, such as accounting, personnel management, marketing, and finance. Each of which has also developed a variety of sub-specialties, such as advertising, product development, human resources, and organizational psychology.

The need for expertise in and coordination of difficult and interrelated activities and projects in modern society, along with the developing need for technical and command personnel in business and other organizational hierarchies of increasing size and complexity, underlies the power that professionals have individually and as a class. As market competition spurs continuing development along these lines, it has been conjectured that the growing power of professionals may even imply a revolutionary shift in the fundamental power structures of modern society. Both socialism and capitalism in their advanced forms are what might be called coordinator societies in this view.[18] Although power did seem to have devolved into the hands of the professional class in the historical socialist experience, capitalists remain the real power in capitalist societies. Still, even there, the power of professionals is a major phenomenon of modern times.

This power is not merely some abstraction of the special status or prestige of the educated class; it is a form of domination. Individuals in professional positions have and exercise power over other people. They can take those power positions primarily because of their having significant human, social, and cultural capital in a world in which these are unequally distributed. Those who lack these things must submit to those who have them. Human capital, as formally gained from general and specialized education, is the critical currency required to purchase professional power positions in modern society. The need for the services of people with special knowledge, and the fact that knowledge is costly, constitutes the main dependency upon which professional power rests.

Human capital and the social and cultural capital obtained with it are the currency of professional power. However, good, old-fashioned financial capital in the form of individual, especially family wealth, is the main foundation of people's ability to attain professional positions in market societies. Money allows access to not only the requisite education but also the requisite social networks and cultural faculties. And as with employer and business power, it is inequality in the distribution of capital that underlies professional power. If everyone had equal access to the capital required for attaining professional power positions or the means to escape subordination to them, no one could be subjected to such power.

Professional power is of two kinds, agency power and managerial power. The latter is exercised by those in hierarchical chains of command over their subordinates. Insofar as managerial power undergirds the ability to command people to the tasks required for fulfilling the goals of capitalist or bureaucratic organizations, it virtually defines the nature of management in such systems. But although in capitalist firms managers must have power over subordinates to manage, and while intermediate-level managers are in turn subject to the power of those managers above them (or, at the very top, that of the owners themselves), managers also have a kind of power directed upwards in the hierarchy. That is, they have a degree of power over their superiors. That latter power derives from their role as agents of their superiors in positions of asymmetric informational advantage. Just as lawyers are agents of their clients, doctors are agents of their patients, and auto mechanics are agents of their customers, business managers are agents of their superiors, and at the peak of the firm's hierarchy, of its owner(s). Modern hierarchical organizations, therefore, embody power relationships both downward and upward.

An effective organization requires that the downwardly directed managerial powers be decisive over the upwardly directed agency powers of inferiors in the hierarchy, that is, the agency powers. Without decisive managerial power, managers would have no place in the hierarchy. Indeed, the latter would be effectively nonexistent. Managerial power virtually defines the status of hierarchical intermediates in the capitalist enterprise. It is the form of professional power most critical to that or any other hierarchical organization. Entire faculties of graduate business schools are devoted to the study and development of managerial power (most often without acknowledging it as a form of power). Economists have perversely expended much greater energy studying agency power (seldom acknowledging that as a form of power either). In fact, it is the need to counter the agency powers that inferiors always have to some extent that actually defines and determines the need for managerial powers in the first place. Thus, it is best to begin with agency power.

Agency Power

Economists have long considered the principal-agent relationship a problem insofar as it may entail efficiency losses. But only rarely do they note that the essence of the problem is a power relationship. The agent has power over the principal by virtue of an information asymmetry, that is, the agent has information that the principal lacks and can use that information to their own benefit at the principal's expense. This follows from the nature of the contractual relationship between the two. The principal employs the agent to accomplish some specific end, and is motivated to employ someone rather than doing it themselves because of ignorance of or a lack of expertise in the techniques necessary to accomplish that end.

The agent thus can extract benefit from their position vis-à-vis the principal in the form of extra income or rent from the principal, that is, in mainstream economics terms, income greater than the minimum necessary to elicit the agent's services. Principals, aware that they may be ripped off, may nonetheless happily offer the extra money or benefits, insofar as that may discourage opportunistic overreaching by agents. Suppose the agent can get extra benefit equivalent to what they could take from the principal by means of some deception, for example, without having to make whatever effort would be involved in the deception itself. In that case, they may well choose to do so, since they do not risk getting caught and suffering possible contract termination or more serious consequences. But even with the extra benefit from the principal, they may take the risk and undertake the deception and take even more from the principal.. Either way, however, the principal is usually aware that the greater the agent's extra benefit from their relationship, the more the agent has to lose by either being caught in a deception or having the relationship otherwise terminated by the principal. Thus may the principal buy the agent's honesty.

Examples of such relationships in modern market economies abound: lawyers or accountants and their clients; doctors and their patients; automobile mechanics, construction contractors, even hairdressers and their customers; corporate CEOs and their stockholders—all involve agency power relationships. Indeed, all employees, not just CEOs and managers but ordinary workers, may have agency power to some extent vis-à-vis their hierarchically defined superiors in the organization.[19] For most ordinary workers, their agency power is too little to be of great consequence. But the incomes of people in many of these professional occupations are significantly inflated by the rent they can extract from their positions, in some cases quite spectacularly, for example, in the case of CEOs of large stock companies.

Principals invariably seek means to minimize the impact of their agents' powers. Economists' inquiries into the principal-agent problem mainly have been about how best to ameliorate that impact. In the context of running a capitalist business, the issue assumes especially great importance. In many cases, the particular knowledge that employees have that might otherwise give them power over their superiors in the business hierarchy may be so easily attained by others that the employees can be easily replaced with more compliant and obedient employees at little cost to the firm. For such employees, simple employer power by itself may suffice to stifle any excessive exercises of employees' agency powers. In other cases, however, employer power must be leveraged to be an effective check on employees.

The leveraging is often accomplished by technological and organizational means within the firm. Today's communications and information processing technologies, for example, enable improvements in the monitoring of subordinates in the business hierarchy. A major organizational enhancement of the monitoring of subordinates is the multiple layering of supervision constituted in the managerial hierarchy itself. Other organizational improvements include such things as group decision-making, improved congeniality, and multiple personnel evaluations.[20] Enhancements in incentives are also possible, such as those discussed earlier, and the use of evaluation-based pay, bonuses, and "efficiency wages."[21]

In effect, since manager power at all levels of the business hierarchy is merely delegated employer power, the latter effectively counters employee agency power throughout the hierarchy, as much among higher-level managers toward the top as among production-level employees at the bottom. But toward the apex of the business, in many instances, top-level managers' agency power over business owners gives top managers near-ownership powers themselves. Their position at the head of large and complex organizations of greatly diverse activity and their many connections with other firms and governmental organizations give them the ability to conceal much from their firms' owners and to organize their firm's information and decision-making processes significantly in their own interest. Thus, being able to effectively run things more to their own choosing, they can vote themselves into impregnable command positions with higher compensation (often including considerable amounts of their firms' stock) that amount to significant extractions from owners' profit income.

As businesses have grown in size, outside stockholding has become so diffused that controlling interest coalitions of outside stockholders have sometimes become impossible to form. Top management's ability to run things at its own discretion has increased even further. Indeed, according to the so-called managerial hypothesis, top managers are the de facto owners of many or most of the largest corporations, running them pretty much as they wish. At the same time, the outside stockholders have been relegated to a position of mere rentiers.[22] This almost certainly accounts for much or most of the increasingly outrageous disparity between top managers' compensation, especially that of CEOs, and that of the rest of the workforce.

Manager Power

Monitoring, supervision, and control by managers are the fundamental approaches to controlling employee agency powers in the firm. As a hierarchy, the firm constitutes a cascading of directives downward with increasing specificity and managers wielding power downward over successive layers of employees. At each layer, the manager is delegated with the employer's power, that of the firm's owner(s). The managers cannot claim power as their own; instead, they have been loaned it. Only owners have ultimate power. As an employee, the manager's job is to ensure that managerial power is best used in the employer's interest. Thus, whatever power the manager has is both by virtue of the employer and is to be exercised on behalf of the employer.

The power of managers consists in their ability to determine the status of subordinates—in promotion or demotion, retention or firing, granting or withholding pay raises. Subordinates, of course, cannot reciprocate. Managers are simultaneously subject to their superior's similar power. The power that managers have over those below them in the command hierarchy is supposed to be in the service of the supreme power of those above, the business owner(s). Their power over inferiors is not really their own. They may nonetheless have some discretion in their jobs that gives them real powers of their own over subordinates. Whatever such power managers have over inferiors exists only to the extent their superiors' powers over them are effectively incomplete. That is, their power exists only to the extent their superiors cannot sufficiently constrain them to abide completely by their employer's wishes. Intermediates in command hierarchies generally do have some such discretion; it accounts for many interesting aspects of life in hierarchical organizations. Thus, the critical aspect of managers' agency power over superiors is that they often can use their management power over inferiors in their own interest.

Their agency power may enable managers to inflate their incomes in two different ways, that is, above what they would receive for simply managing. First, as agents of the employer, they are generally able to take advantage of the employer to whatever extent the latter must offer incentives to assure their correct or honest behavior. Second, as managers with some independent powers of their own, they may be able to take benefit directly from those below them in the hierarchy. The lower the position in the managerial hierarchy, in general, the fewer are the potential economic benefits thus available for possible capture by managers from the exploitation of those beneath them in the firm's workforce. In both ways, managers get a portion of the material benefits deriving from their power over inferiors that would otherwise go exclusively to business owners.[23]

CLASS, CHOICE, AND OPPORTUNITY

Social class in modern capitalist market systems now appears to be far more complex than is suggested in the basic employer-employee power model. The system as a whole now appears as a highly varied and stratified hierarchy of people. Its delineations are not simply between two classes. Instead, the system comprises a variegated layering loosely organized around the two broad classes. The delineations between them are now somewhat blurred. And other social processes now are involved in the constitution of employer power besides wealth disparity and unemployment, notably, the existence of significant poverty, the artificial division and stratification of labor in the business workplace itself, and public policies aimed at appropriately securing the requisite larger economic environment. Other structures of power are foundational in the class system besides employer power. Professional power provides the requisites of the day-to-day operation of the system. Business, political, and cultural power systems will be examined later.

At each level of the class hierarchy and within each collective entity immersed in it, the employment relationship appears as the predominant organizing element. In that sense, employer power is both the linchpin and the distinctive structure of this system. Moreover, despite this additional complexity, the fact remains that the propertied, or more broadly, those with financial and human capital especially, but also social and cultural capital, are different from the rest of us. They are endowed with actual or potential positions of real, immediate power over others. As in all of human history, so too in modern market capitalist economies, the prestige and social status of the propertied are actually derivative of, not distinct from, their positions of economic power over others. The business, political, and cultural realms of modern capitalist societies, contrary to market mythology, do not temper or counter these basic realities of the class system. Instead, they are critical components of it.

A fairly realistic picture has been developed thus far of the basics of the modern capitalist society as a class system. Its economy is structured as a command hierarchy in which class power is not only present but an essential constituent. At this point, it might be useful to step back and try to consolidate things a bit before moving on. In particular, how does all of this jibe with the account of an economy in which people make their occupational choices subject to constraints, taking advantage of whatever opportunities are given them as they seek their best economic prospects in markets?

Class as power does not change our understanding of choice and opportunity. Unless one simply refuses to acknowledge the concept of power (as some have, especially in the mainstream of economics), there should be no major conceptual conflict here. To summarize in concise theoretical terms:

People may be thought of as choosing their occupations according to the human capital model, with compensating differentials and hedonic wages in labor markets, some of which may be competitive People's choices are subject to differential constraints arising from information imperfections and asymmetries, labor market immobilities, discrimination, inequalities of prior endowments of financial and human capital, social and cultural capital, and systematically segmented labor markets. The upshot is major systematic disparities in substantive economic well-being among people, disparities that are considerably above and beyond those caused by any actual differences in innate abilities. These disparities are also systematic in that they reproduce and magnify already given disparities in prior endowments of wealth broadly defined. Briefly then, class is reproduced in this system. The nature of the differential constraints upon people's choices is such that class disparities are not only reproduced but also magnified by this system.

What actually happens in the labor market is not simply people moving about in pursuit of their most preferred occupations and then proceeding to get to work. There is also an allocation of labor at work in processes of control by means of the exercise of power in the workplace. In capitalism, all work is allocated by power. As people choose occupations and move around in the labor market, they are simultaneously moving into one or the other of the two poles of a power relationship. By their lack of capital (broadly defined), most must move into a basic employee position. Others, by their possession of sufficient capital, may choose to move into a professional, managerial, or even a capitalist ownership position. Again, prior endowment or class background is the determining factor so class systematically reproduces class. But class now designates positions of real and immediate power over others, or else subordinacy to the power of others, in employer power or professionals' power relationships.

Consequently, the reproduction of class as power is qualitatively something far beyond that of class as mere economic status. In the latter case, the reproduction of class is the process of individuals' class backgrounds determining their opportunities. Those with higher-class backgrounds tend to end up in higher-class jobs, transferring to their offspring higher-class backgrounds. In class-as-power, however, in addition to that process, those in the upper classes exploit those in lower classes. They derive material benefit, that is, income, from them, in effect reducing the incomes of those in lower classes' incomes and raising their own. They thereby spread the differentials among the classes from what they would be otherwise. In class-as-mere-economic-status, the system passes on class from one generation to the next and magnifies class disparities. In class-as-power, structures of power and those benefiting from them effectively create even further class disparities. In that way, the capitalist market system itself creates class.

6. Business and Politics in the Real World

I t is a basic principle of major power structures in a developed society that they generally tend to reinforce each other, sustaining the entire hierarchy of which they are parts.[1] This chapter and the next will look at three power structures that are closely intertwined with employer power and professional power in the modern capitalist class system but exist and operate mainly outside the production workplace and the labor market. First, in business, structured power relationships exist not only within the firm and the workplace but among firms. Economists have been loath to examine power relationships within the economy. Still, the business power structure—the organization of the hierarchical relationships of command and influence among businesses—is a critical part of the class system of the modern market system. Not only does it guide or steer the development of the economy and society, but it also forms an important part of the skeleton of the stratification of personal wealth, insofar as the latter correlates with individuals' associations with or ownership of particular businesses.

Second, political power is essential to the creation and maintenance of the institutions and processes of daily life in a class system. It affects the rule-making in the public sphere that guides the conduct of all affairs, economic and otherwise, in the capitalist market society. It is a commonplace that money is power in the political realm. Since the converse is true as well, individual political power is closely correlated with class position. Political power is the very linchpin of the class system, and the political power structure is therefore a continually contested realm. However, given the correlation of individual political power and class position, the contest is more or less consistently one-sided in capitalist society on the most critical matters.

Third, cultural power influences and shapes people's attitudes, perceptions, and values sufficiently to align them with the requisites of life in a class society. It has a pivotal place in the panoply of power structures sustaining the class system of today's capitalism. Until modern times, cultural power worked through the institutions in which people associated with their families, communities, and churches. Today it operates critically and perhaps most visibly in the mass media and the education systems. These latter two institutions are loci of power that work to sustain and reproduce the class system and to assure that the messages and habits of thought conveyed in them are those most preferred by elites in that system.

The focus of this chapter is on business power and political power. Political conservatives have mostly tended to fear the power of big government. In contrast, progressives have most feared the power of big business. Where is the power behind the system in today's capitalism? The answer will become clearer in light of consideration of political power. However, an attempt to clarify here a theory of the state will not be undertaken.[2] This chapter will outline the structures of business and political power as they shape decision-making in those two distinct spheres of society and the class system.

BUSINESS POWER

The patterns of development of the modern market economy are guided most importantly by what may be called business power, a pattern of power relationships manifest in the hierarchical structure of the business sector as a collection of distinct but interdependent firms. Power generally lies in the hands of the largest individual business entities, the biggest corporations and networks of financial and nonfinancial businesses. In conjunction with the public sector, these guide or steer development with investments that lead the rest of the business sector.

This "guided capitalism," as it has often been called, is actually descriptive of all variations of modern capitalism.[3] The private sector of the capitalist system, contrary to the account given in introductory economics, is not a mere anarchistic hodgepodge of firms in anonymous competition with each other, all more or less equally disadvantaged in the melee. In their relations with each other, businesses are not like homogeneous particles in random motion, occasionally colliding. Instead, the business system is a highly stratified collection of distinct and greatly differentiated entities in an easily discernible power hierarchy. Influence reaches from the heights of international finance and globalized production down to the remotest, rural small business, and guides, with more or less gentle incentives, the directions of movement—of innovation, investment, and routine production—of all involved. Power in this hierarchy roughly correlates with a business entity's size. At the peak of the hierarchy, the largest transnational corporations dwarf many nations in their economic activity and social, political, and economic influence. At each level in the hierarchy, a firm may be surrounded by many smaller ones that are, as a group, subject to its business decisions. It and others like it may be themselves subject to the decisions of yet some larger entity.

To say that the business system is hierarchical is not to assert that it is inflexible; in fact, its flexibility and dynamism are well known, as is the pervasive competition that is also present. That competition and flexibility make it an effective organizational scheme for national economies. But what enforces specific coherence in its development patterns over time is the power structure that coordinates businesses at each level of the hierarchy with those above them. If the primary means of class exploitation in the capitalist economy is employer power, the main mechanism of economic system steerage is business power. Steerage occurs as profit is gathered by larger entities, including from those businesses lower down in the business power hierarchy and is mobilized in investment and production mainly decided at higher levels.

In this regard as well, the textbook account of mainstream economics is greatly misleading. So-called consumer sovereignty is not the main guide to the development of the system, at least in its larger contours. Consumers do, of course, exercise choices that critically decide certain matters. However, both their tastes and preferences and the available alternatives from among which they may choose are significantly influenced by business advertising and marketing of products and services. Businesses influence public policy in whatever directions are accordingly required, and shape and limit in various ways what choices are made available to consumers in the first place.[4]

In the process, profit concentrates in those entities in more powerful positions in the business hierarchy. Depending on the power relations within any such entity, the extra income is parceled among the business's owners, managers, and workers, and possibly other firms in its sphere of influence or with which it does business. For example, workers more often have successful labor unions in firms with power positions since such firms are more able to accommodate them. In such cases, the extra pay garnered by a union, in effect, derives as a portion of the firm's extra profit.

Similarly, because the managers in such firms often can garner for themselves a portion of their firms' extra profit, they are usually the highest-paid of all those in similar positions of responsibility. Therefore, profit rate studies of larger firms or firms with market dominance have not consistently found major differences in their profitability compared with other firms. In larger firms, excess profits tend to get parceled out by management, labor, and other recipients of the firms' spoils.[5] The hierarchy within the capitalist class itself is strongly correlated with the power hierarchy of their business firms, with those at the top in financial wealth also at the heads of the most powerful firms.

Several specific kinds of power relationships among businesses constitute this system as a power hierarchy. For each, however, an important underlying determinant of which particular businesses actually take power positions is simply their size, measured by their access to investable funds. As is true among individuals, where employer power is undergirded by differentials of wealth (as the wealthy can "purchase" employer power positions over those who cannot), so too is power in the business hierarchy undergirded by differential spending power among business entities. To see how this is so, consider two kinds of power relations among businesses that are especially noteworthy here: monopoly or oligopoly power and financial power.

Monopoly and Oligopoly Power

The textbook case of pure monopoly is the rare extreme of a much more common situation widely found in market systems in which a small number of firms controls an entire market. There are many industries where a single firm unambiguously dominates as the universally recognized leader in pricing and investment among several or many smaller firms. Oligopoly industries, in which a few firms share dominance, often behave in tacit or actual collusion as if they were one, even though each firm may compete against its rivals in other respects.[6]

Aside from the typical striving among all firms to achieve dominance over their rivals in market competition, barriers to entry are the most important cause of market concentration. Barriers limiting the number of firms in most markets to something far short of the textbook case of competition include:

- Scale economies that, often in conjunction with transportation and communication costs, lead to concentration in a large or small region or locale;

- Exclusive access to productive or other resources such as land or minerals;
- Advertising and marketing barriers such as brand recognition and customer loyalty;
- Strategic actions of larger or otherwise advantaged firms to prevent entry by rivals, for example, temporary price-cutting, strategic overcapacity, subsidiary cross-subsidization, and product differentiation in market niches.

Advantageous relations with government also are critical and deserve special attention. Patents and copyrights, trade protections, and special access rights are only the tip of the iceberg. Government contracts and tax concessions ranging from depletion allowances on federal taxes to breaks on state and local taxes for location go to countless businesses nationwide. Many receive generous loan guarantees. Public authorities and even special acts—of Congress, state legislatures, and local governments—routinely give largesse to individual firms.

Such realities hold at every level of market size, from the global down to the regional and local. Traditional public policy dealing with these realities, that is, antitrust and regulation, historically has been ambiguous and wavering in its enforcement.[7] It would be difficult to garner enough public resources and commitment to have much effect on the underlying conditions that lead to market concentration. Not to mention the fact that other aspects of government policy itself are aimed in exactly the opposite direction. Indeed, since the 1980s in the United States, public policy concerning these matters has arguably been downright hostile to even the stated aims of the laws. As discussed earlier (see the Appendix to chapter 2), scholarship and academics in economics have been of no help.

One or more barriers put a business entity in a monopoly or oligopoly power position. The rewards to such a position are well known in economic theory. All of this applies analogously on the buyer's side of markets ("monopsony" or "oligopsony") as well as the sellers'. Also, while often ignored in college economics text-books, the extra profit going to firms with such market power is actually an income transfer or redistribution from customers (or input suppliers) or from competing firms losing or being put out of business.

The critical but mostly overlooked reality behind the fact that substantial size is a requisite for a firm to attain dominance (on the supply or demand side of its market) is that invariably some investment expenditure is necessary to construct entry barriers against rivals. Smaller firms, lacking internally generated funds and thereby lacking access to external funds, are thus less likely to attain such positions. Accordingly, more are likely to be subject to the power of those larger firms that do have access. The smaller firms are forced to give some of their profit to the larger ones in the process of being competed out of business by, or as customers of, or input suppliers to, the latter. Thus, like all the other forms of power discussed in this book, market dominance (on the supply or demand side) both generates and is sustained and reinforced by economic inequality, in this case, significant differentials in spending power among business firms instead of among individuals.

Perhaps even more critical is the fact that today the real world is messier than the traditional models of market power. The biggest firms nationally and internationally are virtually all conglomerated across several or many different industries. They bring to bear in each industry such advantages as investment risk-pooling and the cross-subsidization of subsidiaries in the strategic pursuit of market dominance against rivals. This enables them to further magnify whatever market dominance their subsidiaries may already have in particular industries.

Moreover, given the powers thus associated with size, larger businesses are often the hubs of sprawling networks of legally independent firms that are suppliers upstream or distributors downstream in the flow of production or that produce synergistically related goods or services. Such networks constitute flexible business entities that extend far beyond the legal boundaries of the dominant firms at their core while giving the core or hub firms network power. They assure the firms on their appendages various advantages in competition with non-networked rivals, even as those appendaged firms are invariably dependent and subordinated to the core firm and accordingly surrender some of their profit to it.[8] And core firms are advantaged by such networking against their rivals, for example, in their flexibility of response to market changes and their steadiness of access to inputs or other requisites of production.

Financial Power

In general, investment expenditures are required often in the face of competition for access to inputs, information, or positions of power in the business hierarchy. Businesses have an acute need for liquidity (cash or another asset immediately convertible into it). Working people need liquidity as well: in a market economy, virtually every aspect of material subsistence requires having some money more or less readily at hand. For individuals, getting the funds for expenses incurred in lean or transitional times requires either liquidating other assets, such as savings or even one's home, or borrowing. The same and more holds for businesses, where the need for access to cash is typically continual. At least as much so as for individuals, businesses need a secure reputation of creditworthiness.

Lenders then—wealthy individuals, businesses temporarily with excess funds on hand, and financial firms, with their large concentrations of liquid financial assets and cash—are in a privileged position in market economies. In fact, their position is one not merely of conspicuous privilege but of power as defined in this book. Lenders assume a role in determining the behavior not only of their current borrowers but of those seeking their money. Borrowers and potential borrowers are constrained to do whatever is necessary not only to repay their loans with interest but also to sustain their worthiness of credit in the future. The loss of credit constitutes a major threat for a business or for an individual or family. Like employers vis-à-vis their workers, lenders need not necessarily assume an overt role of dominance over their borrowers. The latter generally obey the imperatives of working to repay their loans and maintain their creditworthiness, just as employees generally obey the obvious imperatives of their jobs.

Lenders often do, nonetheless, overtly intercede in their customers' financial and operational affairs. Thus, individuals who are close to loan default often must submit to financial counseling and change their behavior. In default, they must submit to more than that. Even financially sound businesses routinely must offer a position on their board of directors or elsewhere in their top management to a lender's representatives. And both businesses and individuals are usually required to submit to various forms of monitoring of the financial worth of their loan collateral and their other assets (often by state regulatory agencies).

Lender power per se is very often augmented by monopoly or oligopoly power.[9] Lending institutions of substantial size can augment their position further with network power. Lenders act as the informational hub of a set of economic activities—in a locality, a region, or an industry. They can use this position and their influence in borrowers' finances and operations to coordinate the diverse activities of the various spenders and investors using their money. Hence, lenders may determine the overall pattern of those activities. Those businesses most critically involved in such networks typically share "interlocks" of various kinds, for example, among directors or in stockholdings, with the hub firm.[10]

Although financial power per se has seldom been acknowledged among economists, its face becomes visible in certain instances.[11] In personal lending, redlining is usually discriminatory on class and racial or ethnic lines and a convenient and widely practiced mode of local development planning. And the extra-exploitation of low-income individual borrowers, cash-strapped with greater temporary needs for funds and little access to competing lenders, also is illustrative. In business lending, creditor-based network power structures in urban, regional, and industrial economic development have been extensively examined in scholarly, business, and popular commentary.[12] The submission of even nation-states to the overt power of finance is illustrated in the restructuring of defaulting governments' fiscal and regulatory affairs by lenders' coalitions, with help from their international representative organizations, and in the "structural adjustment" terms on loans the latter make to national governments.[13]

Even more clearly than in the nonfinancial sector, there is a hierarchical structure of finance as a specific sector of the economy in terms of institutions' size, status, and power. In banking, this structure manifests in the national versus state chartering system of banks and the role of large private banks as the "bankers' banks" for smaller, local banks. This hierarchy peaks in the national central bank system itself, the supreme bankers' bank. The power core of the hierarchy is composed of the large national banks officially designated for business with the federal government, foreign governments, and central bank branches. The rest of the financial sector—insurance and investment companies, pension funds—are networked, as are nonfinancial firms, with banks. At levels below national and international finance, sometimes the real power lies not in the hands of banks or even in those of other financial institutions. Often, large industrial or nonfinancial firms lie at the hub of major financial networks.

The bottom line of creditors' power is the interest and related income taken as a cut out of borrowers' incomes. Recall the critique of the idea that interest income is earned. In fact, it is no more than a return on assets owned, like profit and rent. It redounds to owners as the fruit of their power positions, not of any productive contributions they may have made to the larger society.

One of the critical roles of the central bank (in the United States, the Federal Reserve) in sustaining the class system has been to regulate the supply of money or loanable funds to assure a positive volume of aggregate interest income without too greatly stifling nonfinancial investment activity and production in general. In this regard, however, some choking off of the economy's real potential for production is necessary for sustaining interest and profit income. Interest rates are sustained by restraining the supply of money or loanable funds. Profit is sustained by the consequent unemployment, the essential bedrock of employer power, that necessarily follows upon restrained money.[14] Control of price inflation is ostensibly the primary function of the central bank's monetary policy. However, that is simply because unanticipated inflation is both the most immediate threat to real interest rates and an indicator of potential tightness in the labor market and slackness of employer power.

Since the Great Recession, the Federal Reserve has used "quantitative easing" and the monetary "accommodation" of U.S. fiscal spending to bring the economy to recovery. It has been difficult to sustain interest rates at anything near traditional levels. Indeed, real rates may even be negative at the time of this writing.[15] This is so worldwide and appears to be the long-term future of interest rates as well. One might wonder if John Maynard Keynes's "euthanasia of the rentier" will soon be at hand. In response to a correspondent who asked about that, Paul Krugman of the *New York Times* responded simply, "Not if the rentiers can help it."[16] Which, of course, raises the subject of political power.

POLITICAL POWER

Politics is broadly defined as a society's decision-making processes that lead to the creation, modification, and enforcement of its laws, regulations, rules, and mores. More commonly, it refers specifically to social decision-making about and at the level of government. Effective government encompasses rule-making that affects all other spheres of life. As the ultimate expression of the rules applying in all other spheres, government is also the last, decisive determinant of them, and politics encompasses those social processes leading to that determination. What is distinct about government is that it gives the imprimatur of enforcement by the power of the state to the laws, regulations, and policies it embodies. Insofar as the state holds the ultimate means of bringing power to bear—violence—politics is the realm in which those holding ultimate power in the society, those at the pinnacles of the society's power systems, exercise their power most visibly and decisively.

Although modern democratic structures are a major progressive advance over older political systems, politics in the modern capitalist market economy is notoriously the child of money. Universal suffrage, fully representative elected officials, unabridged political, religious, and personal expression, freedom of association—these and the various other specific institutions of the modern polity provide the citizenry a voice in government never before seen in the history of civilized societies.[17] Yet, as students of modern government know all too well, the political structures of democracy, in even the most progressive modern nations, leave much to be done in the direction of achieving real political democracy. Even such a mainstream proponent of the modern system as Robert Dahl insists that this system is not democratic at all but "polyarchic."[18] The system fails to be democratic most importantly because, although it facilitates citizen participation in their own government, money still rules.

The general principles of political power in modern market economies are the same as those of the other forms of power considered herein. Having wealth (more precisely, financial, human, social, and cultural capital) enables one not only to take a position of political power but also to avoid being subject to it, since one has the resources to counter, or to avoid or escape it. Lacking wealth puts one on the short end of political power, unable to take a political power position, and instead being subject to the political power of others.[19] Thus, although the democratic system ostensibly aims to give equal voice in political decision-making to each citizen, in reality, personal wealth is a major determinant of citizen input into the process. Those with more wealth have many more "votes" than those without, even if all seem to enter the polling place as equals. Money's influence in politics works in several distinct ways.

Individual Political Participation

Individual participation in political decision-making takes many forms, ranging from the simple act of voting to turning out for public demonstrations, from joining and participating in or leading civic group involvement in political activities to donating financial or other resources to such groups or to political candidates, from sending letters or other communications to public officials to running for or acting in public office. However, all forms of individual political participation require significant personal resources, and those with more resources are better able to participate.

This is obviously true of participation in the form of monetary donations. But it holds equally for other forms. Volunteering for political activities, for example, joining and participating in groups or campaigns or turning out for demonstrations, requires time, as does the simple act of voting. Indeed, so does the necessary act of registering to vote in the first place. Those on the shortest end of the income and wealth distributions may be completely shut out of politics for this simple reason. For example, their employers may not permit them to leave work early to vote. They often cannot afford transportation to the polls.[20] Informing oneself on the issues is also costly, and attaining what one might consider sufficient competence to participate may be prohibitively so for a lower-income individual. On the other hand, the greater one's affluence, the greater will be the time, energy, and financial or other resources available to participate in politics.[21]

Private Organizations

Politics in modern market societies are conducted through private organizations of various kinds, because individuals cannot accomplish much politically unless they are wealthy. Even some of the more notorious apparent exceptions actually have personal organizations of their own.[22] Private organizations, in effect, bring together and orchestrate individual activities toward common ends. They are highly effective in influencing government action, from legislation to the enforcement of laws, regulations, and policies. However, organizing for political ends is costly and requires financial and other resources. People must be hired as employees to accomplish many of the necessary tasks. Even if all involved are volunteers, their organizing efforts will require communication and material expenses along with their own time and effort. Organizations that represent the political preferences of affluent people, those more able to contribute, join, or otherwise be of help, therefore end up better endowed with financial and whatever other resources are required. Accordingly, they are better able to press their ends upon government. Needless to say, organizations representing the less affluent are more often out of such luck.

Lobbies, advocacy organizations, and research institutes or think tanks are among the most important kinds of political organizations. They may be single-issue or more broadly oriented. They may directly influence political officeholders in legislatures or the executive branch or indirectly influence them by addressing their citizen constituencies. Operating upon all levels of government, the main effect of such organizations is to set agendas, to define for discussion in government and the broader public not only the issues they feel require legislation or other policy action but also the appropriate ways to deal with those issues. To the extent that all such organizations depend on private contributions, money rules in the agenda-setting processes for political discussion.

Political action committees (PACs) and other similar groups channel financial donations to candidates for political office. Although the laws regulating officially designated PACs are stringent, like all other political organizations, these groups are nonetheless more effective in reflecting the preferences of those more able to make financial donations than of those less able.

The legally recognized political parties are similarly subject to regulations on their expenditures and collections of donations. Contrary to a widespread misconception, the affluent donate money and resources, including personal volunteering, of roughly the same order of magnitude to both of the two major political parties in the United States. This makes both parties more responsive to the preferences of the affluent regarding party platforms and office candidates than they are to those less well off. The Democrats receive most of the donations of labor unions and other organizations representing lower-income and working people's interests; thus, they are somewhat more responsive to them than the Republicans are. But such donor groups are less well-endowed than others (and especially so recently), and seldom rule in the Democratic Party, for the party must attend closely to its biggest donors and constituents.

Other private organizations not dedicated to political activity per se are involved, often closely, in influencing political issues. Labor unions, for example, are not mainly about political action (at least not in the United States) but do participate significantly in political activity. Still, the weight of private business in politics far exceeds that of organized labor. At every level of government, business leaders stay closely in touch with political representatives in government legislatures and executive branches, expressing their preferences and needs both directly and through their lobbies. Government officials, both elected and appointed, circulate through revolving door positions in private business and vice versa. While in public office, they also share common social groupings with private businesspeople. Although much of the networking process is highly regulated, private businesses are allowed to make financial and other donations to PACs and other political entities. It is their constitutionally and judicially guaranteed right to "free speech."[23]

Then there are those firms selling their services for direct purposes of political activity, such as political consulting firms, political public relations and advertising firms, and especially the mass media firms themselves that distribute political advertisements.

The services of these private profit-maximizing capitalist entities are costly and far more affordable for wealthier interests. As
such, these entities are inclined as well to bring the same sorts of
biases discussed earlier into public discussions on specific political
issues.[24]

Capital Flight

Government officials, in their relations with the private business sector, are well-attuned to business reactions to government
policy. This is not merely because of their close associations with
business leaders and their dependence on them for campaign
and other funding. More critically, it is because of the particular
kind of threat-based power business has vis-à-vis government in
modern market societies. The wrong kinds of public policies from
the viewpoint of business and the wealthy may incline them to
relocate to other political jurisdictions more amenable to their
needs.

This is a real threat. For one thing, the affected government
would lose important sources of tax revenues. Revenue would be
lost not only from the specific businesses and wealthy individuals
who might leave but also from local businesses and people affected
by their leaving, as purchases of goods and services locally disappear. Along with these losses of tax bases, jobs, and incomes,
sources of political funding are also lost, a not inconsequential
matter from the viewpoint of politicians.

The threat and frequent actuality of capital flight or "capital
strike" is a critical and well-known factor in local government
policy. It can dictate state and local government policies regarding taxes, regulations, zoning, and public services from roads
and infrastructure to education, health, welfare, and research and
development. It leads these governments to compete with other
state and local governments across the nation, and even internationally, for the beneficence of private business and the wealthy,
greatly restricting the possibilities for public policy.

Although capital can move among localities in search of the best offers from state or local government, governments cannot move in search of the most publicly beneficial businesses or affluent residents. They instead must offer incentives to them in the form of subsidies or lower taxes, suitable labor laws and other regulations, or public services such as roads, infrastructure, and public safety aimed at the needs of business and the affluent rather than the broader public. Since middle- and lower-income working people and the poor are less able to move, capital flight leaves them with revenue-starved local governments and poor public services. What is more, they are likely to be ignored even in good times under the mere threat of capital flight.

Capital then has state and local governments and their lower- and middle-income constituencies at a great disadvantage. In the United States, the tradition of states' rights to set important public policies rather than being subject to federal law has helped sustain this class bias in state and local politics. In effect, it forces these governments to compete for business and wealthy residents on matters of considerable consequence for the distribution of income and wealth.[25] Moreover, it should not be thought that the threat of capital flight is mainly a matter affecting only smaller governmental units. Public policies in even the largest of national governments are profoundly affected by it, as will be discussed in a later examination of globalization.

WHO RUNS THE SYSTEM?

The power of the state is certainly the ultimate power. Still, politics is about who wields that power. Therefore, in a critical sense, whoever has political power has the penultimate power. Who then has penultimate power? In view of the realities just presented, it would be difficult at best to make the case that popular sovereignty rules the U.S. polity. We need only ask ourselves what institutional aspects of the polity might constitute sufficient checks and balances on the powers of money to make it so.

If politics is about who wields the power of the state, then the fear of government is to that extent misplaced: the proper fear is simply that of unaccountable power. Where does the unaccountable power lie in the modern capitalist market society? It lies unambiguously in the private sector with the wealthiest individuals and families who run the leading business and financial firms and wield influence at the pinnacle of government. In the modern capitalist society, political power is, to put it simply, an element of the class system. It reflects disproportionately the preferences and interests of those in dominant class positions. Thus, in the directions toward which it inclines government rule-making, it mainly sustains and reproduces the class system.[26]

This is not to deny the truly progressive nature of the democratic states of most modern capitalist societies compared to pre-modern governments of a few hundred years ago and their kindred today.[27] Of course, some democratic states in modern capitalist societies are more progressive than others. But even in the more progressive cases, class—as a power-based hierarchy of command in the direction of economic activity, and the corresponding stratification of status and well-being according to people's place in that hierarchy—rules as much as ever in the modern capitalist democratic state.

7. Capitalist Culture

Culture may be understood as the entirety of the collection of ideas communicated among people as participants in the various social systems of information production and conveyance or communication. A great part of the flow of information occurs simply and directly between individuals or in small groups, for example, families or neighbors, in conversation, or localized artistic expression or entertainment. The accumulation of cultural capital is critically important for individuals in gaining social status as they pursue occupations. What is critical about culture from the viewpoint of power is that the information flow involved in its production and conveyance is mainly one-directional. Major imbalances exist among different groups concerning their participation in the construction of their society's culture. When some people speak or display or act while others attend or listen or watch, it is a one-directional occasion.

In every context in which cultural communication is continually one-directional, power may be implicated as a cause or an effect. In general, the utterances or expressions of some individuals or groups may be better attended to than others simply on their inherent merit. But the powerful are invariably better heard, better

attended to, than others. The fact that people choose which utterances or expressions they attend to does not negate the possibility
that power is involved. As discussed earlier, an exercise of power
does not mean that those subject to it are without choices. The
question is, what kinds of choices do they have? The kind of power
involved in one-directional cultural communication is what has
been referred to as value power, the ability to influence non-recip-
rocally the preferences or values others express or in accordance
with which they behave.[1]

Other forms of power and social influence besides value power
per se may affect people's values or preferences. For example, the
mere fact that workers are under the direction of their employer for
a large portion of any workday gives the employer disproportionate access to their attention. It also may incline them to listen more
closely to the latter's ideas even outside of the workplace and be
more open to the employer than to other people. Thus, employer
power often gives the boss some value power over subordinates in
the workplace. Employers may or may not be aware of this power
and they may or may not exercise it. Similarly, the behaviors of the
rich are widely emulated. Whether they have direct power otherwise over people, they occupy a disproportionate share of public
attention. The rich are typically conspicuous in their riches. For
the moment, cultural power may be taken as "pure" value power.
That is, people's values or preferences are influenced by nothing
other than the cultural communication itself, as opposed to some
other power relationship.

CULTURAL AND OTHER FORMS OF POWER

Still, if people can choose whose ideas they listen or respond to,
then how are they subject to power in merely being on the receiving end of the communicated ideas? Again, as in other kinds
of power relationships, in cultural power it is a question of the
breadth and kind of choices available to those subject to it. First,
if the communication is mainly one-directional, then the receivers

presumably lack opportunities to communicate their own ideas back to those originating the communication. Second, given that the communication is one-directional, if they do not have alternative sources of information (perhaps similarly one-directional) then it is more difficult for them to form critical or contrary ideas. Again, people's expressions or ideas may be attended to purely on their inherent merit (that is, because of their relevance intellectually, scientifically, or artistically). But if they are communicated one-directionally and if those attending do not have other sources of relevant information or ideas, then cultural power is implicated.

Such one-directionality that monopolizes communication generally derives from an imbalance among people of some kind. A power position, for example, that of an employer, may give an individual extra "voice" among people. In principle, the imbalance need not be one of power. Still, the one-directionality and monopoly of communication will yield cultural power to those doing the communicating.

Cultural power is also like other forms of power in that the individual possessing it need not necessarily directly exercise it on subordinates. Larger employers have managers who do the actual hiring, firing, promoting, and demoting of employees. Similarly, the person in a position of cultural power may merely pass on ideas through other individuals selected to actually express and communicate those ideas. In modern economic systems based on wage-labor and advanced, complex, and capital-intensive mass-communications systems, the material requisites for cultural power exercised in such indirect ways are considerable.

As a consequence, having or lacking cultural power in modern market societies—that is, being on the sending side of one-directional communication, or being on the receiving end without alternative communication sources—is generally a function of having or lacking sufficient wealth. Those sufficiently endowed with financial, human, social and cultural capital can "purchase" positions in institutions of cultural power and thus be on the sending side of communications. They also can avoid being on the receiving end and subject to others' such power by accessing alternative sources and perspectives on the ideas communicated. Those lacking sufficient wealth do not have the resources to purchase cultural power positions or escape being subjected to cultural power since they cannot access alternative communications.

How this works in the capitalist market economy may be seen by considering two important institutions of cultural power today. Institutions of cultural communication in modern market societies include the mass media, the educational system, churches, civic and similar organizations, and the family. Business and government also represent major such institutions, but their primary social functions are other than that of cultural communication. The mass media and education systems are singularly dominant institutions of cultural power. They are increasingly involved in the class system of modern market societies as the cultural influence of the family, civic organizations, and churches declines.

THE MASS MEDIA

Television, radio, films, newspapers, magazines, books, live audience speech, theater, and music are the main mass media. Today, these are being supplanted or supplemented by various digital and social media. Digital technologies deliver a great variety of entertainment, commentary, and commercial programming, using such technologies as satellite or cable systems, compact discs and DVDs, computers and hand-held devices. Social media have added an entirely new dimension to the mass media. They allow a considerable amount of bi-directionality in communication for a mass audience that thus has considerable freedom to participate in "the conversation."

Though barely past their infancy, social media suggest breathtaking prospects for the democratization of media culture because of their openness and bi-directionality. Yet whether their promise is positive or negative is not clear. Thus, while hundreds of millions of people worldwide now participate regularly in social media and while political and artistic expression and entertainment have certainly flourished on their basis, the private companies providing social media platforms have become, predictably, monopolies and have begun to use their positions accordingly. The factionalization of popular participation in social media has been widely rued. It is certainly responsible for much of the political dysfunction of these times. And while popular participation is widespread, arguably the quality and overall trustworthiness of its content is lessened relative to the traditional media, with some glaring exceptions among the latter.

The dramatically shrinking costs of producing and disseminating media content has permitted such broad mass participation in social media. Yet the costs of producing and disseminating higher quality content both there and in the traditional media remain prohibitive for most people and generally require considerably larger organizations. Theater-quality film, TV, and video programming for large audiences are beyond the capacity of individual amateurs, a few high-profile exceptions notwithstanding. That remains mainly true in radio where large area broadcasting is expensive, as well as in book, newspaper, magazine, and music publishing. In the latter, various factors, such as promotion, investigative journalism, and printing costs, similarly militate against the dissemination of higher quality communications to larger audiences. Consequently, concentration in both the production and dissemination of content in the digital media likely will continue in the newer media industries just as it has in the traditional ones.

Concentration among the traditional producers and disseminators of content has increased considerably over the last couple of decades. Partly due to extraordinarily lax public policy, only a small handful of firms now control nearly the entirety of the higher quality TV, radio, film, newspaper, magazine, book publishing, and music media, along with the digital media now associated with them. And concentration in social media has even become a public issue in recent years. But if a more careful public policy is renewed, as perhaps seems likely, the vast economies of scale in the mass media industry will almost certainly be little affected. Traditional media industry firms and maybe the few new digital era firms that now dominate social media will continue their dominance. They may even achieve greater dominance in the media as a whole.

Despite Marshall McLuhan's famous phrase of the 1960s that "the medium is the message," it remains as true today as then that the message or content matters at least as much as the medium over which it is communicated.[2] What is communicated in the media should preoccupy students of culture, even in these times of remarkable digital-technological wizardry, at least as much as the gadgetry and the amazing communications feats it can accomplish. Although business concentration is of great concern for economic inequality generally, concentration versus democratization in the media is especially important for the pernicious effects of concentration on media content. The fewer the sources of information competing for audience attention, the more likely is a homogenization or simplification of content, and the fewer are the alternative information sources available to those on the receiving end of the communications.

The typical media company today consists of many distinct media subsidiaries. However, no subsidiary of any such company is independent of the rest. All are subordinate to the head office, and whatever competition there may be among them is typically managed by that office. Concentration in the form of declining numbers of ever-expanding companies has gone quite far in all media sectors. Most local radio stations are owned by a small handful of nationally-based broadcasting companies. Academic and trade book publishing are becoming highly concentrated, as is mass-market book retailing. The music industry at the national and international levels is similarly concentrated. In the United States, just six companies now control 90 percent of all media, the same percentage that fifty companies controlled in 1983.[3]

These facts understate the extent of media concentration. For example, synergies are routinely constructed with common programming and other content not only across subsidiaries of single media companies, and not only across media types and geographical regions as well, but also across independent companies in media joint ventures. Local cultural uniqueness gets washed out of content amassed at a national and international level in highly concentrated media.[4]

However, there are two even more fundamental structural realities of the media industry in modern market economies that foster cultural, political, and social homogenization. First, the media are managed as traditional capitalist private businesses. Second, the primary commodity these businesses sell is not so much content for audiences as it is advertising space or time for producers and sellers of other goods and services, or alternatively, access by advertisers to their target audience groups.[5] Neither owners nor advertisers are disinterested parties in the operations of media companies. Therefore, these two realities result in a bias in media content that favors capitalist private business and the system of private wealth, wage employment, and private personal consumption upon which it is based.[6]

Such a bias would exist even in a competitive, private, advertising-driven media industry. Media concentration, however, aggravates it, especially when the state fails to offer alternatively structured media to compete against private sector media or does not effectively regulate the latter. The critical issue concerning the so-called democratization of the media as the new digital forms and social media potentially compete against the traditional media firms is whether alternatively structured media may arise from the development of the industry. That is, will media arise that are not based on the capitalist business firm maximizing profit from advertising sales?

The new media do provide more heterogeneity than the traditional media, hence at least in principle some diversity of alternatives to the traditional media's mainstream bias. Whether this can continue depends crucially upon the public regulatory stand on the new media as virtual "common carriers" versus their now hugely distorted role in serving a democratic citizenry. The issues here are enormous and far beyond the capacities of this book to address.[7] Whatever the future of the new media, the traditional media will likely remain a critical element in our cultural lives. Given the intertwining of the new media with traditional media, it behooves us to step back and simply consider the question of media bias in general.

Is there really a mainstream media bias? Political liberals accuse the broadcast and publishing media of a conservative bias; conservatives take the opposite stand. At this point, in a highly fractious political climate, at least in the United States, broadcast TV is sharply divided between liberal and conservative networks. Because of recent political developments, certain issues now are occasionally highlighted that have not been traditionally since they are flashpoints of real ideological difference. But is there really an enormous diversity of content in traditional media? Within certain parameters, there is indeed great heterogeneity. Yet it is still far less than could and should exist, for outside of those parameters, what content may be found is limited in scope. Certain dominant cultural elements take up most of what is communicated. Alternative content is minimized. Whatever diversity that does exist does not reflect an acceptance of or tolerance for diversity but instead is offered because of a need to sustain audience interest. This is done by providing some minimal contrast with the homogeneity of the dominant content, giving the impression of a lively competition among ideas.

The class bias of media content is most clearly seen in the United States. In European countries and elsewhere, a long tradition of alternative politics based on traditionally strong labor movements has provided greater balance. Here, except for recent, grudging media attention to the rising progressive tide in Democratic Party politics, one must search long and hard in the dominant mainstream media news, commentary, and programming for significant favorable treatment of:

- *labor unions* as legitimate, indeed critical, organizations repre-senting the interests of working people;
- *welfare benefits* as appropriate public insurance against labor market misfortune;
- *progressive income and wealth taxes* as the moral approach to funding the provision of public goods in an inequitable market society;
- *state enterprise* as an effective alternative to failures of private enterprise (especially in the media themselves);
- *worker-managed production* as a further critical step in the long historical progress of democracy.

Nonconsumerist, cooperative, egalitarian, and ecologically har-monious ways of living in human community are most frequently downplayed, ridiculed, or ignored as nonexistent, quaint, comic or irrational. At best, they are perhaps colorful but unfortunately unachievable.

While these themes are excluded, certain other broad themes dominate in the mainstream media and serve as a supportive mythology for the class system. Rationalizing the class system or simply distracting attention from it with other concerns, these ideas do not hold up very well under serious scrutiny. They often contradict each other. They are mainly sustained in circula-tion simply because of their usefulness to the status quo. Widely accepted as true, or at least true enough, they become not only the defining ideas of the society's self-image but also parameters guid-ing public discussion on policy matters.

A fundamental rationalization of class is the idea of individual self-reliance and personal responsibility for reaping what one sows and the implied legitimacy of most private wealth accumulation as fruit of productive individual effort.[8] Social stratification thus is presented as meritocracy rather than as a class system. Private enterprise, as the most efficient and fair of all possible forms of production and social organization, is an important corollary theme. It serves to secure allegiance to the system and thus prevent encroachment on it. Associated with this theme is the idea that government is inherently undesirable. Besides forming a consistent and coherent whole, in a world of totally asocial individuals, these ideas fit nicely, for as Britain's Margaret Thatcher put it, "there is no such thing as society, only individuals."[9]

Distracting attention from issues that would highlight social class is an increasingly important characteristic of traditional and new media. It is fascinating to watch the parade of distractions advanced one after the other when issues that all too obviously involve class arise. For example, when Occupy Wall Street and the Bernie Sanders presidential campaign insistently raised the issue of rising economic inequality, the media found it useful to divert attention with other issues. Particularly useful distracting ideas in this regard, at least judging by the frequency with which they are brought up, are the need for military vigilance in a world desperately calling for "democratization" and freedom from terror and chaos, and the role of immigrants and subcultures in domestic crime and other issues.[10]

And spectacle of all sorts—crime on local TV news, national and international scandal, the continual extreme hype of the professional athletics industry, the periodic (or continual) hoopla of political campaigning American-style—attracts audiences by the sheer excitement and fascination it generates. It thus attracts advertising and consequently tends to take a much greater proportion of the content of TV, radio, newspapers, and magazines.[11] The new media are themselves incredibly distracting these days, with online gaming and social networking reduced to pocket-sized jewels of enthrallment, leading to addiction for many and apparently moving entire groups to various states of abject delusion on a variety of outlandish fantasies.

Thus, the bias in the cultural content conveyed in the media in modern market societies favors the extant system of class in those societies. Certainly, the media are, to an extent, merely responding to the preferences of their audiences. They do convey, to an extent, the news, commentary, programming, and entertainment that those audiences desire. Yet the media also help form those preferences. They do not provide for significant public discussion of things outside the parameters set by the class system. Hence, they do not provide much, if any, opportunity for audiences to develop their preferences on their own. And in their functioning to distract people from critical matters people might otherwise choose to reflect upon and engage with, the media clearly go beyond merely responding to audience preferences. As now constituted, the media are a structure of class-sustaining cultural power.

They are, of course, closely dependent upon and intertwined with the other power structures of the class system. Those who manage and ultimately control media firms do so by the same employer and professional power extant throughout the rest of the society. They are part of the same wealth-based socioeconomic elite and occupy the same kinds of positions in media institutions as in other industries. And media firms partake in the system of business power with other major firms in finance and other industries. Media companies purchase their inputs from them, and sell to them, as advertising space, the right to access audience attention. Serving to help sustain the class system, not surprisingly, they are integrally a part of it.

There also is considerable overlap between the media and the political power system. Concentration in the mass media is at least as much the consequence of political decision-making (for example, regarding media regulation or the enforcement of antitrust laws) as it is of the economic development of the media industry. Media concentration tends to normalize biases in the content of mass-mediated communication on public issues. This facilitates the widespread acceptance, or at least tolerance, of certain ideas such as that a highly concentrated, unregulated, private capitalist mass-media industry is just fine. Thus, political power and the cultural power constituted in the mass media engender each other.[12]

Class systems almost certainly could not be self-sustaining without accompanying structures of cultural power inducing a high degree of acceptance. In the past, these structures were mainly built upon the family, the local community, and established religion. The mass media industry is one of two relatively recent institutions that have become critical for creating and sustaining the values and preferences that uphold the class system of today's market capitalist society. The education system is the other.

THE EDUCATION SYSTEM

Most people in the United States may not think of the nation's education system as a class structure. It is part of the sustaining mythology that education in the United States is among the best, if not the best, in the world. It is, according to the mythology, mainly devoted to assuring equal access to the American Dream. Universal and free public education is said to provide the skills people need for citizenship in a democracy and for productive work lives. It is widely recognized that many schools, even most, may not live up to the ideal very well. And while there are aspects of the education system that may need serious attention, most people believe that the system as a whole is at least primarily not an institution of class but one of democracy and equity.

Yet there is significant systematic variation in the quality of education institutions at all levels, not only between public and private schools but also among public schools. These quality differences are not random. They are mainly a direct function of differences in income and wealth of the students' families. Thus, the best quality education is found mostly in expensive private schools, even if not all private schools deliver it. In addition, the predominantly local and state tax-based financing of public education provides for more spending per student in wealthier school districts and states than in others. State and federal government expenditures help offset the local and state tax-based differentials among school districts and states, but not nearly enough to fully remove those differentials. Indeed, so-called accountability policies for teachers

and schools and charter schools probably work overall to aggravate them.

Moreover, in primary and secondary schools, family income
and wealth differentials mean that parents have greatly different
capacities for voluntary contributions of time and resources to their
children's schools. In lower-income secondary school districts, disproportionate numbers of students drop out before finishing their
high school diplomas. They drop out to supplement their families'
incomes or because they see little evidence in their environments that
finishing school will yield decent job opportunities. Demonstration
effects on their fellow students, even those who might otherwise do
well in school, can worsen further their schools' graduation rates as
they follow the example of the drop-outs.

Higher education is substantially differentiated in quality, not only between private and public but also among public
institutions. State governments have stratified the latter into a
multitiered system of schools ranging from premier research and
graduate-school quality universities to two-year, remedial-quality
community colleges. Is the real function of the latter to provide a
second chance for those who have made mistakes in high school?
Or is it that remedial schooling, the cheap alternative, is the
only higher education actually available to lower-income young
people? In recent times, moreover, rising higher education costs
mean that the cost differentials among all colleges and universities
are that much more effective in sorting out students by income
and wealth class.

At the very least, it must be true that the education system
accommodates the realities of the class system within which it
operates. Education provides the stratification of quality the class
system requires. People graduating from each level of the education system move into the variously appropriate positions in the
class system. The levels of the education system correspond to the
classes from which people enter it. In at least that sense, rather
than the education system working against the class system, the
latter structures the education system.

Moreover, as an important institution of cultural power the education system is implicated even further in sustaining the class system. That education is at least potentially an institution of cultural power should be clear enough. One could argue that as such, it is merely a matter of adults assuming and exercising power over youth in a process that is presumably necessary for enculturating the latter into any society, even an otherwise egalitarian one. Nonetheless, further consideration strongly suggests that the power structure of education involves much more than intergenerational enculturation.

First, the education system is not disconnected from the larger system of class power, even if the connections are perhaps less overt than in mass media. The mass media are run by privately owned entities that sell advertising for other privately owned entities for the profit of owners of both the media firms and their advertising clients. The education system is only partly privately operated. Most educational institutions in advanced market societies are publicly owned, managed by publicly elected or appointed officials and operated primarily out of tax revenues, not sales of any commodity.[13] Still, although that may represent a step in the right direction, toward separating education from the class system, it is only a step. Decision-making and the management and operation of the education system are disproportionately responsive to higher class interests. Looking at private education, that should be obvious. But consider how it is true even of the public education system.

To begin with, the professionals who manage public education are among the more affluent, not merely by having somewhat climbed the ladder of success but more importantly by the prior endowments of financial, human, social, and cultural capital required to attain their positions in the education hierarchy. They have some powers of agency vis-à-vis the officials overseeing them. Their position, however, is that of managerial power over teachers and others involved in the education process itself to ensure compliance with the commands of higher officials.

Teachers too are professionals, but generally, they are not particularly affluent and mostly occupy a wage-employment position.
Their agency powers vis-à-vis their superiors are significant—they
even have discretion over many of the details of their classrooms.
They are nonetheless substantially subject to their employers'
powers of hiring, promotion, pay, and retention, and especially in
primary and secondary education most have little discretion over
the content and methods of their teaching.[14] Despite significant
rights to tenure, the ultimate threat of job termination is still relevant for them. Those tenure rights are continually under scrutiny
and being chipped away by administrators and education system
officials.

Teachers' unions are widespread in public education. They are
effective in supporting the tenure system and teachers' pay and
relative autonomy in the classroom. Still, like most unions in
other industries, they do not generally participate in other policy
aspects. Unions are not at all widespread in higher education.
Moreover, although teachers' unions are strong, they do not have
a legal right to strike in most states. There is also an increasing
stratification occurring in the field of teaching, both in primary
and secondary teaching with the so-called teachers' accountability
movement, and in higher education too, as administrators create
various kinds of permanent but nontenured positions. This not
only cuts costs but divides and conquers teaching personnel and
their unions. It adds an additional punitive threat to the already
existing one of dismissal: demotion or being denied promotion.[15]

Thus, while public schools are not hierarchical in the same way as
private businesses, they are nonetheless hierarchical. Management
is quite top-heavy in the sense of being disproportionately representative of and responsive to higher class interests, particularly those
of the professional class. Do parents have a countervailing position
in this power structure? In principle, yes, but in practice, only the
most affluent parents have the time and resources necessary to affect
policy and decision-making in their children's educational institutions. School parent-teacher associations (PTAs) are notoriously

ineffective on education policy issues of any significance. Parents do have some exit power. They can find alternative educational institutions for their children if they wish, and in that way express their preferences about their children's schooling. But the ability to do that is strongly dependent on their resources, their own wealth or endowments of financial, human, social, and cultural capital. What influence parents have in the education system is itself strongly and directly correlated with their class positions.

How about at the top, in making public education policy in federal, state, and local government? The highest education officials at all levels are by and large from the propertied or professional classes. They come from and occupy positions with both employer powers and agency or managerial powers obtained through relatively privileged access to financial, human, social, and cultural capital. Of course, ordinary political processes, either direct election or else appointment by elected political officers, put them in their positions at the top of education systems. More importantly, politics informs the policies those administrators follow, and those political processes are broadly shaped by the society's class system. Although a single large area of government activity can be relatively free of such influence—for example, because of a historical tradition of populism—there seems little reason to expect that to be true of education.[16]

A second consideration also strongly suggests the education system, including its predominant public portion, is a class-sustaining, cultural power structure rather than merely an institution of intergenerational enculturation. That is the fact that, aside from what is communicated in the mass media, most or all of the important class-sustaining mythology comes to people through their education. Some of the same elements of the mythology that the mass media promulgate also predominate in the education system. In fact, mass media promulgation of the sustaining mythology is made possible by media personnel having been properly educated in the same education system. Audiences too are well-prepared to accept that same mythology.

Incidentally, the special role of economics in this enculturation process should not go unnoted. Its role in the late secondary
school and higher education curriculum is mainly ideological. It
serves well to distract from class issues in favor of applauding the
virtues of the market. This is indicated by its introductory textual
material, studiously hammered into the heads of millions of young
people as the last and only word on the subject, even as it fails
to rise even to the level of Adam Smith's theory as an account of
today's capitalist market system. It is mostly students who major in
economics who get to peek into more advanced treatments of the
subject, and the field mistreats them too.

Ironically, McLuhan's formulation, "the medium is the message," perhaps applies better in education than it does to the mass
media itself. Indeed, the education system, perhaps more so than
the media system, promulgates class-sustaining mythology not
merely by the content of the messages it delivers (in courses,
textbooks, and other course materials) but especially by the way
they are delivered to their target audiences, mostly young people.
Students, especially in public educational institutions and outside of the more expensive private ones, are well-trained by years
of repetitive experience to accept and respect the legitimacy of
authority (personified by teachers and administrators) and of an
ostensibly merit-based social stratification (in the progression of
levels of schooling and in the grading system). Similarly, they
become gradually accommodated to the behavioral requisites
of wage employment by being continually subjected to work
requirements under the oversight of an authority who expects
students to have enough self-initiative to conscientiously follow
directions but never to critically question the system of authority
and direction itself.[17] After such extensive and intensive experi-
ential training, gaining and practicing more critical perspectives
will be difficult for most people. Alongside the mass media
system, education in the modern capitalist society is a most
effective institutional means of providing the cultural requisites
of the class system.

CAPITALIST CULTURE

Culture, however, is not confined to what is disseminated by the mass cultural institutions of the media and education systems, or by the other traditional institutions of the family, religion, and social and community groups. Much of the actual creation of people's values and preferences occurs outside of intentional communication. Value power exists elsewhere than in the institutions of cultural power per se. Much value power is exercised, consciously or unconsciously, in the contexts of other forms of power, such as employer power. More broadly, the simple habits of living according to the dictates of a particular social context generate particular habits of thinking along with them, and these become, in effect, values and preferences.

Thus, there is a capitalist culture that arises with the modern capitalist economic system, in contrast with cultures based in other systems or traditions. Like all successful cultures, it consists of mythologies, ideologies, manners of thought and expression that are constructed partly by cultural power systems and partly by the mere habits of daily life dictated by the various institutions and practices of the society, all of which tend to bolster the power structures of the class system. This is not the place for a thorough explication. Still, some particular features of capitalist culture can be noted, insofar as they arise from daily life in that system rather than from institutions of cultural power itself.

For one thing, capitalism's restless dynamism continually disrupts existing social structures, as in a state of perennial revolution. Atomization of community and family relations proceeds, as people are in constant movement. Individual identification by locality, family, and community disappears. In its place arises the well-known individualism of this system, a worldview in which the person, and not the social context in which every person's life is lived, is the individual's primary guiding principle for every aspect of daily life. The need for wariness and a self-protective attitude in market exchange and competition in a system based on individual private property greatly strengthen this individualism.

The extension of this attitude to one's nuclear family is the last vestige of the individual's immersion in larger social groupings that once prevailed in the human experience. Atomization and mobility in a private property system not only give rise to individualism. They also offer some promise of betterment for individuals and their families to "move up," an ever-present enticement and an important distraction from whatever other disappointments, frustrations, and injuries life may bring.

This economic system's restless dynamism also has notoriously given rise to another related kind of distraction from the realities of class. The material affluence brought about by technological development and the all-enveloping commercialization of the advanced capitalist societies have led to a nearly universal consumerism, a quasi-addiction to the continual purchase of an ever-expanding stream of personal commodities as a way of self-fulfillment and the construction of self-identity. Insofar as individual consumerism is guided by emulation of other, more affluent people's lifestyles and consumer choices, it is especially effective in negating the resentment and other negative feelings people might have about economic stratification and class.[18]

Individualism and consumerism dovetail nicely with a view of the class system as based on meritocracy rather than power. These are highly serviceable mythologies from the viewpoint of those privileged by this system. Not only do they help sustain the system by diverting attention from its invidious side; the system's particular kinds of individual material successes also serve to strengthen these very mythologies. Some might even argue that there is no class system at all in this society. The worldview thus generated by daily life is then explicitly promulgated by the mass media and the education system. This further reinforces the status of both these mythologies and their promulgators as critical sustainers of the class system.

Has modern market society and its cultural power system

created conformist automatons of people? Does an analysis of cultural power imply that people are, in effect, brainwashed into lockstep with the requisites of that society? There is plenty of room for diversity even within the parameters set by capitalist culture and cultural power. Within that framework, the members of this society are, after all, individuals. But those parameters nonetheless form a constricting framework. Those who have struggled at its edges know it all too well. The capitalist parameters constrain what people are able and willing to think and therefore what they can do.

Moreover, it is not required that a successful class society be perfectly effective in inculcating its values and preferences in all its members. A majority suffices, or even a small minority, if those who are out of the loop are not sufficiently empowered to do much about it. Moreover, it could be that many who are in the loop and follow the social line do not really believe in that line at all but simply go along because it is in their material interest to abide or simply not think about it.[19] But in a world where most people are too busy working or distracted by the many diversions the system offers to give it much thought, how many true believers does the society require to keep it sustainable?

8. More Inequality, Less Flourishing

Class is the power-based hierarchy of command that directs productive labor and other economic activity; it stratifies status and well-being according to one's place in that hierarchy. This is quite a different picture of the distribution of income and wealth from that of the naive choice theory.

Economic inequality is not about different people making different choices. Instead, it is about different people having different choices available to them. Moreover, while it is an advance over simple choice theory to acknowledge that the different opportunities available to people matter, that is only a first step. It must also be acknowledged that power is involved in determining exactly what opportunities are available to a person. In a nutshell, class is about power and how some have it while others are subject to it. Because those with power generally take material benefit from those without it, class and power cannot be ignored or glossed over in any analysis of economic inequality.

In this book, the class system of today's capitalist market system has been analyzed as comprising five power structures, each defined by a particular kind of power relationship. The primary power structure defining the class system of capitalist society is employer power. Delineating the two major class categories, employer power structures the relationship in which most work is directed. Professional power may be thought of as the secondary power structure; it delineates other classes that are intermediate or intersecting or even outside of the two main classes, and it structures much other work accordingly. Business power structures the private sector as a collection of firms in a stratified hierarchy of influence and command in the direction of investment. Similarly, it stratifies the incomes and wealth of the people associated with the various businesses. The positioning of people in these first three power structures forms the main and proximate basis of the stratification of their economic status, that is, their class rankings in the distribution of income and wealth.

Political power and cultural power are closely intertwined with the other three power structures, with people in political or cultural power positions also often having power positions in business, professional or employer power structures. Political and cultural power play essential support roles for the class system, which could not flourish without them. Political power determines the system's rules: its laws, regulations, institutions, and policies. Cultural power serves to make people amenable and even allegiant to the system who might perhaps not be otherwise.

People's positions in each power structure are most critically determined by their wealth broadly defined—including all forms of capital, financial, human, social, and cultural. And just as those with wealth get power, so too do those with power get wealth. Individuals' actual positions in the strata of monetary income or wealth and class per se are greatly varied in reality. But it is their place in the five power structures that may be said to be the main determining factor.

Although economists used to be among those least concerned about economic disparity, the causes of increasing inequality have come to preoccupy a significant segment of the economics profession. Theorizing about the causes of the phenomenon is now thriving. This chapter will focus upon some of the current thinking about increasing inequality that is congruent with the main themes in this book. A small but significant fringe of the economics profession, along with many analysts in the other social sciences, has forcefully contended that power and class are at the very heart of the problem of rising inequality. Thus, this chapter outlines some of the most critical elements in what may be called a power theory or class theory of the recent trend of rising economic inequality. It contrasts this with several of the more salient mainstream economic theories. To so studiously avoid acknowledging that power has been the predominant factor in rising inequality, as the mainstream of the economics profession has done, is a truly momentous mistake.

DISPARITY AT THE TOP OF THE DISTRIBUTION

Most recently, public and academic discussion on rising inequality has focused primarily on how so much of the increase has occurred at the very top distributions of income and wealth.[1] However, it would be a mistake to suppose that rising incomes and wealth at the top are all that is happening. That is perhaps not even the most critical aspect of increased inequality. "Extreme" poverty has also been increasing. So too has the disparity in the overall distribution of wages and of labor compensation. But for the moment, consider this increase at the very top of the distribution.

To begin with, the trend of increasing wealth inequality seems to be mostly the result of increasing disparity at the top of the income distribution. Until the Great Recession of 2008, many commentators instead attributed the increasing wealth inequality to the corporate stock and housing markets.[2] Stock prices were inflating faster than housing prices. Since the wealthy are the main stock owners while the middle class are mainly housing owners, the wealthy got wealthier faster than the middle class. However, it was clear all along, and especially so after both of those markets collapsed in 2008–2009, that the real long-term impetus behind the rising wealth disparity was the increasingly top-heavy disparity of income. Specifically, what must have fueled the rise in both markets, even as the stock-to-housing price ratio increased, was the speculation and credit-over-expansion of the pre-Great Recession boom years. The rise in the ratio was fueled by the disparity in income growth. As incomes rose strongly at the top, they were disproportionately invested in stocks, bringing stock prices up quickly. Housing price increases, on the other hand, were fueled mainly by purchases out of slower-growing or stagnant middle-class incomes, with the help of mortgage credit overexpansion.[3] Thus, increasing income disparity at the top and not wealth inequality seems to be the primary issue.

Looking at the top income receivers both pre- and post-recession, consider first the top salary earners. These, of course, are at the very top of the business hierarchy: CEOs and other high-level managers and related professionals in those firms at the pinnacle of what has been referred to in this book as the "business hierarchy," that is, the biggest and most powerful firms, including and perhaps especially those in the finance sector. One fairly promising and much-discussed explanation of why these groups have gained such disproportionate income increases may be called the "superstar" theory.[4]

As most people probably know, incomes among top celebrities of all kinds in professional sports, film, and music have grown way out of proportion to the average incomes in other occupations, and relative to the averages in their own fields. According to the superstar theory, this has happened because of the expanding scope of "mass-mediation" in these fields. As the audiences of athletic spectacle, for example, have grown with the vast improvements in mass communication to include the whole world, the world has begun to contribute to the star athletes' salaries. Some top celebrities are among the top 1 or 2 percent in income distribution, and perhaps something similar is happening among others in those other groups. For example, similar vast improvements in communications and information technology have given financial firms far more "reach" than they had previously for marketing as buyers, sellers, or brokers of the financial assets and securities in which they deal. Indeed, the same technological changes—along with similar great innovations in transportation and the production scale economies of all kinds that have also followed—have expanded in all directions the scope of effective operations, purchases, and sales of most businesses of all kinds. CEOs are, in effect, brokers of their companies' positions, and top financial professionals are brokers of various financial assets. Those in the largest companies especially would be expected to benefit from expanding their companies' market scope.

However, the superstar theory leaves unanswered an important question. Referring to professional sports for analogy, why should athletic superstars be the ones whose incomes are most dramatically raised by the expansion of the market for athletic spectacle? The latter expansion implies greater incomes for the industry, but why for these particular people? Many others are involved in bringing, for example, ballgame entertainment to the public. Program production staff, photographers and their assistants, food service workers, maintenance people, and many others working at the stadium and in the media and communications sectors bring the game to viewers. Why haven't they participated proportionately in the greater income generated by the expanding market for athletic spectacle?

The question is not about the moral issue involved, but simply the facts as they are. It may seem obvious that more talented athletes should get the biggest income increases. Still, followers of team sports know that it is mainly the superstars who get such increases, not their lesser-known teammates, not even necessarily those who are also directly involved in their teams' successes. Again, as a merely factual question, why should not, for example, the TV production people and even the food service workers at sports events also get proportionately the same income increases as the athletes themselves? Generalizing, why haven't the proceeds of the expanding industrial and financial corporations, instead of going to huge windfall incomes for CEOs and top managers and professionals, been more evenly distributed, at least to a larger fraction of those responsible for generating those proceeds if not among all their employees? Before returning to this question, consider first another theory about the top 1 or 2 percent of salary earners' recent windfalls.[5]

As we have seen, a major reality of the modern large corporation is the rising power of top managers vis-à-vis their companies' stockholders. The dispersion of stock ownership among growing numbers of people and institutions has made it increasingly difficult for any one of them or any coalition to assume decisive control over their firm. This leaves a control vacuum filled by top managers who can manipulate the memberships and decision-making processes of boards of directors to their own ends. As the typical corporation's size has grown, its management has become more complex. It is often opaque to outsiders, especially those without sufficient education and training in corporate management and connections with middle-level managers. In effect, top managers' power has risen relative to that of stockholders not only because of stock ownership dispersion but also because of a stronger position in their principal-agent relationship with even those stockholders who have controlling interest. This is known as the "managerialist" theory. It is considered a relatively heterodox idea among economists.

One particular theory about the rise of top managerial compensation focuses on top managers' social interconnections or networks and the positive effects this social capital has on their effectiveness as executives.[6] This theory is almost certainly true. In effect, it supplements the basic managerialist model with the insight that the networking referred to in superstar theory has been rising in recent decades. Increased networking implies, moreover, that top managers may take advantage of broader "old boys" connections with each other's memberships across boards of directors. This enables them to manipulate board decisions, including those concerning each other's compensation.

The result is that the disproportionate influence of managers on boards of directors is responsible for their dramatically rising compensation. That increasing managerial power derives partly from the same trends as those underlying managerial control itself, namely, growing corporate complexity (for example, with increasing conglomeration and networking) and corporate stock dispersion. It also derives from the communications and information technology trends underlying the expansion of networks of all kinds, facilitating the social networking of top business managers. The greater agency powers of top corporate management vis-à-vis stockholders enable management to siphon off a greater share of what otherwise would go to stockholders.

Yet this power theory of top corporate managerial compensation, while seemingly an advance over the mainstream economists' theory, cannot suffice as a theory of rising economic inequality overall, and in part for the same reason as the superstar theory. Two important facts about increasing inequality are simply beyond the capacity of the managerialist power theory or the superstar theory by themselves or in combination to explain. First, among top incomes, not only top salary incomes but also property incomes have risen. Second, while top incomes have risen, incomes of those further down have stagnated or worse.

But neither theory is even about the second fact. Moreover, both are partial theories, and as such, neither theory, even supposing it to be true, can fully explain even the particular portion of the distribution at which it is aimed, the top. This is because what happened to the rest of the distribution also must have mattered for what happened to the top. That is, had incomes in the lower portions of the distribution not stagnated but instead continued increasing as they had after the Second World War, there may not have been sufficient left over for the increase at the top. Thus, since the stagnation of the lower portions at least partly caused the increase for the top portion, a complete explanation of the latter requires an explanation of why the lower portions stagnated. To understand why the top portion did so well, we need also to know why the bottom portions did so poorly.

Still, the first fact must be addressed too, that property incomes have risen, that is, the share of rent, interest, and profit in total personal income. Here, one factor that should be noted is the attention economists are now giving to the recent increase in market concentration. Monopoly market power has always been acknowledged along with "monopsony" power as concerns by the mainstream of the economics discipline. But both issues have been slighted in recent decades because of political and theoretical misdirection. More recently, though, they have come back into vogue among some in the field, and new research in this area is just now beginning to come into its own.[7] Firms with market power rip off both their customers and their employees relative to how more competitive firms would behave. Hence, people get squeezed both coming and going. That monopoly/monopsony income, or economic rent, as economists prefer to call it, as it is taken from customers and employees, accrues as property income to owners of the properties associated with those firms (stockholders, lenders, and landowners). When market concentration increases throughout the economy, as it has over the past few decades, most famously with the recent rise of the "new tech" sectors, the effect is an increase in inequality in the distributions of income and wealth.[8]

Rising market concentration would seem to go a considerable way toward explaining the increasing inequality of these times, but it can be only part of the story of worker income stagnation. First, consider again the famous wedge that has come between the long-term growth in labor productivity and the lesser rate of growth in labor compensation that developed after the mid-1970s (as shown in Figure 1.1 in chapter 1). Although labor productivity has continued its historical growth trend, total labor compensation has not. In earlier decades, labor compensation grew at about the same rate as productivity. More recently, its growth has fallen relative to that of productivity. In earlier decades, as productivity improved, the increases in output produced by the labor force went proportionately to the labor force. Accordingly, business and property owners and managers took income increases of about the same proportion as those that employees received. But since the beginning of the last quarter of the twentieth century, the increases in output produced by the working class have not gone to its members. Instead, they have gone to owners and managers, in the form of disproportionate income increases for these higher-income groups.[9]

The wedge illustrates both the dramatic increase in property incomes of those at the top and the income stagnation of those further down. A proximate cause of both is rising market concentration and the consequent shift in the power relations between labor and capital. Again, however, there is much more to the story.

UNEQUAL WORKERS, UNEQUAL SKILLS?

It is true that top incomes—those of property-income receivers, top management of large companies and financial firms, and international celebrities—have risen astronomically. These enormous incomes exert a huge influence on measured inequality. One might blame nearly all of the measured increase in inequality in recent times on income increases at the top.[10] But the fact is that inequality has increased throughout the distribution. That is, looking at the last forty or fifty years, at all levels of the distribution, disproportionately higher increases in income occur in higher-income categories. The closer to the bottom, the smaller are the income increases proportionately, and near the bottom, they are negative (decreasing). The incomes of the vast majority of the population below the top of the distribution are wages and salaries. Thus, the increase in inequality of recent decades is not strictly or even mainly a phenomenon of the very top. Instead, empirically it significantly involves the entire range of the wages and salaries of the working class. Thus, a third important fact needs to be taken into account: increasing inequality is apparent up and down the distribution of income, particularly in the distribution of wages and salaries alone. This is shown graphically for middle-class wages in Figure 8.1. Although the increase in inequality is apparently greater the higher up the distribution, it is also apparent at all levels of middle-class wages.[11]

The explanation for this most critical aspect of increasing inequality that has had the widest agreement among mainstream economists is "skill-biased technological change," that is, the fact that technological change in recent times has altered the distribution of skills required in production. Especially the digital revolution in communications and information processing has had an enormous impact on industrial and other production, for example, in robotization and digital control in mass production, in the coordination of geographically more specialized production units, in the control of inventory and transportation systems, and in countless other specific processes. The consequence of these changes for the workforce is a raising of the skills required in upper and some middle brackets of the skills hierarchy of the workforce. In contrast, the skills required in other middle brackets and lower brackets have declined and the number of jobs available for lower-skill employees has declined as a proportion of the total. According to the mainstream economic theory of human capital, labor compensation is, in long-run equilibrium, a function of the education and training costs workers require for their jobs. At the lower end of the job skills hierarchy, those costs may not have changed much, or they may have fallen. The higher tiers of the skills hierarchy are increasingly taken by occupations requiring both more education and more costly education with the advent of the new technologies. Thus, wages and salaries among higher tiers of the skills hierarchy have risen, while those toward the bottom have changed little or have fallen.

The skill-biased technological change theory of increasing inequality is popular in economics and elsewhere. Studies based on the theory, however, have had mixed results. For one thing, there seem to be difficult empirical inconsistencies with the theory. The beginning of the increases in inequality predates by about a decade the major technological changes highlighted in this theory.

Figure 8.1: Increasing Middle Class Inequality

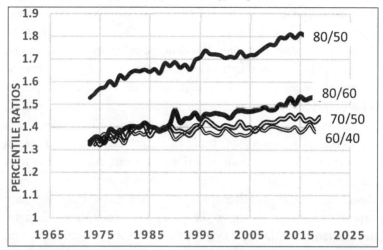

Wage percentile ratios, for example, 80/50 is the ratio of the 80th percentile wage to the 50th percentile wage. Source: Economic Policy Institute, *State of Working America Data Library*, "Wages by percentile and wage ratios," February 2020, https://www.epi.org/data/#?subject=wage-percentiles; author's calculations.

Also, the skill-biased technology theory suggests a corresponding increase in inequality in the distribution of education and training. Instead, that distribution has become more equal. Pay inequality has increased not only between different skill groups in the hierarchy of the labor force but also within each given skill group. Hence, even if the skill-biased technology explanation is correct, the question remains of why this intragroup inequality has also increased. Casual observation and some empirical study seem to support an explanation of increasing inequality that involves technological change. There must be, however, something else going on.[12]

There are profound theoretical shortcomings in any explanation of distributional matters based primarily on the human capital model and the presumption of well-functioning markets. That approach, because it tends to minimize the roles of market "imperfections" and of social and cultural capital, may lead theorists to forget the significance of opportunity differentials among groups, and especially among economic classes.[13] For present purposes, the most critical shortcoming in most mainstream economists' explications of the skill-bias theory is the failure to incorporate issues of power. If technological changes have indeed been skill-biased, then certainly one of the greatest enduring economic consequences has been their effect on the balance of power in the workplace.

The new digital and communications technologies have bolstered the powers of traditional professional (and semi-professional) classes with additional information asymmetries above and beyond those they had before those technologies. Their agency powers relative to clients have probably been greatly strengthened—for example, the powers of accountants, doctors, technicians, and managers versus their clients, patients, superiors, managers, and stockholders. The powers of managers over those below them have almost certainly been strengthened as well.

These changes in the power of people in workplace hierarchies would result in the same kind of change in the distribution of labor compensation as has actually been observed. Inequality increases up and down the distribution, as higher-ups increasingly siphon off larger portions of what would otherwise be stockholders' incomes. Similarly, independent professionals also are more able to secure higher incomes from their clients and customers. At least some portion of the increased inequality in labor compensation could easily be caused by the effects of technological change on these power relations.

However, a more critical aspect of the changes in power relations resulting from these technological innovations is their effect on employer power. At least two immediate impacts may be discerned, one direct, the other indirect. The direct effect of these technologies is in the workplace, specifically, the improved monitoring of employees' work and in measuring, comparing, and evaluating the work of different employees. Better monitoring makes managing workers easier by reducing the latter's "slacking" and occasional deliberate disruption. Easier evaluation of employees helps facilitate the invidious distinctions among workers so effective for dividing and conquering them. It also makes it easier to legitimize the firm as a bureaucratic authority by making measurement, comparison and evaluation more reliable and "objective." On both counts, employer power is strengthened.

The indirect effect has to do with the macroeconomic impacts of technical change. These technologies have generated unemployment, and those made redundant by them have mostly suffered lasting income reductions that have put downward pressure on wages economy-wide. First, the disequilibria brought by such changes represent turmoil in labor markets, whether or not officially measured unemployment significantly increases. They most often bring income declines for the people directly affected, even if not for the labor force generally. Second, although it has been seldom noted in mainstream economics discussion until recently, since progressive new technology almost invariably improves labor productivity, it poses major difficulties for the achievement of system-wide full employment even in the long run. Indeed, there has recently been widespread discussion among economists and policy analysts of long-term and possibly permanent technological unemployment, especially in light of the continuing revolutions in digital and artificial intelligence technologies. Economists now have accepted the possibility of such technological unemployment, to an extent nearly unheard of in the field just a couple of decades ago.[14]

The consequence for employer power in the firm is straightforward. The threat of job termination is now considerably more credible than before these technological changes. Property income and upper management income would rise relative to labor income with increased employer power. And with sufficient increases in employer power, stagnation further down the distribution also would be expected. The leveraging of increased employer power, further stratifying the labor force in the firm to take advantage of divide and conquer effects, would result in increased inequality in the distribution of labor compensation among middle-income groups in particular.[15]

Finally, unemployment exerts greater downward pressure on incomes in the lower income distribution levels, further increasing inequality. To the extent it affects the entire economy, like any other unemployment, technological unemployment strikes lower income levels harder. They are generally the last hired, first fired regardless of the technologies involved. James K. Galbraith's *Created Unequal* carefully and forcefully argued that unemployment due to "tight money" and a refusal to exercise a sufficiently stimulative fiscal policy were the primary causes of rising wage inequality toward the end of the twentieth century.[16] The proximately causal role of these particular policies must be seen against a backdrop of rising, technologically induced unemployment.

However, these pernicious effects of technological development are not all. They are compounded in the context of the increasing internationalization of the modern market economy, which is also brought about, in part, by the same new technologies at issue. Indeed, the internationalization of capital may have played even more than a strong supporting role. Consider the role of internationalization in increasing inequality.

GLOBALIZATION

The growing international orientation or globalization of the economy is often singled out as a culprit in discussions of rising inequality. Leading the trend among nations, the United States has embraced globalization and abandoned controls of cross-border movements of capital. Not only have imports and exports of goods and services increased dramatically as a portion of U.S. GDP, so too have the flows of real and financial investment across its borders. A dramatically globalized specialization of "American" production has occurred, as U.S. companies, both industrial and financial, have spread subsidiaries and employed independent, foreign-based suppliers of inputs and services worldwide. The same is happening with companies based in other countries. In the United States, workers now are much more likely than ever before to be employed in operations owned by foreign companies. Similarly, the banks, credit unions, pension funds, and insurance companies with which Americans do business are increasingly invested in the financial assets of foreign-based companies and governments. And, conversely, the latter are invested similarly in American production, assets, and land.

It is important to be clear about the causes of globalization. Contrary to popular mythology, the processes that have brought about globalization are not irresistible, natural outcomes of technological change. Without question, technology has been a critical element. Globalization could hardly have occurred without the radical cost-reducing and scope-expanding changes in transportation, communications, and computation in recent decades, including those to which the skill-biased technology theory refers. However, international trade and international capital and investment flows have always been, and will remain, at least potentially subject to control by state policies. They are the real heart of globalization as a social and economic issue. Globalization is thus at least as much the result of a convergence of national governments' policies, specifically, those favoring freer, less regulated international markets in goods, services, finance, and real investment, as of technological change.[17]

What are the effects of globalization on the distribution of income? Mainstream economists' views on this question have been mixed. Economic inequality may fall in developing countries but increase in advanced countries as both participate in international trade and investment. Or, the opposite may happen, depending on various factors, few or none of which are easily incorporated into statistical models to yield incontestable conclusions on their importance. Most economists concerned with rising inequality would probably concede that globalization has at least somewhat aggravated the trend overall. However, globalization is a fundamental factor in the trend of increasing inequality, indeed, it may be the single most critical factor of all insofar as it has been and remains at least partly subject to policymaking. For along with the new technologies, globalization has fundamentally altered the power relations of the class system of the modern capitalist market society.

Globalization has brought a considerable increase (often driven by necessity and not choice) in labor force mobility across international borders. It also has brought a much more dramatic increase in the international mobility of capital investment, both real and financial. People indeed find it easier to chase the available jobs elsewhere. By and large, however, people's mobility as labor is restricted by the full costs of moving relative to their incomes. Meanwhile, firms and especially finance find it easier than ever to seek and find the lowest-cost locations for production and investment across the entirety of the planet. If the labor costs of production in a particular location are too great—both *private* labor costs (wages and benefits per unit of output) and *social* labor costs (the taxes and regulations costs for public education, transportation, public health, and environmental sustenance)—then production can be relocated more easily to a more accommodating location, either directly or by importing from other producers whose costs reflect more accommodating locations. Capital, especially with its rising scale economies in both production and transportation, can more easily than ever before roam the world, seeking the most productive investment opportunities, which are, of course, those with the lowest labor costs.[18]

At the same time, as the ability of capital to move and globalize increases, the need to move and spread out internationally increases in step with the expansion of product and service markets beyond national borders. Firm expansion and relocation overseas are both easier to accomplish and a more pressing need in the face of rising competition from imports. Imports in these times are both more accessible everywhere in a globalized world economy and cheaper as capital investment finds less costly locations for production for export. Economies of scale and scope also play an increasing role in this cheapening of products and services as production expands and firms diversify and specialize across borders.

Once more, we have a change that results in a pernicious shift in the balance of employer power. Production relocation and import competition generate increased unemployment and labor market turmoil in an affected region or nation. By also directly raising the threat to workers of job termination, they strengthen the power position of employers over those remaining at work. This effect is independent of the strengthened employer power due to the new technologies discussed earlier. If the latter is occurring also, then globalization magnifies or augments its effect on employer power since the range of low labor-cost options for any particular technology-plus-skills match available for use in production now extends beyond borders.

EMPLOYER POWER RISING

There are additional important consequences of the momentous shift in the balance of power in the firm and the workplace. Not only does power yield wealth; wealth also yields power. Thus, increased disparity between those with sufficient wealth to assume power positions and those without such wealth tends to strengthen those initial power positions. It is also true that structures of power feed on or reinforce each other. Not only does each power structure foreclose options for those subject to other power structures, strengthening them by making it harder for people to avoid them. Superiors in each power structure, by accumulating wealth, may become superiors in other power structures. Thus, the declining share taken by labor out of the economy's total added value and the rising share taken by top management and property in general (profit, interest, and rent) largely occurred because of strengthened employer power consequent upon the globalization and new technology trends. But additional consequences further strengthen all the power structures involved in the class system, especially the core of the system, employer power. In a mutually compounding spiral, each of the power structures strengthens and is in turn strengthened by the others. And each moreover strengthens and is in turn strengthened by the consequent rising inequality of wealth, which strengthens all the power structures of class.[19]

Consider first the impact within the firm and workplace itself. The shift in the power balance toward employers due to technology and globalization has given employers the ability to implement in the firm such things as work speedup and reduced break time and the use of contingent labor (part-timers, temporary workers, contractors, "gig" workers). Increasingly, with spreading globalization, contingent labor is international in scope and ever cheaper. Labor costs are progressively cut by improvements in labor productivity or by direct cuts in labor compensation. Not only can wages and salaries be frozen or cut even in the face of continuing inflation. Concessions of retirement, health, or other benefits can also more easily be overtly or covertly forced on employees. Efforts to strengthen management—with expansions in the managerial workforce, better workforce monitoring (especially with new digital technologies), or greater stratification and bureaucratization—are more easily and effectively enacted. Perhaps most important of all, however, the power shift has enabled employers to take a more aggressive position vis-à-vis the one countervailing power workers have—labor unions.

Unions are directly weakened by the loss of active membership when a unionized plant closes or relocates (for example, due to robotization or globalization). Indirect effects are at least equally pernicious. When overall union membership declines, unions generally (not merely those directly affected) now have less credibility in their negotiations with employers over workers' pay, benefits, and working conditions. The threat of layoffs or plant relocation is now ever more real. Unions are now less able to elicit better pay and working conditions for their members, and employees see union membership as less desirable than nonmembership.[20] This spiraling decline in union effectiveness and membership removes barriers to even further managerial encroachments on whatever influence workers may have had in the firm. Nonunionized workers feel these adverse effects as well, since the threat of unionization is no longer as credible (or even present) to inhibit employers from exercising their "prerogatives" among workers, unionized or not.

Moreover, the ramifications of the decline of labor unions extend far beyond the workplace and the labor market. Unions are the only effective, organized voice of working people not only in firms but also in politics, culture, and society. When their influence wanes in a firm, it declines in political decision-making in the society at large.[21] The ability of unions to make financial contributions to politicians, campaigns, and political organizations, to lobby, and to pay for political advertising in the media declines with falling membership dues. Losing clout financially and in the workplace, they lose credibility in the media as newsworthy organizations. They never really had much clout in the capitalist media system, but in these times of media concentration, they may virtually disappear from the public's consciousness. The decline of labor unions and their visibility in the culture of modern market society affects both politics and the workplace. Unions may now just not seem "right" to people. Today, voting and other activities by union political constituencies and supporters have become confined to the 9 or 10 percent of the full-time workforce who are actually union members. For increasing numbers of people, organizing unions in the workplace has come to seem far-fetched.[22]

The decline of a union presence in the culture, and especially union influence in politics, have broad ramifications. It is in these processes that the rules of the game are created or given legitimacy by the state. As the disparity of wealth expands with growing employer power, the influence of wealth in politics and culture, now increasingly unchecked by organized labor, grows as well. Ongoing alterations in rules of the game consequently tend to strengthen employer power even further. The disparity of wealth cannot but expand as employer power rises. Labor rights and incomes are further squeezed while property and top management incomes, hence political and cultural powers, grow, in what is now a vicious circle.

The role of labor unions as working people's only means to

counter the power deriving from wealth cannot be overstated. In a social system of great wealth disparity, working people, lacking wealth themselves, have no other means of countering or escaping the power of the wealthy (not only employer power but also political and cultural power) than to organize themselves. Unions are the means of making the case both in words and in actions that working and lower-income people matter. That they have done so effectively in the past is shown in Figure 8.2.

A dynamic interplay between private wealth and cultural and political power also strengthens the professional power system, and even that of business power. Again, the increasing disparity of wealth means those on the short end of these power relationships are all the more subject to them. As doctors' patients, lawyers' clients, auto mechanics' customers, and so forth, working people are especially subject to the agency power of professionals. Of course, they also are increasingly subordinate to professional managers in the workplace. The shift in the distribution away from working people thus tends to benefit not only employers but also professionals of all kinds. Professionals' expanding powers yield them growing wealth, hence, their influence in politics and culture grows, further bolstering their power positions.

In the business power system, smaller businesses are subordinate to bigger ones. As the concentration of personal wealth proceeds, those who benefit most tend to be associated with bigger businesses. The disproportionate influence of larger corporations, politically and culturally, is most likely to favor rules of the game that bolster rather than undermine the system of business power. This tends to be detrimental generally to smaller businesses as bigger firms' positions of monopoly, financial, or network power are strengthened. Many smaller businesses share somewhat in the benefits to the business sector from the general squeeze on labor, but many do not. Those that share in the benefits forego some or all to the larger firms higher up in the business hierarchy with whom they do business and whose power over them is strengthened.

Figure 8.2: Unionization Rate and Inequality

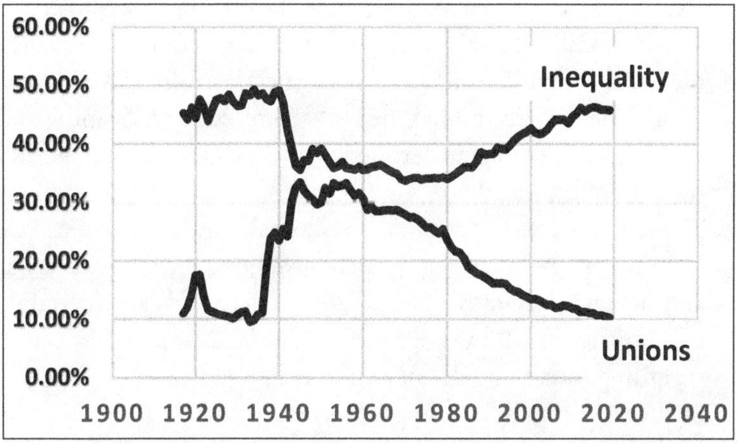

Union membership rate and share of total income taken by the top 10 percent. From H. Shierholz, "Working People Have Been Thwarted in Their Efforts to Bargain for Better Wages by Attacks on Unions," Economic Policy Institute, August 2019.

CHANGING THE RULES OF THE GAME

The rules of the game in the age of globalization and digital technology are progressively stacked in favor of capital over labor. They also favor professionals over their subordinates and clients, and big businesses over smaller ones. A list of some of the changes in state policy that have occurred in recent decades might help make the point:

- Total erosion of federal government enforcement of workers' existing rights in labor law, as the National Labor Relations Board fails to prosecute employers' violations of union organizers' and leaders' rights to their jobs and of workers' rights to organize.
- Decline in the real federal minimum wage. Even when the most recent wage was set (over ten years ago!), the minimum wage in real terms remained substantially less than it was in the 1960s, keeping the wage floor low.

- Welfare reform,   that is, replacing Aid to Families with Dependent Children (AFDC) with Temporary Assistance for Needy Families (TANF), raised the costs of job loss and made the threat of job termination more effective. With TANF, work requirements were added, benefits were cut significantly, and the real value of benefits eroded over time by inflation (as with the minimum wage).
- The rise and consolidation of neo-liberal "anti-antitrust" as U.S. government policy, as indicated instances such as the arguably lenient resolution of the 2001 Microsoft case (certainly in comparison with the European Union's case), and in policy regarding media and financial and banking mergers.
- Failure to bring adequate government initiative to bear in the health care industry as it evolves in the direction of private big business medicine. This has allowed the privatization of public and nonprofit hospitals, the rise of big private corporate health insurance, a mega-pharmaceutical industry, and a progressive undermining of the Affordable Care Act.
- Decline in the federal subsidies of state and local public education that were intended to help balance regressive, property-based local tax systems, with the near cessation of federal revenue-sharing with state and local governments.
- Continual decline in the progressiveness of federal income taxation, especially with cuts in effective tax rates on capital gains, inheritances, and corporate profits, the latest chapter being the Trump-GOP tax cuts of 2017.
- Deregulation or slackening of enforcement of existing regulations on industry and finance more or less across the board. Examples include trucking (leading to independent "small business truckers" and the decline of the Teamsters Union); securities, banking, and lending (leading to the housing collapse and the Great Recession); electric power (leading to the California energy crisis of 2001); offshore oil drilling (leading to the Gulf spill of 2010) and other environmental restrictions (for example, on mining on public lands); fast food, especially

in schools (contributing to mass obesity); TV advertising, including but not exclusively that aimed at children (leading to hegemonic schlock broadcast TV).

As noted earlier, globalization, as a collection of rules of the game written by political units large and small all over the world, spread not merely as the outcome of technological change but especially as the result of state policies, in particular the deregulation of international financial flows. The application of political and military power in international relations by the developed nations, especially the United States, along with the economic power of their international agencies, such as the World Bank and the International Monetary Fund, have been critical factors in bringing about the requisite coordination in national government policies.

More than anything else perhaps, the anti-government cultural and political sentiment of these times has provided the background necessary for the successful implementation of the above list of policies, including those involved in globalization itself. That background, however, far from being merely a reaction to big, corrupt government, is a created mythology engendered by and undergirding the power structures of the class system, both a consequence and an instrument of the strengthened dominance of wealth over working people. Fox News and other reactionary TV and radio networks have been perhaps most pernicious in the promulgation of this recent development.[23] Yet the rise of "anti-governmentism" in the United States predated these mass media. It should not go unsaid that its rise in the field of economics, under the leadership of the "Chicago school," is a central piece of the story.[24]

As of this writing, a change in the general direction of these trends seems to be occurring. Public reaction is growing, in response to the developments listed earlier, to the Great Recession of 2008, and to the general rise of inequality itself. The political balance seems to be shifting. Yet it will take a good deal more than public reaction to bring about significant and lasting change in the present direction of things. An enduring change in the balance of powers in the class system itself must occur. How can it happen? That is the question of our times. As a leading U.S. presidential candidate recently put it, "it will take a political revolution." Undoubtedly it will take at least that.

9. Economy, Community, Biosphere

The inequality associated with class has usually been presented as a necessary evil for the economic strength of human societies. It is said that unjust though it may be, inequality is nonetheless essential for economic growth and indeed even for minimal economic viability. Therefore, human societies must make the unpleasant trade-off of "equity versus efficiency" or suffer the even more unpleasant consequences of dissolution.[1] As applied in the context of modern capitalism, this idea is, at best, an exaggeration. In previous cases in the history of civilization, such ideas have been a convenient element of the sustaining ideologies of ruling classes. It is simply not true that the kind of inequality present in today's capitalist market society is necessary for economic growth or viability. Indeed, it has already done great damage to this economy.[2] It is now acknowledged in mainstream economics that the "equity-growth trade-off" of the standard introductory economics textbook is off the mark. In fact, the correlation is of the opposite kind. Statistically, at least in the twentieth century, better economic growth tends to go with less inequality. What follows here is an account of why growth and equity thus go together.

Much more is at stake than justice alone when equity is sacrificed for efficiency's sake. Forgoing justice is no small matter, but some of the most important other values of human community and survival in the natural world itself hinge upon proper arrangements in human society. Human individuality and personal development require the densely cooperative and congenial social arrangements of real community. Community, however, is undermined by inequality and the power relationships of class. The ecological sustainability of human societies requires a similar congeniality in human relationships with the natural world, but that too is undermined by life in a world of class. How these other important values are vitiated by the class-based inequalities of modern market societies will be considered after a critical look at the equity versus efficiency argument.

IS INEQUALITY GOOD FOR THE ECONOMY?

To begin with, there is the critical question of whether any of the general economic improvement that supposedly follows from inequality actually devolves to those on the short end of that inequality as subjects of the power structures associated with it. If those who have been made worse off for the sake of economic improvement for the larger society cannot share enough of that improvement in the future to offset their immediate sacrifice, then justification on the grounds of economic improvement fails.[3] Indeed, those closer to the bottom of the income and wealth distributions may be willing to sacrifice for the sake of future generations of their own and others' offspring. Even strong critics of the capitalist economy have been willing to accept it as historically necessary on such grounds.[4] Those at the bottom, however, have seldom actually been asked their own feelings about their sacrifices. In this light, through most human history, justifications of inequality and social power on economic grounds have sounded a bit hollow.

There is also the pressing question of whether economic growth is a real value at this stage of human life on the planet. Most of humanity today would probably appreciate economic growth in their own societies, assuming that they or their offspring may expect to share in the fruits of that growth. But in the already developed world it is not clear that further economic growth in the usual sense of the term would be of any lasting benefit. Indeed, given its damaging consequences for both community and environment (in fact, the long-term ecological viability of the global environment is now called into question), it may well be time to bring economic growth to a halt.[5]

Before turning to that important issue, assume that growth, like efficiency, is a good thing. Is there a necessary conflict between economic growth or efficiency and distributive justice? Does more of one require giving up some of the other? The argument that there is such a trade-off is usually made in terms of three distinct, presumptive effects of economic inequality on the requisites of efficiency and growth: inequality strengthens work incentives; it improves aggregate saving and investment; and it increases technological innovation. Consider these supposed effects.

Work Incentives

It is argued that in market systems, economic inequality provides individuals with incentives to work more and better and seek self-improvement to make the most of their occupational aptitudes. Given that individuals have economic mobility, these incentives include both the positive incentive offered by the prospect of greater economic reward and the negative incentive of the possibility of economic loss. That is, the prospect of moving up or down the income or wealth ladder makes people more conscientious about their work. Better work and work that accords with people's best aptitudes are the essence of economic efficiency in labor. Efficiency implies a larger surplus available for economic growth or for more leisure or consumption. Similarly, people working longer and harder may be thought to contribute more to society's capacity for economic growth.

However, in general more work per se, that is, more work hours per day or per year, may or may not provide more surplus available for growth, depending on how much more material subsistence and production resources are also required. In addition, while longer and harder work may add to the economic surplus, they are not necessarily more efficient in the sense in which economists usually use that term. That depends on whether the disutility of the leisure or rest and relaxation foregone is or is not exceeded by the utility of the additional consumption goods obtained.

Moreover, the work-incentive effect may go in the opposite direction. Leisure is generally a "normal good," that is, one for which an individual's demand increases with increasing income, other things being equal. (For an "inferior" good, a person's demand falls with rising income.) Consequently, pay increases that yield increases in income and consumption per unit of work may induce people to work less or less hard, or less productively, since they may use their extra pay to take more leisure. This has been empirically shown for some income levels, and it holds in neoclassical theory as well. In such cases, presumably attaining a higher income translates into weaker work incentives.

Of course, other motivations may be involved than simple material satisfaction. It might be the prospect of economic status, that is, people's standing relative to others, rather than merely their own isolated, individual economic well-being, to which people respond when economic incentives are offered for work. In that case, greater inequality might be thought to induce more and better work because it implies greater status differentials, that is, a longer income ladder. But status is a function of more than just income or wealth. It includes all sorts of social norms and perceptions about occupations and social groups. Significant status differentials may exist regardless of the amount of the income or wealth differences associated with them. Status differentials may be insignificant or nonexistent even when great income or wealth disparities exist. The argument that income and wealth inequality is necessary to induce status incentives for work does not hold because income and wealth do not necessarily correlate closely with work-inducing status.

A critical issue regarding the putative work incentive effect is the fact that it requires economic mobility. Consider the extreme case: great economic inequality without mobility cannot stimulate stronger work inclinations. Indeed, it will diminish work incentives or leave them simply unaffected, for people on lower rungs of an income ladder that cannot be climbed must certainly experience feelings of hopelessness, apathy, and indifference to the work they must do. In reality, some small amount of mobility always exists. There is always room for hope, even in the worst cases. On the other hand, significant immobilities abound in capitalist market systems today. To that extent, greater inequality may undermine work incentives for many people.

In fact, this suggests a kind of trade-off between economic mobility and inequality as stimulants of work. The less mobility is available to people into and across occupations as they seek their best jobs, the greater is the amount of inequality that may be required to induce a given level of work in the society.[6] Conversely, the greater the degree of mobility, the less inequality is required. Thus, societies that strongly attend to people's human capital investment needs with universal high-quality public education and training do so at some expense to their wealthier classes and accordingly are more egalitarian (the Scandinavian countries are the perfect example today).[7] Yet they do not seem to suffer from diminished work incentives because by providing a strong human capital base for people, they are also providing them sufficient economic mobility that relatively little income incentive is needed.

Finally, market systems and the inequalities they bring disproportionately reward other things besides better and more productive work, for example, competitive greed, self-seeking miserliness, opportunistic back-stabbing, and pure, conspicuous, accumulation-based status-seeking. To the extent these are rewarded instead of honest, productive work, they are an important and effective route to individual economic betterment. Yet they diminish the incentive for those who would otherwise commit to honest and productive hard work. Not only do they tempt with an alternative and easier route upward, they also arouse a rightful resentment in others who choose the more ethical route. They thus undermine the quality of the work done and are conducive to anything but productive efficiency.

There is then quite a bit of uncertainty about the work-incentive effects of inequality. Accepting that some inequality might be good for work incentives, it is almost certainly also true that too much inequality harms them. Exactly how much inequality is necessary for a positive work incentive? The underlying sources of the inequality are critical. Inequalities arising from some kinds of activities or circumstances may be harmful to work incentives. In principle, once established, a minimal amount of inequality may be all that is required for a strong work ethic. This is especially valid if other less meritorious behaviors and circumstances are not also similarly rewarded, and if other kinds of positive rewards like social recognition and self-respect are attained by diligent work.

Aggregate Savings and Investment

The growth process requires that a portion of productive resources be devoted not to producing consumption goods but instead to accumulating capital, those goods needed for producing final goods since growth requires that increasing amounts of the latter be produced over time. Thus savings, the forgoing of consumption, and the channeling of the income thereby released into capital investment are critical for growth. Savings and investment are closely intertwined in market economies, but it will be convenient to focus on them separately. Also, it is important to look at both physical capital goods investment, as is usually done in economic growth analysis, and human capital investment, as is unfortunately often not done.

It is often argued that the aggregate savings rate is improved by increases in inequality. Since the rate of saving out of personal income is greater for people with higher incomes, a dollar taken from a lower-income person and given to a higher-income person will yield a higher aggregate saving rate, that is, a greater portion of aggregate income saved. But there are several problems with this as an argument for greater inequality as a means of stronger economic growth.

First, although the affluent save a larger portion of personal income and spend a smaller portion on consumption, their personal consumption expenditures tend to be more wasteful. Consider that superfluous multiple homes and fleets of automobiles, massive collections of clothing, conspicuous and trivial travel, and so forth, use resources that otherwise could be available for investment in both physical capital and human capital accumulation. From the perspective of economic growth, making resources available for both kinds of investment is the whole point of savings. Thus, although redistributing to the rich may increase the saving rate, the accompanying increase in wasteful consumption by the rich works against the intended effect of improving the saving rate.

This may be critical from the viewpoint of the importance of human capital for economic growth. Saving for investment in human capital may be especially sensitive to the distribution of personal disposable income between affluent spenders on wasteful consumption and less affluent people who may spend on things that advance their productive capacities, that is, things that improve their human capital. This is so because, as discussed earlier, individuals' human capital is developed both in formal education and training and in their homes, families, neighborhoods, and communities. Its accumulation requires resources to pay for schools (for taxes for public schooling or tuition for private schooling) and for the various perquisites of healthful and intellectually stimulating non-school environments. To the extent that personal disposable income is distributed to affluent spenders on luxury goods (whose human capital may already be more than sufficient), less is available for the critical consumption and

government expenditures necessary for human capital development among the rest of the population. From the perspective
of the need for human capital investment then, this is wasteful
consumption, and in the aggregate, it is larger the greater is the
disparity between the affluent and the rest.[8]

The second, more fundamental problem with the argument
that increases in inequality raise the savings rate is that in modern
market economies, the vast bulk of private-sector financial saving
occurs in corporations and other businesses in the form of retained
earnings.[9] Business savings are motivated more by market competition among firms than by the personal savings inclinations of
their owners and, accordingly, are not responsive to the distribution of personal income.

Even more critically, public sector saving—that portion of total
government tax collections that is available for and devoted to
publicly provided investment in capital goods and human capital (roads and transport, research and development, education,
and health care)—is also a considerable portion of total saving.
Therefore, increasing the aggregate personal savings rate among
individuals can have relatively little impact on aggregate savings,
that is, total private plus public savings.

Finally, and perhaps most importantly, the whole point of highlighting the effect of inequality on aggregate savings is that they are
critical for investment in physical and human capital, the linchpin
of the process of economic growth. As has been argued, aggregate
savings (public plus total private) are unlikely to be much affected
by regressive redistributions of personal income. Yet, even were
savings significantly improved, thus releasing resources available
for investment in economic expansion, it is not clear that greater
investment would necessarily follow. A presumption that investment spending would rise just because of increased availability of
investable funds is contradicted directly by Keynesian economics.
Investment is determined by profitability expectations that depend
on many other factors.

In that regard, in fact, to the extent that the aggregate personal savings rate increases, the aggregate consumption rate would fall, that is, aggregate consumption as a fraction of aggregate income. But private consumption demand is the ultimate driver of investment in capital goods in the long run, aside from government spending.[10] Thus, with a higher personal saving rate, it would seem less likely that strong profitability expectations may prevail in the long run in the face of weakened consumption spending when investment in capital goods production is ultimately motivated by the prospect of final goods sales.

Some of the adverse effects on human capital investment that follow from increasing inequality have been noted. Looking at them from a slightly different angle, the labor market supply-side effects of increasing inequality may be harmful when inequality reduces for the majority of the population their income available for personal investments in improving their own human capital. To the extent that government spending on human capital development (for example, public education and training) is also generally less in societies with great inequality, it is difficult to imagine that incentives toward self-improvement for most people can be much strengthened by the presence of such hurdles against them. In effect, increasing inequality thus reduces economic mobility, at least for the majority. This in turn not only reduces the efficiency with which the labor force is productively employed but also may negate any work-incentive improvements that might otherwise be expected.

Innovation

Economically useful technological innovations are typically embodied in physical capital goods of one kind or another. Thus, the first question about possible connections between economic inequality and the innovation process is that of capital goods investment. As just discussed, the latter is not significantly, if at all, improved by inequality. Yet, a strong investment environment would seem crucial for strong technological advances, at least in the private business sector.

It is often said that economic inequality contributes to technological advancement insofar as the affluent have the time and resources to pursue innovation. Some freedom from the necessities of work and access to the material requisites of invention and intellectual activity are critical elements in the technological innovation process. But it is not clear that denying most people these requisites so that elites may have them is necessarily conducive to innovation. Presumably, much innovation could otherwise come from the majority who are so denied.

Might inequality be conducive to innovation insofar as it provides positive material incentives to those who innovate? If inventors and discoverers of new knowledge are motivated by personal material advancement, only an environment of economic inequality can provide the prospect of such advancement. But as with work incentives, perhaps even more so with innovation incentives. There is a real question about the extent to which material reward plays a role in motivating innovators and how much material reward is necessary. The promise of recognition and respect are probably the most important external motivations of scientific and technical work. Simple curiosity and the joys of intellectual inquiry are major critical internal motivations, widely acknowledged by both innovators and observers. Among the various other motivations that may be relevant, exactly how important is material reward?

Perhaps most critical for theories of innovation based on individually motivated behavior, the vast bulk of innovation today is corporate, in both the general and specific senses of that term. It occurs predominantly in business, government, and university environments and is accomplished mostly by people in wage employment. In these settings, most of the material reward generated in the innovation process goes not to the innovators themselves but to others, namely, their superiors or business owners. It can hardly be a great incentive for those who supposedly respond to such rewards when others get most of the material benefits.[11]

Second, given the importance of nonmaterial incentives in the innovation process, what would seem to matter most is not so much the material incentives provided by these institutions—either for technical employees or for superiors or owners—but instead the environment these institutions provide the employees involved in the work of innovation and discovery. Especially important are those aspects of the environment that stimulate intellectual work by providing the cooperative social surroundings required for fruitful mental synergy. For that, great material reward and to a great extent even status itself are largely irrelevant, indeed even to some extent destructive.

Among these innovation institutions, the pay and status inequalities in university and government environments are significant. It may be a part of what positively motivates innovators in those contexts. Yet it is nothing at all like that found in business environments, where one might well question whether it is essential for owners and higher-level managers to reap unimaginable riches from the technical innovation of their employees so that innovation may proceed.

Therefore, there is little reason to believe that economic inequality improves the pace of innovation. But what about the directions of innovation, that is, the particular kinds of goods and production processes developed in capitalist technological change? The capitalist economy itself profoundly determines the direction of modern technology. Thus far, we have considered mainly the early phases in developing a new technology, discovery and invention, rather than later phases in which a new process or product is advanced toward implementation and dispersal into widespread use. Regarding these later phases of the development of a technology, it is usually supposed that, in the capitalist market economy, profit expectations determine which particular discoveries and inventions get advanced to further development.

Moreover, given the corporate institutional settings in which most discovery and invention occur, profit is an important motivation in the early phases of technological development as well.

This is not to say that the people involved in the technical and intellectual work in these early phases are mainly profit-motivated; instead, as we have seen, other motivations are critical. Yet the questions asked of them, the tasks they are given, the projects in which they are employed, and therefore the directions of their intellectual work are strongly influenced by profit-motivated investors. New technologies in capitalism therefore tend to be of certain kinds and not others. Notably, innovations that directly affect production or administration processes tend to be those that strengthen management in its control over workers and not those that might empower workers. Perhaps most obvious among these are the many "speedup and intensification" technologies that have come into common use in capitalism, from the mechanical clock itself to the assembly line to numerically controlled machines and digital production flow control. From management's viewpoint, the digital technology revolution has brought salutary changes in the monitoring and supervision of workers. Supposedly benefitting everyone by increasing material production through scientific methods in the workplace, such technologies have degraded both working people's lives and incomes. Inequality and class are built into capitalist innovation.[12]

Aside: Wealth and Risk-Bearing

Concerning the distribution of wealth as opposed to income, it is sometimes argued that greater wealth inequality generates a greater capacity for risk-bearing since the wealthy are most able and willing to bear risk. To that extent, upward redistribution of wealth would be good for both investment and innovation. Yet more wealth for the already affluent may have little or no additional effect on their willingness to take risks. The affluent tend to be already risk-neutral or risk-seeking. And since the diminished wealth of those on the shorter end of an upward redistribution would, on the same reasoning, increase their risk aversion, the overall effect could well be the opposite of that proposed.

In addition, the analysis here suggests that increased wealth inequality implies a greater necessity for many to enter wage employment as opposed to private businesses of their own (or other forms of self-initiated and self-managed activity such as cooperatives or worker-managed firms). Not only would risk aversion thus be further increased among those so forced into wage work but so too would the incentives toward quality work and innovation thereby be diminished as well.[13] This effect could easily more than offset any increased ability or willingness of those on the top end of the distribution to bear risk.

PROGRESS, POWER, AND CLASS

Although inequality harms economic growth, there is a separate but related argument about the connections between class and economic growth. First, growth is not the same as real human progress. Still, both involve uses of society's economic surplus. The surplus may be understood as that portion of a society's total potential for material production that is available for investment in additional or new kinds of capital goods (growth), or luxury goods or overconsumption, or wasteful and inefficient production, or more leisure time, were society simply to refrain from producing it. In that regard, it should be clear that everything said up to this point about the effects of inequality upon economic growth can be extended *pari passu* to the effects of inequality on society's capacity to produce an economic surplus. Inequality is not necessarily conducive to producing a greater economic surplus; instead, too great a level of inequality, such as exists today in the United States, most likely adversely affects the economy's surplus productivity.[14]

However, looking at human society in history, perhaps the ability to produce economic surplus is closely tied to the strength of the power structures that constitute society. Historically, civilization seems to be a function of the great centralized power embodied in strong class systems. Great economic inequality may not be conducive to economic productivity. But what about the power structures of class associated with inequality, as both its effect and underlying foundation? Are not those structures necessary for surplus productivity?

An influential strain of thinking about power and class argues that they are necessary for progress in the human condition, which never would have occurred without the structures of power that historically have been fundamental characteristics of civilization. Most of this thinking comes down to the belief that humans cannot be motivated toward economic activity except by material or physical threat, in conjunction with positive incentives attached to appropriate behavior. Class power structures, it is said, are precisely what is needed here, as some people are then in a position to get the rest to do what would otherwise never get done. Power is often seen also as a kind of glue holding the many disparate strands of society together, without which it is impossible to conduct any great complexity of interdependent activities in the cooperatively integrated forms required for progress as usually understood. Finally, it is argued that class creates economic surplus in the first place, by depriving a portion of the population of whatever level of consumption they would otherwise get and making it available for investment, luxury or excessive consumption or leisure for elites.

This is a complicated set of arguments, and all we can do here is speculate. But human progress depends on what is done with the economic surplus. Historically, merely wrenching a surplus from the working classes through social power has not typically facilitated even simple growth in the material consumption of any but the elite classes themselves. Might the reason not lie in the use of power as the primary or sole means of generating a surplus?

The history that suggests the necessity of social power and class for human progress must be taken skeptically. True, there seems to be very little documented history supporting the contrary view that humans do not need class societies for advanced material existence and may even thrive and develop without them. But it should be recalled that history is mostly written by and for elites, whose cause is generally best served by sympathetic accounts. The nature and logic of social power suggest that whatever the failures of more democratic societies in history, the reasons may lie not in their inherent economic shortcomings but in the use of power by elites or outside contending societies in constraining or crushing them and suppressing their remaining records.

More democratic societies certainly have existed throughout all of human experience, both historical and pre-historic. Classless societies apparently were the rule for that 90 percent of human existence that is prehistoric, that is, up until state societies came on the scene five thousand or six thousand years ago. More democratically organized societies have survived, and many have thrived, even alongside more aggressive and imperial state-societies ever since, at least according to many historians and anthropologists.[15]

Modern democratic societies are fundamentally structured by class and power. That, however, is certainly not the only lesson to be taken from the mere two centuries of experience humans have had with modern democracy. Modern democratic societies bring into the political equation a kind of accountability, limited though it may be, that earlier monarchical and oligarchical forms did not. They do represent a real diminution of social power and are, in this sense, progressive. Perhaps the most important lessons of the modern experience are that people really do want to get past the historical tedium of social class and that this is a viable goal. Perhaps social class really is the greatest of hindrances to human progress.

COMMUNITY AND HUMAN FULFILLMENT

But what is real human progress? Religious tradition, philosophical inquiry, and modern empirical social science suggest that, given the basic material requisites of life and health, human happiness derives from things other than simple material well-being. Economic efficiency and growth may be essential for ensuring the fulfillment of the most basic human wants, physical survival. But the human animal has other fundamental wants, too, that require more than mere access to an adequate gross amount of material goods and services. Among those wants, justice in the distribution of material well-being matters as well. This is not the place to begin an exploration of the material conditions necessary for human fulfillment and happiness. Some discussion, though, is needed about how economic inequality and its correlate power structures militate against the fulfillment of one particularly critical human want, in contexts of great material affluence and otherwise: community.

Humans are social animals. Every aspect of our being involves relationships with other humans, so much so that in these times, much of the world's human population is now effectively knit together into a single vast collective of communication and production, a global community. Even in our earliest prehistory, humans survived only in bands and tribes. Their individual members were so tightly held together in interdependent task specialization, coordinated by dense webs of communication, that people barely thought of themselves as individuals.

The intellect and consciousness that distinguish humans from other animals are completely social phenomena, aspects of our being in which each of us individually participates only insofar as it is in a social context. Nothing shows more clearly our profoundly social nature, the extent to which each of us needs many others for all aspects of our conscious being, than our use of and dependence upon language. Scientists today believe that the very physiology of human vocal capacities and even our brains themselves evolved because of our use of language for social communication—rather than the other way around. Either way, language and the human community it represents are hard-wired into our nature.[16]

Humans want not merely connection with other humans but real community, a rich density of connection with a diversity of others who are mutually supportive and share common circumstances in extensive, thoroughgoing, and intricate cooperation. Every dimension of our personal development—physical, intellectual, emotional, psychological, spiritual—depends critically upon our immersion in community. Our individualities and identities, those unique things by which we feel as if we stand out from our communities, are in fact conceived and constructed only in and through those social contexts. Denied community, we experience detachment, drift, a lack of meaning, a sense that important urges to expand toward our fullest capacities are thwarted. In other words, we suffer alienation and all of its attendant individual and social maladies.[17]

Power relationships in general and class, in particular, militate directly against the fulfillment of this most basic of human needs, for the powerful and their subjects are immediately and unavoidably estranged from each other. And economic inequalities, whether they involve power structures or otherwise, also segregate groups from each other. In modern market societies, the segregations of class are profound. They are easily recognized by the different places and activities of consumption and recreation in which people engage, their different occupations, their different residences and neighborhoods, their different identities as expressed in social behaviors, clothing, and cultural tastes. Those closer to the bottom of the economic hierarchy are denied access to the most basic material privileges, rights, and life possibilities taken for granted in the larger society. The lack of common experiences undermines mutual concern, understanding, and sympathy among people across different economic groups. The materially privileged are especially inured in their insulation from adversity in general, particularly from the kinds of hardships and rigors experienced by the rest.[18] The injustice of the economic inequalities associated with power structures as either cause or effect rightly leads to withdrawal, apathy, resentment, or rebellion on the part of those on the short end, while the powerful practice a willful indifference, which they consider, from their own viewpoint, sometimes even necessary.[19]

The system of class segmentation that segregates people into groups by economic position also militates against cooperative and congenial social relationships among individuals within groups, especially in capitalist market societies. People are both forced and drawn into a self-centered or nuclear family-centered competition with others over jobs, promotions, and decent places to live. These and most other aspects of their material security depend upon their self-aggrandizing struggles against others striving for the same things. Moreover, they find themselves separated and individualized by their private properties, for the most fundamental nature of private property, indeed its very essence, is the exclusion of others.

The confining nature of private property is especially pronounced today when public space in capitalist societies has been nearly totally privatized. Those physical and social spaces in which individuals may experience the social side of their lives are progressively more encroached upon by the seemingly insatiable expansion of the private sector into every remaining unclaimed nook and cranny of common life. This applies not only to the ownership of physical space but in all dimensions of social life having anything to do with discourse—the media, politics, local community, the bar, and the bowling alley.[20] As privatized consumption has expanded into what used to be public space, a kind of hyper-individualized private consumption has reached previously unimagined extremes, as residence, recreation, and entertainment become increasingly personal affairs. And as the virtual realm of personal life expands, all the more do entertainment and spectacle become the source of individual identities. Meanwhile, the realm in which the dialectical self-construction of individual identity in the rich reality of actual (as opposed to virtual) social interaction shrivels. Correspondingly, so does the realm of interaction with the natural world.

The consequence of all this is a considerable narrowing of the individual's social relationships, in quality, depth, and breadth. An individualized ambition follows, a competitive striving for oneself, or at most for one's immediate nuclear family. The most critical relationships with the larger society, those of which the individual is most immediately conscious and upon which they expend the most energy pursuing and sustaining, consist of *pecuniary emulation* and *conspicuous consumption*. Such a social life, in which the minutest attention is devoted to the details of one's personal or family consumption in comparison with that of others, can be at most a pale imitation of the immersion in real social connection that people need for the fullest development of their own potential.[21]

Thus, the presence of such a consequential ladder of pecuniary reward in people's lives, and the system of economic inequality and class of which it is constituted, and the fractured semblance of real community existing in such a society, form real barriers against more congenial—that is, less self-centered, less striving, less competitive and predatory, more cooperative, and socially aware—individual behaviors and social relationships. The kind of social character generally arising in this system, the disposition most representative of individuals in this society, is helpful neither for the fullest intellectual, emotional, and spiritual development of the individuals manifesting it in themselves nor for that of others having to associate with them.[22]

Aside from the incalculable costs of all this in lost human potential, there are also more directly measurable or at least observable costs in the form of the economic resources devoted to correcting some of the grosser consequences of this extant alienation. A world ruled by competitive striving, individualized ambition, pecuniary emulation, and conspicuous consumption requires large expenditures on police, courts, and incarceration to counter the criminal activity of the many who would attempt shortcuts up the ladder of success. Not only do the private security industry and gated communities thrive, but the locational and economic segregation of society and its breakdown before the forces of individuation are aggravated all the further, as opportunism and lack of trust are more widespread, albeit perhaps better hidden, than even what is found among outright criminals. When society tends toward a Hobbesian free-for-all, people must defend themselves in various ways against others vying for resources and positions. Since markets cannot work well without trust, engendering it in such circumstances necessitates costly efforts at regulating and policing behavior to assure a minimum of basic honest conduct. How ironic that it is often those most enamored of competitive, individualistic striving in a free-market context who most bemoan the costs of the loss of congeniality and trust.[23]

All of this may seem merely speculative complaining. Social scientists, however, have observed and commented upon the self-centered and narcissistic culture and politics of these times. The symptoms and at least the proximate causes are widely acknowledged.[24] Self-indulgence in cultural, entertainment, and recreational consumption is exemplified in the escapism found in the mass media and entertainment industries. The latter are all too happy to oblige their public's self-indulgence.[25] In politics, entitlement and narrow interest-group approaches on public issues stifle discourse and action, providing fertile ground for the more delusion-based (for example, "faith-based") approaches now arising everywhere. And through it all, the ideology of individualism, convenient enough and preferred for the needs of those with class privilege, both thrives in and helps undergird this society of asocial individuals.

COMMUNITY AND BIOSPHERE

Connections between the threatening global ecological crisis and the capitalist class system are seldom highlighted in mainstream public discussion, even as awareness of the crisis heightens with news of each new environmental catastrophe. The connections with capitalism are now more often noted, even in mainstream media.[26] What class has to do with this, however, is mostly swept under the rug. These connections are profound and critical for a satisfactory approach to the crisis. Increased recognition that a truly worldwide ecological sustainability crisis is in progress raises profound questions about modern industrial life and its social features.[27]

Obviously, high-output production—the massively energy-using and materials-transforming processes that constitute globalized mass production, distribution, and consumption—is the proximate source of the crisis. The unavoidable entropic byproducts—air and water pollution; soil, forest, fishery, and wildlands depletion; ecosystem imbalance and species decimation and extinction; environmental disorder and deterioration of all kinds—accumulate to levels that cannot be sustained by nature. The result is a critical threat not only to a great variety of living species but to human life itself. Climate change is perhaps the most all-encompassing of the various dimensions of this threat, with its large-scale extreme weather events, such as heatwaves, droughts, wildfires and floods, polar and glacial ice melts. Rising sea levels have dramatically affected millions of people worldwide already. [28] Micro-particulate plastic pollution now exists everywhere and in every creature on the planet, not just in the notorious Pacific garbage vortices. And certainly, the now ongoing species declines and extinctions, including those of such critical species as birds and insects, will have a momentous effect on human agriculture and life in general.[29]

It is well-known and widely acknowledged that features of normal business competition in capitalist markets are to blame for all of this. First, mainstream economists noted during the twentieth century that the problems of externalities and the commons (or, more accurately, open access resources) are inherent in market systems.[30] Market prices can only reflect costs that are themselves determined by the pricing of inputs in markets. Those costs that are not so determined do not get "internalized" or accounted into product prices, and the latter therefore are distorted, as is product use based on those distorted prices. The pollution and resource, environmental, and ecological deterioration that arise in production for capitalist markets are the best-known examples of such side effects. They are real costs of production, and since markets cannot internalize them, they are not accounted for as costs and hence are uncorrected. When the production of goods involves such side effects, the goods are overused or overconsumed, relative to what would be socially optimal, since their prices do not reflect those external costs. Similarly, open-access resources, since they are not anyone's property, get overused relative to their usage by a single owner or in the common interest, which would employ them more sustainably.

Equally well known, albeit somewhat less widely acknowledged, is that only public action and policy can prevent, repair, or otherwise correct such problems. The market itself can initiate neither regulation nor incentives to correct or prevent environmental destruction; these require public action to internalize the costs involved or regulate open-access resources. Traditional government approaches include simple regulation, taxing pollution and other environmental damage, fines, and access fees. They also include subsidization of pollution or environmental damage control to induce the necessary business and consumer behavior. Conservative economists have urged government to create novel property rights and markets as alternatives to the traditional approaches, for example, "cap and trade" systems in which pollution rights are created that can be exchanged in markets. It is not clear that there are any major benefits of such market-like approaches over traditional approaches like regulation, taxation, and subsidization. Even market-based approaches require substantial government involvement to create and enforce property rights, oversee compliance, and regulate pollution levels and the exchange of pollution rights.

Even less widely acknowledged is the fact that appropriate levels of policy action are difficult or even impossible in the social, cultural, and political environment of capitalist market systems. Government environmental policy in such systems will generally tend to provide less than is necessary for real sustainability, as some environmentalists have noted. The reasons boil down to essentially this: the capitalist market system is *growth compulsive*, ever endlessly expansionist, propelled into new geographies and locations, new and more productive methods of production, new products and new variations on old ones, and perhaps most egregiously, new consumer wants and new ways of expanding them. A continually rising flow of new materials, processes, and products is the result, and with them, even more ecologically damaging external side effects. Although capitalist government could perhaps, in principle, correct for the latter, it does not, because its most critical role is not so much to regulate or oversee things in the public interest but to facilitate business. Thus, in every possible instance, government in a capitalist market economy tends to side with growth, not ecological sustainability.

A complete account of the growth compulsion of capitalism is not possible here. Still, a few simple points can be made. Government is most responsive to business, but not just any business. Business is, in general, growth compulsive in the sense that dynamic competition both in product markets and in finance rewards those businesses most committed to growth. Those businesses that are not so committed fall out along the way sooner or later. Government is most responsive to those that are biggest and have developed based on the strongest growth compulsion.[31] Government even emulates capitalist business values in a market society—as do all other realms of that society—and economic growth is an assumed and even stated goal of government policy.[32] As for the citizenry, jobs depend on growth in a system that refuses to consider other ways of providing them, and that will not provide real economic security otherwise. So most people (and certainly politicians) tend to side with business on the need for economic growth.

But the class system of economic inequality and its associated power structures in modern market economies are a critical part of this problem, which goes much deeper than merely the politics of growth versus the environment. Analyses of the breakdown of developed societies caused by ecological unsustainability in the historical and prehistoric past suggest that social class structures are important elements in most if not all social collapses. The ecologically suicidal consequences of those structures are compounded multifold in the social and economic context of capitalist market systems, where class and all its ramifications have been hyper-developed.[33]

First, although it is widely held that rampant consumerism in individual behavior is the proximate cause of resource depletion and ecological destruction, consumerism is itself a consequence of more fundamental things. Certainly, the advertising and marketing that are pervasive features of modern capitalist business, devoted as it is to expansion in competitive markets, and the hegemonic culture of consumerism built on this commercialism, are to blame here. Yet that still does not quite get to the heart of the matter. To be successful as business investments, advertising and marketing must appeal to other propensities than the simple need for goods and services. The idea is to get people to want more yet. It must therefore be asked, to what propensities do those efforts so successfully appeal?

In modern market systems, even aside from the all-encompassing commercial environment, people are well-prepared to be wholly receptive to and seek and find gratification in consumerist behaviors. To begin with, because most people as wage employees are subject to employer power, they must seek their personal fulfillment elsewhere than at work, insofar as the time and effort spent there are not their own but their bosses'. This alienation, from which people seek some escape, taints their social lives generally, and indeed their intellectual lives and relationships with the natural world.

On the other hand, businesses are all too willing to offer customers gratifications of all sorts for profit in the form of commodities to be purchased. Thus, it is natural in modern market systems to seek commodified gratifications in compensation for lives unfulfilled at work and in the community, especially where other, noncommodified or nonprivatized gratifications are hard to find (that is, in public goods consumption or in the commons). Consumerism thus has roots in the alienation at the heart of production in modern capitalist market systems. The commercial advertising and marketing industries build on people's need to seek gratification where it is available—in personal consumption, which becomes a kind of compensation and is often felt as such.

These industries find easy targets as they appeal to, exploit, and encourage consumerist approaches in people's pursuit of personal fulfillment and identity.

Moreover, pecuniary emulation and conspicuous consumption, which probably are inevitable behavioral features of any class system, are strongly compounded in modern market systems by people's need to pursue gratification in personal consumption, as well as by the individualism and competitive striving and ambition that capitalist market systems induce. Pecuniary emulation and conspicuous consumption are key elements of the consumer psyche to which all advertising and marketing efforts strongly and overtly appeal. Thus, it is commonplace in advertising to encourage the emulation of other consumers at or above one's own level in society's economic status hierarchy. The "Joneses" must be "kept up with" or surpassed if possible and are always a necessary benchmark for comparing and measuring one's own status position. And this is not possible without the specifics of one's own possessions, like those of everyone else being at least as conspicuous to others' eyes as theirs are to one's own. The advertising and marketing appeal to these propensities is perhaps nowhere better exemplified than in the clothing, automobile, housing, and related industries.

Consumerism, therefore, is not the ultimate source of today's global ecological crisis but only the most obvious one. It has its roots in the alienation and pecuniary emulation that were recognized as part of this system long before the advertising and marketing industries rose to the outlandish extremes of today. Individual efforts to resist these propensities will certainly help the cause of dealing with the ecological crisis. Ecological sensitivity, conservation, humility, and moderation in people's personal consumption are, after all, the ultimate goal. But that goal is unlikely to be reached except by a small minority when the larger context of class in the capitalist market economy still eclipses other more congenial qualities of life.

Consider the implications of conspicuous consumption and pecuniary emulation for the politics of dealing with the ecological crisis. Public action on this crisis will require a broad and strong constituency favoring it, but that will be even more difficult to attain than is suggested by the politics of growth versus the environment. Emulation by the broader population is, unfortunately, emulation of those with the greatest material consumption. Moreover, it is emulation of those whose views, values, and behaviors most tend to conservatism in the face of developments requiring a wholly different attitude. For it is the most affluent who have, first, the greatest material interest in the status quo, insofar as their positions most depend on keeping things as they are, not changing them. They are the rentiers, the top-level managers, and especially the owners of the businesses most profiting from environmental exploitation. And second, it is the most affluent who are best able to avoid the many inconveniences and life disruptions arising from the ecological crisis by their consumption and residential location choices. Accordingly, they are least inclined to be affected by the material consequences of environmental decline.[34] Theirs are the attitudes and values most emulated by the broader population, not a promising political constituency for dealing with the crisis, even supposing the emergence of strong political leadership.

Historically, class-based societies have been the harshest on their natural environments and, at the same time, least adaptable to the consequences. In effect, the modern capitalist market society has greatly magnified the first of these two realities, for its footprint on the biosphere has been incomparably greater than that of all other prior societies combined. Although it is heralded for its adaptability in other ways, there seems little ground for confidence in capitalism's ability to successfully adapt to the requisites of ecological sustainability in a world it has itself so profoundly dislocated.[35] Contrary to the drift of most mainstream discussion on the matter, the problem of social class is a fundamental element of both the global ecological crisis and modern market society's difficulty dealing with it. The crisis will not be dealt with satisfactorily unless that problem is engaged as well.[36]

10. What Could Be Done?
What Can Be Done?

What can be done about inequality and class in the modern capitalist market economy? The parameters within which that economy may function adequately permit a wide latitude of possibilities, as history makes clear. The fact that so little seems possible in the United States and other such societies today merely attests to the present powers that be. Exactly what could be done needs to be stated and reviewed—not only to guide any movement for progressive change, but also to demonstrate, by contrasting the simplicity of what is possible with the array of opposing forces, the real source of the difficulty of achieving progress, entrenched social power.

Even in the face of that power, although it may not seem so, these times may be most propitious for advancing progressive change. In the long wake of the Great Recession of 2008, vast numbers of people were left out of jobs and homes, while most of the middle class experienced great material insecurity and only a precarious relative comfort. Gradually rebounding economic growth since then yielded enduring and secure returns almost exclusively to the topmost layers of the income distribution. And although a job recovery had been in full swing up until the COVID-19 pandemic hit, and even wages finally appeared to be rising slightly, the sense of material insecurity and precariousness among working people still remained.

Post-pandemic, it is now clearer than ever that the traditional foundations of working people's economic security have been thoroughly undermined, and working people know it. A multifaceted crisis of historic dimensions is thus developing, as this deterioration of the institutional underpinnings of the economy is aggravated by an increasingly threatening disaster of longer-term ecological decline and most likely an inexorable long-term increase in the cost of energy due to rising fuel scarcities.[1] In the course of the pandemic, the politics of all of this have nearly come to a head, and the times are fraught with momentous dangers. But there are now also possibilities for mitigating the system of inequality and class, the legitimacy of which may be more and more called into question as it becomes clearer that an adequate resolution to all aspects of the crisis will require repairing or perhaps even replacing that system.

I will not attempt a thorough survey of the great variety of progressive institutional changes that are possible. Instead, I will only highlight a few of the more critical ones without which successful mitigation of economic inequality and class stratification would not seem likely in the context of the modern market system. The analysis of this book has been about how economic inequality is tied up with power in all the various social structures in which it is to be found—power especially in the economic realm, but also in the social, cultural, and political spheres of life. The problem of class is the combined problem of economic inequality and power, so mitigating class must involve mitigating both aspects. Not only are significant adjustments of income flows and assets necessary, redirecting these from the top downward, so too are significant institutional changes in decision-making and executive powers in various social, cultural, political, and economic contexts, making these more accountable to the people affected.

Because power begets inequality, and inequality begets power, the problem of class inherently requires a broadly "totalist" approach. Not only are economic institutional alterations required but also alterations in the social, cultural, and political parts of life. It is all of a piece. For example, progressive income taxes and a minimum wage would be critical elements of any real commitment to significantly reducing economic inequality in the long term, but so too must be such noneconomic institutional changes as just-cause employment dismissal and union certification reform and reforms in both mass and social media.

WHAT CAN BE DONE?

We can broadly conceptualize three kinds of possible progressive institutional changes in modern market systems. Traditional policies that have been tried successfully in various countries, although many have been rolled back in the reactionary political climate of recent times for the convenience of the privileged and power elites. Newer policy changes that have been proposed and discussed but not generally or widely adopted, especially in the United States. More radical proposals that would provide alternatives to the core capitalist institutions of the modern market economy, some of which have been employed in limited contexts in advanced market systems but not generally envisioned for large-scale use. Let us consider each in turn.

Traditional Measures

A major mainstay among the traditional measures for mitigating inequality and class in the modern market society has been the progressive income tax system. If the market economy cannot even pretend to channel personal incomes equitably and if its particular inequity is to favor further those with prior accumulations, then equity requires significantly higher effective tax rates on higher incomes. This cannot be emphasized strongly enough.

For example, the argument that the so-called flat tax is fair, with its single tax rate applicable to all, simply fails when the capitalist market system dispenses incomes so unfairly in the first place.

In the United States, progressivity in the federal personal income tax system has gradually diminished over time with each successive major political cycle since the 1960s, a trend carried on in the 2017 Trump-GOP tax-cut.[2] Compounding this is the great variety of loopholes, deductions, and work-arounds available to the rich and the affluent, and at least equally by the regressivity of the Social Security tax system, which collects flat taxes on incomes, and only up to a certain amount, around $135,000 a year presently. Whether the federal tax system is sufficiently progressive to offset the significant regressivity of state and local tax systems is not clear. State sales-tax systems, for example, though usually exempting food and similar necessities, still apply a fixed rate on all other consumption goods and are thus regressive at higher income levels.[3]

Reestablishing older levels of progressivity in the rates applied to personal income generally, ending special treatment for capital-gains income, adding in perhaps a recently suggested "billionaires' tax," and closing such loopholes as the tax deduction for mortgage interest on second homes, could easily be done.[4] This would also lessen any budget deficit problem, which conservatives are always harping about, since the overall squeeze on the revenue side of government budgets at all levels has been aggravated by the decline in personal tax progressivity.[5]

Estate and gift taxes contribute only negligibly to government revenues, yet they can be significant in mitigating the intergenerational concentration of personal wealth and the rigidification of a class of super-rich. Idiotically misnamed the "death tax" (for example, by *Forbes* magazine), it actually affects only about 1,900 people out of all those who die annually in the United States. A number of other comparable advanced countries have lower exemptions (our individual exemption is now around $11,000,000) or higher tax rates in their estate or inheritance tax systems than the United

States (while our top marginal rate is 40 percent, our average effective rate is 16.5 percent).[6] Many countries even have wealth taxes, that is, taxes levied annually on personal wealth itself, a policy suggested for the United States by at least one 2020 presidential candidate and still being seriously discussed.[7]

A third important progressive economic measure has been the minimum wage, the effect of which is to bring up the bottom-most portion of the scale of labor incomes, both those earning below the minimum and those earning somewhat above it. This might redistribute income a bit from business profit incomes, but although some small businesses are often greatly affected, in the aggregate the infringement cannot be great, since it is only the lowest of all wages that are affected. Moreover, as a downward redistributive policy, its positive effect on profits by means of improvements in both aggregate consumer demand and worker productivity may more than offset any negative impact.[8] In the United States, the minimum wage is not automatically adjusted for inflation, but only as Congress sees fit. Its current level of $7.50 an hour is far short of its 1968 maximum level of about $10.50 an hour in 2018 dollars. Further, significant increases here (there is a bill in Congress for a $15 an hour minimum as of this writing) clearly could be accomplished without even setting new legislative precedent, and significant expansions of coverage could be made as well, especially for agricultural and tipped restaurant workers.

In fact, there is a whole panoply of important purely economic traditional redistributive policies besides the minimum wage, any of which could easily be strengthened from their current practices. Here are a few that are particularly important for lower income people:

- The Earned Income Tax Credit has been a singularly successful redistributive component of our personal income tax system, providing a major tax break for lower income employees. Increasing the credit or allowing more to qualify for it would reduce their effective tax rates even further.

- Social Security is certainly the most effective anti-poverty program we have. Still, many low-wage retirees who must rely on it for their retirement income remain in poverty. With appropriate changes in the system, the benefits could be raised such that no one retires in poverty.
- Medicare and Medicaid provide medical care insurance for elderly and low-income people. These programs desperately need major reforms. With reform of the current public/private health care system in the United States, that is, the Affordable Care Act, they could be folded into a more comprehensive national health insurance system.
- Temporary Assistance for Needy Families (TANF), the U.S. welfare program, is stingy by the standards of other countries. Minimum benefit levels should be removed from state determination (they vary widely from state to state) and brought back up at least to previous levels in real terms (having fallen due to inflation), then set to automatically adjust for inflation.
- Unemployment insurance and workers' compensation provide benefits for the unemployed and those injured at work. Both could be expanded in coverage and the benefits increased.
- Affordable housing and housing assistance are desperately needed at this moment. The pre-COVID-19 pandemic so-called economic boom has certainly gone bust. Even during the boom, there were many without shelter lining the streets of major cities in tents and cardboard boxes, having been priced out of their own homes by galloping urban gentrification in a period of stagnant working-class wages. America's promise of a roof for everyone was totally broken with the post-1980s conservative revolution in government spending.

One other traditional set of economic policies has important progressive redistributive impacts even though it is not often discussed in such terms. Antitrust, the set of policies aimed at reversing and preventing excessive market concentration, has also been significantly rolled back since the early 1980s, and could just as easily be reexpanded. It is essential for mitigating the concentration of capital and profit taken by firms from consumers and other firms and from the employees of these firms with their considerable monopsony power in labor markets. It can also be critical in helping prevent or at least mitigate the rise of family dynasties. The need for a return to serious antitrust policy in the United States is apparent not only to mitigate market power in the new network industries (Facebook, Amazon, Google) but to address the clear direct effect of market concentration on the concentration of income and wealth. This is now being acknowledged even among mainstream economists, as discussed earlier in this book.

Class is more than a purely economic phenomenon. It involves power in the social, cultural, and political realms. Thus, affirmative action law is a policy that has been critical in mitigating inequality and class, for class in the United States is always mediated racially. Efforts begun in the 1960s made some important inroads toward closing the gap between whites and African, Hispanic, and Native Americans by addressing discrimination and residential and educational segregation. Yet an "achievement gap" has remained as great as ever and is now expanding. The biggest impact of the Great Recession was predictably on new homeowners among these groups, many of whom were wiped out by both the housing and the job market crashes. Meanwhile, residential and school segregation are measurably as great or greater than ever across the nation. Affirmative action is weaker now than ever, in the sense that it can no longer be racially preferential as it was in its earlier years.

Given this, for it to be effective in helping close the Black-white gap, for example, in principle it must now more than ever be affirmatively fair (that is, preferential) at the level of government enforcement. Yet it is questionable whether even the most rigorous affirmative action can help much, given the enormity of the residential segregation that underlies the educational and cultural disparities that now exist. Although nothing short of real affirmative action would help matters, some new thinking will also be necessary. In the meantime, a simple enforcement of current law would be a positive thing, since at this moment even that has been lacking.[9]

One of the most important issues in recent decades has been the regulation of broadcast television advertising and public interest programming. As commercial radio and TV broke into the American cultural milieu in the mid-twentieth century, their power as mass media was immediately evident. Studies of the effectiveness of TV advertising in garnering consumer "dollar votes" for corporate products showed it to be wildly successful. Soon, however, questions arose about various other effects of TV on viewers, including children. As there also was a need for some balance in political advertising, the Federal Communications Commission mandated various content and time limitations on commercial and political broadcast advertisements. These clearly had the effect of constraining the extent to which the media could become subservient to commercial interests and provided a measure of balance and improved quality in political advertising. Both of these effects were limited as long as the media obtained the vast bulk of their revenue from commercial advertisers, and regulating the extent and content of advertising was probably in the TV media's self-interest anyway in helping to sustain viewing audiences' involvement in programming. But the conservative turn in American government reversed all that, and now the media mostly regulate themselves in this regard, with mostly dire consequences. Even in the age of digital and social media, television and other broadcast media should facilitate a diverse and accurately informed political discourse and quality programming. The history of the media in all their various transformations suggests a need for regulatory oversight to sustain those things. It is easy to imagine better progress on critical contemporary public issues if there were a more rigorous regulatory environment for broadcast advertising and public interest programming. Of course, the newer digital and social media present a whole new set of problems.

New Thinking

It might be thought that some of these traditional measures are outdated. Would it be better to move past such approaches to the problem of inequality and class and look for other ideas? Major changes have occurred in recent times, but this is still a capitalist market economy, the fundamental institutions of which are essentially as they were fifty or seventy-five years ago. Both socially and economically, this system has certainly done little better than in the decades after the Second World War, when traditional approaches to mitigating class were largely in place.[10] New approaches to the newer problems that have developed are certainly called for. But although many of the older approaches may need serious refurbishing, they mostly need to be strengthened, not abandoned out of a misguided preference for novelty.

Fresh approaches are needed, however, in the face of some of these newer problems. Consider a few such approaches that have come into the limelight in recent policy discussion in the United States. First, as we have had a floor on wages for many decades, why not a ceiling on executive compensation as well? In the run-up to and since the Great Recession, CEO compensation has been off the charts.[11] This is partly the result of deregulation in financial markets. Many financial firms receiving bailouts from the government's post-Great Recession stimulus spending continued to dole out embarrassingly high bonuses to their officers. Moreover, as was discussed, globalization and the top-heavy position of higher-level executives as agents of the owner-principals of firms across the spectrum of industries make this a general phenomenon.

After great public outcry, President Obama's administration jaw-boned some firms into retracting some of those corporate bonuses. There is thus strong precedent, at least in public discussion, for tying some kind of maximum executive compensation—in absolute terms or relative to a company's average salary—to eligibility for federal government contracts, special protections like loan guarantees, bailouts, or other government largesse. Some breaks could also be given for good compliance records with EPA, OSHA, anti-discrimination regulations, and the like. This could easily be written into law and enforced through existing government agencies.

Certainly, the biggest and most important bill passed by the U.S. Congress in recent years is the Affordable Care Act, an effort to approach something like universal health care. In strictly legal terms, it is perhaps a strange sort of entitlement. Employees of large firms are required to buy health insurance from private companies of their choice or be penalized, while lower-wage employees and those of smaller firms pay lower premiums or get subsidies from government.[12] (Nonemployed people are insured under Medicare or Medicaid.) The economic theory of cost incidence suggests that employers pick up a portion or even most of the cost of the medical insurance in higher wages paid to covered employees. However, there is no evidence of this.[13] There have been some changes recently, as certain features have been rolled back by the Trump administration. There remains some oversight of private insurance companies by government. At one point, a "public option" was proposed in a separate bill, which would have provided some competition to the private sector to help keep premiums down and quality up, but unfortunately it did not pass. Otherwise, some competition among health insurance companies remains in the insurance exchange that was created as a market-like component of the ACA.

Overall, however, the ACA has shown a number of obvious problems that by now are crying for either repair or wholesale replacement of the system itself. The issue will certainly loom large in future politics, especially insofar as a major portion of the public remains uninsured. From this point onward, at least a presumption has been writ into public thinking that medical care for every individual is a matter of public concern, and that some provision should be made to assure its provision to all. It is now more and more thought of as a full-fledged right, like retirement security, and as part of a basic entitlement income.[14]

Labor unions have suffered major losses of membership and power in recent decades, attributable to an unrelenting attack by business and in the political realm, to globalization, and, in the view of many, to the class collaborationist strategy of many unions.[15] Their losses have been critical in the power imbalances at work in increasing economic inequality and class rigidification. The erosion of those traditional measures mitigating inequality and the effects of class is importantly a consequence of the decline of unions' political and cultural powers. Indeed, it cannot be stressed enough that labor unions' organizing of working people is essential to accomplishing any progressive agenda.

Reversing their decline and rejuvenating labor unions could be accomplished to some extent without legal changes. Simply enforcing existing laws by providing sufficient enforcement resources (for example, assuring union organizers some freedom from employer harassment and persecution) would go a long way toward accomplishing that goal. Yet labor relations law should not be presumed to be neutral in its dealing with labor versus management. Management has resources it can bring to bear that labor can only dream of having, and the relationship is not even remotely balanced. Lacking any other means of countervailing the power employers have over employees in the capitalist business firm, unions constitute the only means available to workers for dealing with it. In a democratic society in which the economy is constituted by a capitalist market system, it is the state's responsibility to assure working people are fully vested with those means.

Most recently, labor unions have pressed for changes in the law regulating how union certification elections are conducted, that is, elections that create a new union in a workplace. Rather than secret balloting, union leaders want a simple card-check process to determine the outcome of the election; stronger penalties for violations of rules on elections and other aspects of labor law by employers; revisions in the definitions of employees versus supervisors or contractors to keep firms from avoiding labor law protections; and a broader scope for workers to participate in collective or class litigation. They should have at least these things, and stronger monitoring and enforcement of all labor laws. Employers have misused existing law, biasing election outcomes with impunity for many decades, a situation that could easily be corrected.[16]

As noted earlier, Social Security is our most successful antipoverty program. Without their Social Security benefits, about 40 percent of all seniors 65 and older would be poor as officially defined; with those benefits, about 9 percent of them are in poverty.[17] Yet polls show Americans are more concerned now than ever about their retirement security. The problem is that with Social Security as it now exists, retirement at a standard of living significantly above poverty typically requires additional income from either pension or employment, yet only about half of all private sector employees retire with a pension. (Virtually all public sector employees have one.) In light of the evolution of the private pension system in the United States in recent decades, we need a universal pension system, that is, a system that will provide retirees with guaranteed incomes sufficient that they need no longer work and may actually retire.

The current private pension system is increasingly a defined-contribution system rather than a defined-benefit system. Hence, it is inherently less secure for retirees, especially in these times of great financial market instability. In addition, since the mid-1980s, fewer and fewer private sector employees are now covered by pensions at all.[18] These changes were caused by the decline in labor union membership (most union members had union pensions), the increasing use of contingent labor by firms (part-timers, subcontractors, and gig workers seldom get pensions), and important changes in pension law. A universal coverage system would have all employees covered by fully portable and publicly insured pensions with at least partially defined benefits guaranteed to provide a retirement above the poverty line. In principle, it could do so by merely supplementing Social Security, or more ambitiously in the U.S. context, by replacing it with something sufficiently bigger.

This book has emphasized the critical importance of wealth

as opposed to income. Accumulated family wealth immediately determines access to whatever schooling or training is required for the occupations that family members enter. Similarly, a person's prior accumulation of wealth immediately determines that person's ability to move into a position of power (for example, employers' power or cultural power in the media) or to avoid being subject to others' powers. The wealth bias of unequal opportunity in so-called free market systems—the economic foundation of class in modern market societies—could be significantly mitigated by a progressive public subsidy of individual asset accumulation.

The standard here is the individual development account, in which the government would match an eligible poor or lower-income individual's deposits. Government may also subsidize a bank's or other institution's additional matching funds, in an account to which the individual at age twenty-five, for example, then gets access for a down payment on a home, or higher educa-tion tuition, to start a business, or later on upon retirement. In principle, the extent of the matching can be adjusted to the indi-vidual's financial need. Advocates for this or similar policies point out that in the United States governments already subsidize asset accumulation by the nonpoor with "tax expenditures" (that is, tax breaks) of hundreds of billions of dollars annually. These include home mortgage interest deductions, capital gains and government bond interest exclusions, individual retirement accounts (IRAs), and lower capital gains tax rates.[19]

Public education is essential for providing even an attempt at equal opportunity, so it is paramount that it be provided cheaply, universally, and at high quality. However, the promise of univer-sally available higher education is vanishing as state university systems find it expedient to price their better institutions beyond the means of the middle class. With continuing suburbanization, public elementary and secondary school systems have become more stratified, with lower quality urban schools and better-qual-ity suburban schools. In conjunction with the rise of the charter school system and the increasing use of school vouchers, the national education system is therefore moving decisively in the direction of even greater class stratification than in the past.

Steps can be taken to help prevent that. A major source of the problem is that state and local governments tend to cut taxes and "unnecessary" services and service quality in their competition with each other for the location of businesses and homeowners. Significantly increased state and federal compensatory spending on local public schooling to offset property-tax-base differentials would aim at bringing the lowest-spending districts up to par with the highest. Similarly, increased federal support for higher education at all levels would go a long way toward offsetting developing educational stratification.

The new ideas discussed so far are not greatly out of line with the spirit of the traditional measures for mitigating inequality and class. Consider a few institutional alterations that are aimed more directly at recent changes in the cultural and political realms of social life and that are perhaps a little further from tradition.

First, a narrowly-decided U.S. Supreme Court case (the vote was five-to-four) appears to have finalized a decades-long history of Court decisions granting the American business corporation constitutional rights of personhood. The Citizens United case expanded rights to free speech, in this case, specifically political speech in the form of political advertisement spending.[20] It is not clear whether it would require only legislation or a constitutional amendment but abolishing corporate personhood is an important prerequisite for real equality of free speech rights, equality of access to the means of political speech, and the public's right to quality information about important public matters. As long as corporate spending on lobbying, political and commercial advertising, and political campaigning is unrestrained, corporations will extend the already considerable cultural and political powers of their owners and managers far beyond their appropriate bounds in a democracy. Reining in the corporation is a critical part of reining in the powers of the elite classes.

Second, a momentous crisis is developing that may well require a major reform of the news media and journalism. For decades, media of all kinds have been concentrating into ever bigger international conglomerates. Local newspapers, for example, have been saddled with debt as they were bought out by larger entities using leverage. This meant that they now had to contend with more rigid profitability standards, and as they began to find it necessary in addition to compete with the new digital media severe cost-cutting became the norm in the newsroom. As journalists were laid off and "work intensification" grew in newswriting, and as the numbers of competing newspapers shrank (most large cities now have a single outsider-owned paper, if they have any at all), readership fell off, and readers turned to online alternatives. Aside from the online offerings of the dying newspapers, ever weaker in content given the declines in journalist staffing, the available online alternatives are themselves highly concentrated news sources. The same story extends to news magazines and broadcast news, and pertains worldwide.

Lest it be thought that this is merely another industry shake-up in progress, the issue is critical. Reliable news information requires vetted journalists, full-time employed individuals paid to dig up and check facts and events thoroughly, report them, and be judged by readers or viewers and superiors for the quality, reliability, and impartiality of their work, preferably by comparison with other competing researchers doing similar work. As readers of newspapers in many a large city can attest, what is happening now constitutes a real crisis. Where will we—not only we "old media" people but also young "onliners"—get our news information? Will it be thorough, adequate to our needs as citizens? Will it be unbiased?

The media function as a vast and variegated propaganda device, in effect, filtering certain kinds of information, especially about the realities of class, government, and war. Yet as is true of our political and educational systems as structures sustaining the class system of the market society, the media system has not been unambiguously or solely malign. Things are not completely black and white, without important positive elements and at least the potential for real and broad liberation. Important aspects of our political system do allow for some popular participation and provide at least a promise of real political democracy. Our educational system does permit intellectual liberation for some people. Similarly, our media have provided the informational requisites of real citizen participation in public decision-making for many people. And truthful information is essential for the daily operation of any complex society, especially one that aspires to and could actually become democratic. When journalism as an occupation and, in effect, a public service collapses, that possibility fades.

As the numbers of news journalists and the number of news-gathering institutions decline—alongside rising numbers of various fact-checkers involved in the news and online in social networks and blogs, many of which are themselves informally and perhaps dubiously vetted—a delegitimization of the mainstream media is occurring. Perhaps that will induce public action. If not, the class system of the modern market society cannot much longer pretend to be democratic without coming to terms with this frightening movement toward a big-brother-like propaganda apparatus without even a semblance of a verifiable, reality-based citizen check over government and business. There will be no way to combat such a thing, as an anarchic hodge podge of competing, invidiously motivated "fake news" makers and "influencers" thrive, seeking "hits" and audiences of their own for a truly threatening confusion of both commercial and political ends.[21]

A democratic society would aspire to something substantially different: a pluralistic public/private media system. Such a system would begin with (1) a major antitrust movement against the current conglomerates, (2) building up public media to compete against them, (3) strengthening the regulatory environment on advertising and on honest reporting in all the media, and (4) public subsidization of independent, small competitive media and of watchdog journalism across the entire spectrum of media types.[22]

Suggestions for reform of various aspects of our political system have been fairly routine in recent decades, and the need is desperate. Some important strides have been made in voter registration and in campaign financing. However, it seems that on the latter, for every step forward, something appears that takes the system two steps back. Pure public campaign financing may be the next step, but major reform will surely be needed in political advertising. Voting holidays would permit many to participate whose employers or circumstances otherwise disallow it. One of the most stifling aspects of the American system is its two-party monopoly, which probably cannot be broken without a system of proportional political representation, or perhaps instead, given the radical changes required to accomplish that, at least instant runoff balloting.[23]

It needs to be stressed that this and the preceding list of traditional and more novel measures for mitigating economic inequality and class rigidity by no means exhaust the important ideas available. One set of critical institutional alterations involves the assurance of adequate jobs for all. The failure to attain something close to full employment has proved one of the most profound problems of the modern market economy. Its resolution may well be beyond the capabilities of that system. The system tends to generate unemployment sufficient to assure enough employer power to sustain profits, that is, through the technological and business-cycle dynamics of market competition. Moreover, the dynamics of both fiscal and monetary policy, subject to the powers of the larger class system, generally affirm those tendencies as well, in what may aptly be called a political business cycle.[24]

The issue is critical. It does not seem possible to get at the heart of class power in this system, employer power, without addressing unemployment. It is not clear that the changes discussed here can go very far in mitigating inequality and class rigidity while employer power remains intact. Either unemployment must be eliminated, or the cost of job loss must be lowered sufficiently to make it mostly irrelevant through sufficient increases in the basic income entitlement due to people regardless of their employment situation. Neither approach is a part of the ordinary repertoire of capitalism.

It may be possible alternatively to change in some other fundamental way the basic institutions of the system. Although it remains mostly in disrepute, despite an upsurge in its popularity, socialism is the most promising and important set of modern institutions alternative to those of the capitalist system. It would be a serious error to ignore it here.[25] No other approach is aimed so directly at resolving or at least mitigating unemployment and inequality, and class rigidity generally. And insofar as progress is ever made in dealing with these momentous issues, it will most likely be by means advocated at one time or another by the socialist movement, whether they are acknowledged as such or not.

More Radical Changes

Some of the institutional alterations discussed above may seem radical. Still, none deal with the locus of power in modern society, the capitalist economy itself, for none directly confront the processes of capitalist production or investment. As a movement, socialism has advanced many of the perspectives and ideas on mitigating class and economic inequality elaborated in this book. The various advocacies of socialism, including both the historically successful and the utopian, propose approaching the capitalist roots of these problems head-on. Socialism aims to alter the form of the two main aspects of the modern market economy: the capitalist productive enterprise and the capitalist investment allocation system.[26] Consider first the allocation of investment.

Socialized investment stands in stark contrast to the free competitive market of (neoclassical) textbook economic theory. In textbook theory, the investment process is guided by sovereign consumer wants as reflected by purchases in markets, the processes of competition assuring that investment proceeds in accord with consumer demand for final products. The consumers whose demands count most are those with the most dollars to "vote" in markets, and consumer sovereignty is, therefore, even in the hypothetical best case, a biased affair. And given the substantial market imperfections of the real world—market concentration, information problems, externalities—sovereignty in reality devolves from consumers to producers who direct the broad course of investment. Financial power presides at an even higher level in the economy, while production and investment in competitive sectors and smaller businesses mostly just follow along in the directions determined by the big financial and corporate powers. Government at all levels is an important player in this, smoothing the way for private investment with breaks, subsidies, and public commitments. On that count, many have referred to the investment process in the advanced capitalist economies of modern times as already highly socialized, even in the most supposedly laissez-faire of those economies.

One may propose, however, that the broader directions of real socialized investment ought to be determined by the public interest. In socialized investment of the capitalist variety, the public in whose interest investment is guided consists of the major capitalist powers, that is, the biggest financial, industrial, and commercial corporate concentrations. It is, if anything, socialism for the rich. One might hope that a broader public might be represented instead. To take it a step further, suppose that by socialized investment, we mean investment determined by democratic public decision-making processes. At least in theory and as understood by those committed to these ideas, that has been the aim of most varieties of socialist investment as envisioned in the socialist movement worldwide. In actual historical practice, everything comes down to the details of how democratic processes are defined and implemented. But, at least in general terms, socialist investment is state-controlled or state-guided, where the state is democratically representative of the public.

In the modern capitalist economy in which investment is (partially) socialized, a kind of compromise exists in which partial control by the state is thought sufficient to guide the overall directions of public and private investment. There, the state directs merely a significant portion of the total social investment, invariably including public goods investment (infrastructure, education, health care, research) and sometimes strategic industrial sectors. A widely recognized example is that of automobiles in the guided capitalist economy of post–Second World War Japan. But both Russia and China today, insofar as they are capitalist, are guided capitalist economies. And all advanced capitalist economies today involve government sector guidance to one degree or another. Thus, as alien as socialized investment may seem to citizens of advanced capitalist societies, it is abundant right there.

In principle, because investment in a socialist economy can disregard strong profit motivations, it can be targeted in ways that private capitalist investment cannot. For example, it can stimulate employment in regions, groups, or sectors where unemployment or low income is problematic. This contrasts with capitalist investment, which not only invariably flees excessively low unemployment areas but also shuns high unemployment areas (since products cannot be sold there), and in any case will not guarantee a well-paid job to anyone anywhere. And since socialist investment aims to provide an adequate supply of capital for producing consumer necessities such as housing and health care, it can assure a decent minimum standard of living. Capitalist investment responds only to the effective demand of those with money to spend.

In Soviet-style investment, the state owned all capital goods, including housing and most major agricultural land. Buying and selling occurred in many of these things. Money itself was mainly a device for accounting and for stimulating efficiency among producers and users rather than a medium of free exchange since where exchanges were allowed, the prices were mostly fixed. All production and distribution were done in state-owned enterprises, and everyone was an employee of the state. The latter was, in effect, one big conglomerate corporation from which all goods and services were sold, *sans* private owners.[27]

For example, all housing was public; there was no private housing, neither owner-occupied nor privately rented. Rents were
charged to tenants by the state and were set low enough that everyone could easily afford a place to live (for example, at 5 percent
of income). The state assured that investment in the production
of housing stock was plentiful enough to provide housing for all.
Similarly, in clothing and food. Consumer goods were adequate
for all then, albeit hardly luxurious for any but top party people,
enterprise managers, and other powerful persons. Capital goods
expansion (industrialization), militarization (in the Cold War
conflict with the West), infrastructure, education, and health care
were the main investment priorities. Given the huge emphasis on
expansion, as well as a good deal of inefficiency, the production of
consumption goods suffered. But once the economy had recovered
from the Second World War, there was no real destitution nor any
significant unemployment, homelessness, or illiteracy.[28]

The Soviet experience, both its achievements and failures,
spurred sympathetic theorists worldwide to envision alternative
approaches to socialism, many quite plausible. Scores of variations
were attempted in the Soviet Union itself, some after its breakup.
In light of a gold mine of historical evidence, theoretical variations
on what came to be called market socialism now appeal to many
as another approach to socialized investment. As an example,
the theory offered by David Schweickart in his *After Capitalism*
may be especially helpful both for its focus on mitigating unemployment and for highlighting the role of planning even in a free
market variation of socialism.

Schweickart envisions the whole of society's investable capital as,
in effect, publicly owned (exceptions may include private housing
and automobiles) and "borrowed" by those using it for production, that is, in production enterprises. Given that this is a market
system, enterprises "interact with one another and consumers in
an environment largely free of government price controls . . . goods
are all bought and sold at prices largely determined by . . . supply
and demand."[29] In exchange for access to society's publicly owned

investable capital, production enterprises pay a flat-rate capital assets tax (a tax at a flat rate on the enterprise's total assets value) that functions as an interest charge. The proceeds of this tax go to a national investment fund that is then dispersed to the nation's regions on a per capita basis and to whatever national public projects need funds.

Regional legislatures allocate a portion of their allotted funds for region-level public investment and disperse the rest to communities on a per capita basis. In turn, community legislatures similarly allocate a portion for community-level public investment and the rest of their funds to their local public banks, making investment grants (not loans) to local enterprises. These grants are based on the profitability and employment prospects of the local public banks' investment proposals. They are used by the banks' entrepreneurial divisions to encourage and develop new business startups.[30] Note that in this version of market socialism, centralized planning must be used to allocate whatever capital investment funds are to be used for national and regional public projects. Critics of schemes such as Schweichart's and especially of the actual experience of the Soviet Union refer to an "impossibility theorem" according to which the central planning necessary to allocate capital for an entire economy is simply unworkable. Too much data is required and too much processing and calculation, hence too much error and waste will be the outcome.[31] In some interpretations, the Soviet experience does seem to verify the critics in this so-called socialist calculation debate.

Yet, on the other side of the debate, large investment projects have always involved centralized planning—think of the American canal system, the transcontinental railroad, the Tennessee Valley waterway system, the interstate highway system, the space program. So too have large corporations and banks and their associated business networks for their own day-to-day operations. Especially in these times, the digital revolution allows companies like Walmart and Amazon to plan globe-spanning and highly diversified operations of production, distribution, marketing, and administration involving millions of employees, tens of thousands of contractors and vendors, intercontinental transportation networks, and hundreds of millions of customers in a great variety of different product and service lines, and all this in an astonishingly effective way (in terms of their goal of profitability). In fact, it appears that planning is extensive and more or less routine these days.[32] The real question is, in whose interest is it being done?

Theoretical accounts like Schweickart's, along with the historical experience of the many variations on "guidance" in both capitalist and socialist economies, suggest that it may be possible to avoid the draconian approach of the Soviet model in socializing investment to mitigate inequality and class rigidity. The other of the two great socialist visions, also with extensive support both in theory and in historical practice, aims to reorganize the capitalist workplace into a democratic worker-managed workplace. Here too there is extensive historical evidence from an even greater variety of experiences, ranging from the small, scattered production cooperatives found all over, even in the capitalist world, to broader specialized cooperative networks such as that of the plywood producers of the U.S. Northwest, or highly diversified networks like the Mondragon network in northern Spain or those found all over Italy. Other examples include the kibbutzim of Israel, the worker-self-managed firms of Yugoslavia during its Communist period, the codetermination models of German and Scandinavian corporations today, and worker participation schemes in capitalist firms in many places worldwide.

This history shows that democratizing production workplaces to any degree is not only economically viable but materially progressive as well. Rather than reviewing this evidence, or alternatively, outlining broadly the varieties and degrees of workplace democracy that may be envisioned for the production enterprise, a major task indeed, consider the idea instead from the theoretical viewpoint on power and class advanced here.[33]

The idea that a democratically organized workplace should be economically viable and highly materially progressive should not be surprising. People working subject to employer power are not running their own show but someone else's. They do not own their enterprises, their products, or the resources and other inputs involved, hence can take neither responsibility for them nor whatever reward may come from their best use. They can be punished, however, for their managers making poor use of those things when their firms shut down or lay off employees. Whatever initiative they may take at work becomes, in effect, someone else's initiative, and whatever benefit may accrue becomes someone else's too. This is known as alienation. Why should employees of capitalist firms be well-motivated to work at maximum effectiveness when they participate in neither management nor profit? A vast and expensive system of management is required—virtually a managerial industry, with complex techniques that are the subject of an entire sector of higher education, and whose personnel comprise the largest cohort of college degrees of all in the United States—to get people to work well and long in the capitalist firm.

Would not firms democratically owned and operated by those who work in them thus be significantly more productive? Surely, working people with a real and immediate stake in their firms' success or failure would attend closely to running them in an economically efficient and progressive manner. They would organize their work to maximize their economic payoff. Given their democratic organization, their profit would be their own, not someone else's. It would be distributed using rules they have decided democratically. Self-organizing, they would save the considerable expense of a managerial staff that is much inflated in size and cost by the daunting complexities of both the principal-agent problem faced by capitalist owners and the managerial problem of controlling alienated workers. Between the greater efficiency of their production work itself and the lower cost of their self-organized as opposed to outsider-organized labor, shouldn't their firms be more profitable than their capitalist counterparts?

The objections to this line of thinking have stood up to neither theoretical scrutiny nor actual experience.[34] It is often thought that in democratic workplaces, people would spend too much time and energy in the extensive discussion and related processes presumably required for decision-making. Yet this behavior has seldom been observed in actual cases. And it makes little sense theoretically, either. If workers own their firms, take their firms' profit or loss themselves, and organize their work and other activities themselves democratically, they must be aware of their own stake and the real costs of all aspects of their production operations, including those of decision-making itself. Accordingly, though they probably would spend more time in democratic decision-making processes than occurs in a capitalist firm, in deciding for themselves just how much time to spend in such activities, they would most likely not let their consultations impinge any more upon their firms' economic success than they themselves would prefer. They would define their firms' success and failure themselves, not by the preferences of outside owners with no personal stake in the workplace. They would attend closely to their firms' viability as competing units in the larger economy.

How about "shirkers"? Aren't there always people who would avoid their share of the work, decision-making, and organizational responsibilities, especially where no managers are looking over anyone's shoulder? In a capitalist firm, where working people have no stake in the organization of their own work nor in the economic rewards of well-organized work, shirkers abound; indeed, most workers, including many managers and technical professionals, are probably secret shirkers to some extent. But wouldn't democratic owner-workers be far less inclined to shirk? And whatever shirking would still occur would then be monitored and reprimanded not by outside-owner-appointed managers but by their fellow workers. The stake in quality work by everyone involved should motivate plenty of mutual oversight and the requisite peer pressure when it is needed.

But wouldn't democratically self-organized workers be likely to misspend or withdraw for mere personal consumption their firms' investable retained earnings? Certainly, the spending priorities of worker-managed enterprises will differ from those of owner-managed firms. For example, worker-managed firms have been more inclined to provide childcare and health and other insurance for employee-members, things considered amenities for workers in capitalist firms, at least in the United States. Naturally, self-organized and self-managed working people will bring their own preferences to bear. But why should not people in such workplaces be motivated to use their earnings carefully when their economic success depends upon it? Given a legally constituted financial environment that appropriately discourages shortsightedness and nonproductive investment, there is no reason to expect any more such behaviors in democratic firms' financial management than in capitalist firms.

One might consider the most telling criticism to be the observed fact that in free-market societies, few cooperative and other worker self-management arrangements are actually found. If such arrangements are so desirable and economically viable, they should do quite well not only in product markets but also in the labor market, as people would naturally gravitate toward work in such firms. So why does this not happen?

For one thing, the competitive viability of such firms in capitalist market systems depends critically on supporting legal, economic, and social structures, as do ordinary capitalist businesses. Where such structures are found—and they are found in countries with more sympathetic legal and financial systems and public policies—more cooperative workplaces are also found. Thus, public financial subsidies and tax breaks help, just as they do for capitalist firms. Some examples are small business loans, loan guarantees for various industries, depletion and similar tax allowances, and the great variety of similar subsidies by and contracts with federal, state, and local governments that exist in the United States. In countries where some such specific targeting of worker-managed firms exists, the latter have thrived.

To a great extent, the viability of worker-managed firms depends on what kind of managerial training the society's system of business schools provides. In capitalist systems, of course, managers are trained for capitalist firms, not for worker-managed democratic firms in which management is a totally different affair. In democratic worker-managed firms, managers represent the preferences of the member-employees, not outside owners. The entire culture of capitalist society, in everything from commercial entertainment to political discourse, is organized around the idea that some people, a tiny minority of rich outsiders, are supposed to own workplaces and select managers who represent them. The vast majority are supposed to work at those owners' behest and under their duly selected managers. That's just the way it is, and rightly so, supporters of the system say, for the majority simply could not run things themselves. Democracy is for political affairs (at most), not for the workplace.

But perhaps the most important factor militating against a larger sector of worker-managed firms in capitalist economies is the distribution of private wealth. Without sufficient personal wealth to go into business for themselves, workers cannot make arrangements, capitalist or otherwise, for financing their own firms without bearing substantially greater risks than do investors in capitalist firms. In the latter, such funds come from widely dispersed sources, and are of sufficient size to benefit from being diversified. Were the workers of a firm to undertake the bulk of its capitalization themselves, their personal portfolios, lacking much size and hence diversification, would involve far more risk than most capitalists are generally willing to bear. Nor can working people generally get sufficient outside funding based on their own personal collateral. Outside funding would still not resolve their own risk problem (although a very few lenders might be satisfied), and would in any case dilute or overwhelm their own control over their firm.

Thus, the relative rarity of democratically organized production enterprises in capitalist market systems is not evidence of their economic inferiority. Instead, not only the bulk of the empirical evidence but also the theoretical argument suggest precisely the opposite. All that is shown by the relative rarity of democratic firms is the overwhelming dominance of the existing system of wealth inequality and class rigidity and the structures of power that undergird it.

That overwhelming reality would not necessitate, however, that the radical step of democratizing the workplace need necessarily be undertaken in a revolutionary way, any more than socializing investment would need to be undertaken in such a way. Just as socializing investment has already proceeded partially in the modern capitalist system, a movement toward democratizing the workplace could proceed partially. Significant public sources of investment funding for worker-managed firms' startup and capitalization, along with state subsidization of related services, especially financial services and management training for worker-managed firms, could in principle accomplish the creation of a viable sector of such firms. Assuming this were done in the context of a broader commitment by the state to a more egalitarian redistribution stance, a sizeable sector of democratic worker-managed enterprises could be made sustainable, even in the setting of an otherwise capitalist economy.[35]

FREEDOM, AUTONOMY, AND POWER

Stepping back then to reflect, obviously, it is possible to conceive the mitigation of economic inequality and class rigidity using a great variety of policy prescriptions, small and large, more or less progressive or radical. There is reason for optimism, even for making a commitment to help bring any or all of these possible changes into actuality.

Nonetheless, this rather skeptical question still might be asked: are things really so critical? Is our subjection to power in the class system of the modern capitalist market economy really so bad? We are not slaves, nor feudal serfs. The traditional measures for mitigating inequality and class rigidity, and even some of the newer ideas, are one thing. More radical ideas are another matter entirely.

Do we really need to consider socialism yet again? At least in a relative sense, are we not, in fact, already the freest people in all human history?

Although socialism has been discussed in the context of a recent U.S. presidential election—one of the most promising and successful candidates was a self-proclaimed socialist, a remarkable event indeed—it does seem clear that the thing itself is not even remotely on the agenda for the majority of U.S. citizens. No, for the majority, it would seem, things do not appear to be that critical. Still, the fact that some of the policy approaches discussed here are even being considered part of the agenda suggests that things are perhaps not as they generally appear.

And are we really the freest people in all of history? The distinction often made between freedom and autonomy matters here. Arguably, we in the United States have more autonomy than almost any other people in human history, at least, most of us do. That is, the space within the constraints to which we are subject in our individual actions is larger than that to which any other people have ever been subject in all of history. We are certainly better-off in that sense. To put it clearly and bluntly, we are definitely among the most affluent.

Yet the constraints to which we are subject are just as binding as ever. As far as freedom goes, those constraints are, for most of us, just as subject to the power of those in superior positions in our class system as the constraints to which any other people in history were subject in theirs. If by "free" one means free of power, that is, free of domination or subordination in a class system, in which the parameters of life are largely set by the preferences of a few, then we are not free. We have not abolished nor transcended class or power. Class and power are as much with us in this affluent society as in any other society in human history.

How about the accountability of those with power over us? Do they really rule as if they are accountable to us? We do have some voice in accepting or rejecting the decisions of our ruling elites, via the vote and our representatives in government, our rights of free speech and assembly. Yet that accountability, though an advance over earlier sociopolitical systems, is deeply flawed in multiple ways. Our representative democracy is, in fact, neither very representative nor very democratic.[36] Most importantly, what representative democracy we do have exists only in the political realm, not in the workplace, where most of us spend much of our lives. There, life is demonstrably undemocratic; those with power there do not even pretend to be accountable to us.

Some may not feel that they are subject to power in a class system, even some in positions or groups that have been described as subordinate or partly so. Given people's awareness of the circumstances and events of their life, can they be subject to class power if they do not feel it? On the other hand, might those who feel as if they are subject to class power actually not be? Are any of us really subject to class power then? Readers might be reminded that the realities of power and class, like those of gravity and ultraviolet radiation, are not necessarily things one feels but are realities nonetheless. If one has difficulty experiencing them directly, consider people more obviously on the short end of the class spectrum. We should picture ourselves there, see how it feels.[37] For some of us, perhaps it is merely that the chains that bind us are cast in gold.

HOPE FOR EGALITARIANISM? HOPE FOR DEMOCRACY?

But how can there be hope for greater equality and democracy in times like these? If rising inequality begets increasing class rigidity and concentrating power at the top, while the latter in turn beget rising inequality, what hope can there be for democracy and egalitarianism in coming decades? On what grounds can one make any kind of realistic commitment to work for them?

Yet today's trend toward greater inequality is not unassailable. In some advanced economies, it is even nonexistent. Where it is happening, there are oppositions and possibilities for reversal. In an inherently and perhaps increasingly uncertain world, there is as much ground for hope as for despair. Progressive change can occur but will not occur if people do not commit to working for it. Why not, in good conscience, commit to these things?

Notes

1. The Crisis Underlying All Other Crises

1. Pope Francis, *Encyclical on Climate Change and Inequality: On Care for Our Common Home* (Brooklyn, NY: Melville House, 2015).
2. Thomas Piketty, *Capital in the Twenty-First Century*, trans. A. Goldhammer (Cambridge, MA: Harvard University Press, 2013).
3. Chuck Collins, "US Billionaire Wealth Surges Past $1 Trillion Since Beginning of Pandemic," *inequality.org*, November 25, 2020, https://inequality.org/great-divide/u-s-billionaire-wealth-surges-past-1-trillion-since-beginning-of-pandemic/.
4. Tommy Beer, "Largest Increase in United States Poverty Recorded in 2020," *Forbes*, December 16, 2020, https://www.forbes.com/sites/tommybeer/2020/12/16/largest-increase-in-us-poverty-recorded-in-2020/?sh=398c237e32bd.
5. According to the United States Census Bureau, in 2016 the "deep poverty rate" was about 5.8 percent, or about 45 percent of the total United States poverty population. "What is 'deep poverty'?" *Center for Poverty and Inequality Research*, University of California, Davis, https://poverty.ucdavis.edu/faq/what-deep-poverty.
6. "Half-million" is the government's gross underestimate. See Op-Ed, "How Many Americans Are Homeless? No One Knows," *New York Times*, January 28, 2021, https://www.nytimes.com/2021/01/28/opinion/homeless-america-data.html, where it was noted that, among other things, a 2017 survey by school districts across the United States found 1.35-million school students homeless.

7.   Historical graphs of wealth or income concentration such as this one, first made prominent by Thomas Piketty, *Capital*, have appeared in numerous publications, for example, the *New York Times*, the *Washington Post, Forbes Magazine*.

8.   Cameron Huddleston, "Survey: 69 percent of Americans Have Less Than $1,000 in Savings", GOBankingRates, December 16, 2019, https://www.gobankingrates.com/saving-money/savings-advice/americans-have-less-than-1000-in-savings/.

9.   Neil Bhutta, Jesse Bricker, Andrew C. Chang, Lisa J. Dettling, Sarena Goodman, Joanne W. Hsu, Kevin B. Moore, Sarah Reber, Alice Henriques Volz, and Richard A. Windle, "Changes in United States Family Finances from 2016 to 2019: Evidence from the Survey of Consumer Finances," *Federal Reserve Bulletin* 2020 Vol. 106, https://www.federalreserve.gov/publications/2020-bulletin-changes-in-us-family-finances-from-2016-to-2019.htm.

10. Raj Chetty, David Grusky, Maximilian Hell, Nathaniel Hendren, Robert Manduca, and Jimmy Narang, "The Fading American Dream: Declining Mobility and Increasing Inequality," April 27, 2017, https://evonomics.com/the-end-of-upward-mobility-america-concentrated-wealth-chetty/ show a dramatic decline in upward income mobility from one generation to the next from 1940 to the present. They attribute the decline mostly to increasing inequality and secondarily to declining economic growth. Note that in Figure 5 the equation for the trend line is $y = 1.1253x - 0.0202$ with $R^2 = 0.5934$.

11. Ibid.

12. Thomas Piketty, *Capital*, gives some of the modern history of the United States and the Western world. Walter Sheidel, *The Great Leveler: Violence and the History of Inequality from the Stone Age to the Twenty-First Century* (Princeton, NJ: Princeton University Press, 2017), discusses the human experience of inequality and social violence.

13. This is not to say that there was no one else trying to provide some such perspective. For example, Michael Harrington, *The Other America* (New York: Simon & Schuster, 1962) and Ferdinand Lundberg's encyclopedic *The Rich and the Super-Rich* (Dering Harbor, NY: J.T. Colby & Co., 1968). And among economists themselves, the Union for Radical Political Economy was formed in 1968 precisely to help shake things up along these lines. And of course, there was *Monthly Review*, founded in 1949.

14. Jan Pen, *Income Distribution: Facts, Theories and Policies* (New York: Praeger Publishing, 1971), was another example showing that not all economists had ignored the subject of inequality.

15. Garrett Parker, "10 Things You Didn't Know about Broadcom CEO

Hock E. Tan," *Money, Inc.*, 2018, https://moneyinc.com/broadcom-ceo-hock-e-tan.

16. "The Highest-Paid CEOs in 2017," *New York Times*, May 25, 2018, https://www.nytimes.com/interactive/2018/05/25/business/ceo-pay-2017.html.

17. "Class Matters: A Special Section," *New York Times*, 2005, https://archive.nytimes.com/www.nytimes.com/pages/national/class/index.html.

18. Originally it was three-times the minimally sufficient food budget for the specified family size. The income amount is adjusted for consumer goods inflation annually. A detailed account is Gordon M. Fisher, "The Development and History of the Poverty Thresholds," *Social Security Bulletin*, Volume 55 no. 4: 1992, https://www.ssa.gov/history/fisheronpoverty.html. Today, there is much concern that because of the way the threshold income-level is adjusted for inflation it has failed to keep up with the actual costs of even that level of sustenance, and that in fact the official threshold should be 10–20 percent higher than it is –see Lawrence Mishel, Jared Bernstein, and Heidi Shierholz, *The State of Working America 2008/2009* (Ithaca, New York: Cornell University Press, 2009). The relationship between poverty and poor health is widely known and well documented. See John Mullahy, Stephanie Robert, and Barbara Wolfe, "Health, Income and Inequality," in *Social Inequality*, ed. Kathryn M. Neckerman (New York: Russell Sage, 2004).

19. But see n 5 above; and Alastair Gee, Liz Barney, and Julia O'Malley, "How America Counts Its Homeless—And Why So Many Are Overlooked," *The Guardian*, February 16, 2017, https://www.theguardian.com/us-news/2017/feb/16/homeless-count-population-america-shelters-people.

20. According to USDA data, between 2004 and 2019, 18–24 percent of Blacks experienced food insecurity at some point in a particular year, 17–27 percent of Hispanics, and 8–12 percent of whites. See Christiana Silva, "Food Insecurity in the United States by the Numbers," *NPR Special Series: The Coronavirus Crisis*, September 27, 2020, https://www.npr.org/2020/09/27/912486921/food-insecurity-in-the-u-s-by-the-numbers.

21. To the "classical" economists of an earlier age, distributional matters were of prime importance, but to twentieth-century neoclassical economists they mattered hardly at all. While the larger public was concerned enough about poverty to have declared a "war" on it, and many economists—mainly on the "fringe" of the field—were sensitive to such matters all along, the neoclassical mainstream mostly ignored them.

22. I showed this in my book, *Inequality and Power: The Economics of Class* (New York: Routledge, 2011). That theory forms the "entry point" for the analyses given in that book and this one. Samuel Bowles and Herbert Gintis, "Contested Exchange: New Microfoundations for the Political Economy of Capitalism," *Politics and Society*, 18:165–222, 1990, rigorously demonstrated this using mathematical methods widely accepted among economists.

2. Economic Fantasies

1. The Cambridge controversy has implications for Thomas Piketty's approach to income distribution. As I have stated, his approach is thoroughly neoclassical, and in fact, blithely ignores many important concessions made by the American school in those debates. (Specifically, he disregards the critiques of aggregating heterogeneous capital generally in macroeconomic models and of the Solow growth model specifically.) On the other hand, he does allow for the wage-profit distribution to play a critical role in the determination of the rate of profit (what he calls the "rate of return on capital")—a thoroughly "classical" or Marxian assumption à la Piero Sraffa (of the Cambridge school). For among other things, he suggests public redistributive tax and spending approaches to mitigating the problem of increasing inequality, specifically as means of altering the rate of return by altering both wage and profit incomes. What follows is basically the account given by the "father" of modern economics himself, Adam Smith, a model that continues to rule the world of textbook college microeconomics. At more advanced levels, despite the modern mathematical rigor of its mode of theorizing, the field of "high economic theory" today has not moved much past this model. Generations of economics students, graduated under its influence, have been thus inclined toward a choice theory perspective on the causes of inequality. For more expanded accounts of this model, see any mainstream text in labor economics, for example, Ronald G. Ehrenberg and Robert S. Smith, *Modern Labor Economics: Theory and Public Policy*, 13th ed. (New York: Routledge, 2018).

2. A number of heroic simplifications and abstractions are being made here that need not be dwelled on just yet. Note that regarding the concept of labor productivity in particular, neoclassical theory refers mainly to the "marginal product" of labor, and not to the much more widely used and easily measured "average product" of labor. Here and elsewhere, unless noted, I use the latter concept. See the Appendix to this chapter.

3. Readers familiar with the present value of a stream of incomes would

recognize the fairly tedious algebraic formulae involved, which fortunately can be skipped here.

4. In N. Gregory Mankiw's best-selling economics textbook, the new classicals play a major role. Robert Lucas is most notable here as the father of the school. At the least, he, Finn Kydland, and Edward Prescott are among the better known new classical Nobel Prize winners. New classical economics has been mainly concerned with macroeconomics; it has of course gone the way of all such conservative macroeconomics in the attempt to revamp the field since the Great Recession, that is, not into ignominy perhaps but greatly under siege these days.

5. Note also that in the neoclassical model the wage in each occupation is also equal to the value of the marginal product of that kind of labor in all industries (see the Appendix to this chapter). Discussion of this and other important elements of the neoclassical economic model are omitted here for brevity, but again see, for example, Ronald G. Ehrenberg and Ronald S. Smith, op. cit.

6. It should be clear that amenities and dis-amenities encompass far more than matters of mere taste—health and risks of danger, for example. Other kinds of risk also matter, such as the risk of loss or unevenness of income. Moreover, amenities and dis-amenities on the cost side of the human capital investment decision, that is, in the particular schooling or training involved, also matter.

7. Actually, it is the number of people "preferring" the occupation relative to the demand for labor in that occupation that is the critical determinant of its wage level. There is a considerable literature in economics on both hedonic wages in particular and compensating wage differentials in general, and an unfortunate lack of strong empirical support for *either theory*, although there is support for the returns to education aspect of human capital theory. See Ronald G. Ehrenberg and Robert S. Smith, chap. 8, on hedonic wages.

8. It should be noted, however, that most economists claim to be more concerned with efficiency than equity. On the other hand, regarding efficiency improvements, the economic "theory of the second best" is frequently forgotten in policy contexts, namely, that an improvement in a variable affecting some market may worsen conditions in one or more others and could lead to a decline in overall economic efficiency. (The theory was formally introduced by Richard G. Lipsey and Kelvin Lancaster, "The General Theory of Second Best," *Review of Economic Studies* 24/No. 1 (1956): 11–32.) An interesting example is that of a polluting monopoly, which, if broken up by means of antitrust (in order to improve overall economic efficiency), would lead to more pollution (because of increased competition and greater regulatory

enforcement costs). An overall decline in economic efficiency would follow if the increased pollution led to more harm than the benefits of greater competition in the market affected. The theory of second best has devastating consequences for neoclassical economics as a basis for public policy.

9. I discussed some of the many complexities involved in understanding aptitude and intelligence and their roles in this model in depth in my book *Inequality and Power: The Economics of Class* (New York: Routledge, 2011). This is certainly not the place for elaboration on this topic and the fast-changing research on "nature vs. nurture" that is relevant to it. It should be pointed out, however, that the recent upsurge in genetic approaches to understanding human behavior and individual attributes are far from completely credible in light of equally compelling recent research that highlights the profoundly critical role of "nurture" in human life. For example, on the use of twin studies to sustain the genetic approach, see Jay Joseph, "The Trouble with Twin Studies," in *Mad in America: Science, Psychiatry and Social Justice*, November, 2018, https://www.madinamerica.com/2013/03/the-trouble-with-twin-studies/. Similarly, on the importance of the new field of epigenetics in stressing the role of heritable environmental influences on individuals, see Ethan Watters, "DNA is not Destiny: The New Science of Epigenetics," *Discover*, November 22, 2006, http://discovermagazine.com/tags/epigenetics.

10. And, of course, those who would espouse this theory would be among the strongest defenders of the institution of inheritance!

11. For example, a "short time-horizon" that is often seen as causing a low-savings rate among African Americans is easily argued to be the *consequence* not the cause of poverty. See Emily C. Lawrence, "Poverty and the Rate of Time Preference: Evidence from Panel Data," *Journal of Political Economy* 99:1 (February, 1991): 54–77, https://www.journals.uchicago.edu/doi/abs/10.1086/261740.

12. It is in fact both the fairest and scientifically the soundest supposition to make. Adam Smith, father of conservative "choice theory," himself averred it as well, as in this passage from early in Book I, chap. II of *The Wealth of Nations*: "The difference of natural talents in different men, is, in reality, much less than we are aware of; and the very different genius which appears to distinguish men of different professions, when grown up to maturity, is not upon many occasions so much the cause, as the effect of the division of labor. The difference between the most dissimilar characters, between a philosopher and a common street porter, for example, seems to arise not so much from nature, as from habit, custom, and education."

13. This is not at all to suggest that inequalities due to the actual de-industrialization experienced in the United States in recent decades should be blamed solely on "imperfect information." More on this later.

14. Business and political scandals, frequent though they are these days, are merely the tip of the iceberg here, as this sort of thing is more or less continual at all scales from the international down to the small-time local, and the vast majority of it almost certainly goes unreported in the news. A major fraction of it too is probably legal; indeed, participants may not even think of themselves as having benefitted from being "inside." Ferdinand Lundberg, op. cit., is a classic on how some of the biggest of the "old established" fortunes were built and sustained on inside connections; there is little reason to think that many if not most lesser fortunes are built otherwise. Also interestingly, that to which insiders perhaps most often have their inside information connections is government.

15. The average household spent about 17 percent of its budget on transportation in 2019, according to the U.S. Bureau of Labor Statistics, "Economic News Release, Consumer Expenditures–2019," https://www.bls.gov/news.release/cesan.nr0.htm.

16. It may be discriminatory locational segregation that impoverished them in the first place, but in that case, they then suffer further substantive income declines with the rise of other, increasingly distant areas of economic growth. Note that an additional consequence of this kind of locational entrapment is the increasing vulnerability to monopolistic pricing of goods and services in such neighborhoods, including the rents on housing.

17. Some would insist on pointing out—and along with Adam Smith, they are correct in this—that government-organized impediments are important too, for example, government jurisdictional borders. However, as Smith was also aware, government may equally be constructive in removing privately constructed barriers to mobility, for example, in precapitalist Europe, in the form of tariffs and toll roads through nobles' lands, and in modern times antitrust enforcement. Here, we are looking at private interference in free markets in order to focus on those problems that markets themselves present.

18. Some labor unions also effect a similar outcome, for example, in construction. Labor unions will be discussed in some detail in a later chapter. Note that what is being referred to here is not equivalent to the restriction of information discussed in the last chapter. Although in this and other cases the two distinct effects are obviously closely intertwined, the restriction of the supply of labor in the field can occur by other means (and in the example of medicine does occur by other

means) than restricting access to knowledge of the craft, for example, restricting certification per se.

19. See, for example, Ronald G. Ehrenberg and Robert S. Smith, op. cit., chap. 12, for the standard labor economics textbook treatment of the subject.

20. "Audit" and "correspondence" studies are particularly strong evidence here; although subject to criticism, they have been improved upon. See David Neumark, "Detecting Discrimination in Audit and Correspondence Studies," *NBER Working Paper* No. 16448 (October 12, 2010), https://www.nber.org/system/files/working_papers/w16448/w16448.pdf.

21. The statistical analysis of gender wage gaps is fairly conclusive on the importance of "institutional differences" across countries, although not on the finer details of such differences, nor on the importance of the institutional impact of "cultural" differences across countries in attitudes about the sexes. Still, it is strongly suggestive: see Francine D. Blau and Lawrence M. Kahn, "Female Labor Supply: Why Is the US Falling Behind?" Institute for the Study of Labor, 7140 (January, 2013), http://ftp.iza.org/dp7140.pdf.

22. The Black Lives Matter demonstrations had the effect of dramatizing for all the world just how profound a racial dilemma American society faces. Among other things, those demonstrations highlighted the critical importance of discrimination in criminal prosecution, from street-level profiling and police brutality to the judicial and incarceration systems, in maintaining residential, educational, and occupational segregation.

23. John Kenneth Galbraith, "Power and the Useful Economist," *American Economic Review*, 63, no. 1, (March, 1973): 1–11.

24. One of the nicest accounts along these lines is Robert L. Heilbroner, *Behind the Veil of Economics: Essays in the Worldly Philosophy* (New York: W.W. Norton, 1988).

25. John Kenneth Galbraith, op. cit., 1973.

26. This point has been argued in a rigorously theoretical way—using neoclassical methods—by Samuel Bowles and Herbert Gintis, op. cit., 1990. I also presented an extensive argument in my book *Inequality and Power,* op. cit.

27. On incorporating power into the neoclassical framework, see Samuel Bowles and Herbert Gintis, op. cit., and Eric Schutz, *Inequality and Power*, op. cit. On the mainstream's eschewing of power, see Randall Bartlett, *Economics and Power: An Inquiry into Human Relations and Markets* (Cambridge University Press, 1989). Also, Eric Schutz, *Markets and Power: The Twenty-first Century Command Economy* (New York: M. E. Sharpe, 2001).

28. For example, in Robert H. Frank, *Microeconomics and Behavior*, 7th ed. (Irwin: McGraw-Hill Irwin, 2008), one of the relatively progressive mainstream texts, no mention is even made of the concept of "market power" or "monopoly power" in the chapter on monopoly! Recently there is some hesitantly increasing interest in the distributional aspects within the field, however; see Asher Schechter, "Is There a Connection Between Market Concentration and the Rise in Inequality?" Stigler Center, University of Chicago, https://promarket.org/2017/05/05/connection-market-concentration-rise-inequality/. And in the popular press there is clearly a rising concern over distributional issues in the context of the new "tech" giants—Amazon, Google, Facebook—that is bound to percolate into economics eventually.

29. In Paul Samuelson's famous and influential piece "Wages and Interest: A Modern Dissection of Marxian Economic Models," *American Economic Review* 47 no. 6 (December, 1957): 884–912, the business firm itself is power-free. Samuelson's work, practically memorized by a whole generation of post-Second World War economists, set the tone for the field thereafter. But see instead Gregory Dow, "Why Capital Hires Labor: A Bargaining Perspective," *American Economic Review* 83 no. 1 (March, 1993): 118–134.

30. See their review, "Piketty and the Crisis of Neoclassical Economics," *Monthly Review* (November 1, 2014).

31. See Suresh Naidu, "A Political Economy Take on W/Y," in *After Piketty: The Agenda for Economics and Inequality*, ed. by Heather Boushey, J. Bradford DeLong, and Marshall Steinbaum (Cambridge, MA: Harvard U. Press, 2017); Romaic Godin, "How Thomas Piketty Ignores Class Struggle," *Jacobin Magazine* (October 1, 2020), https://www.jacobinmag.com/2020/10/thomas-piketty-class-struggle-book-review; and Paul Mason, "Capital and Ideology by Thomas Piketty Review—Down the Rabbit Hole of Bright Abstractions," *The Guardian* (March 1, 2020) https://www.theguardian.com/books/2020/mar/01/capital-and-ideology-thomas-piketty-review-paul-mason.

32. Alternatively, if one's inquiry is about the supply side of the labor market, and one is assuming the latter to be in long-run equilibrium, then one may ignore the demand side as irrelevant.

33. Any undergraduate microeconomics textbook should give an adequate account of this theory, for example, Walter Nicolson and Christopher Snyder, *Microeconomic Theory: Basic Principles and Extensions*, 12th ed. (Boston: Cengage, 2016).

34. This is so only under certain assumptions that should have given pause to every aspiring young economist. This is where the famous "Euler theorem" solution of the "problem of the exhaustion of the total

product" arises, with which every economics graduate student should have been thoroughly familiarized. A graduate level microeconomics text will be required for this one, such as Hal R. Varian, *Microeconomic Analysis,* 3rd ed. (New York: Norton, 1992). Once familiarized with it, graduate economics students ought to have then at least questioned their career choice!

35. Wikipedia has an extensive and quite useful, albeit very difficult entry on the controversy: https://en.wikipedia.org/wiki/Cambridge_capital_controversy.

36. Edwin Burmeister, "The Capital Theory Controversy," in *Critical Essays on Piero Sraffa's Legacy in Economics,* ed. Heinz D. Kurz (Cambridge, England: Cambridge U. Press, 2000). Avi J. Cohen and Geoffrey Colin Harcourt, "Whatever Happened to the Cambridge Capital Theory Controversies?" *Journal of Economic Perspectives* 17 no.1 (Winter, 2003): 199–214, maintain that the debates should not be over yet, there are still many critical issues to resolve.

37. Suresh Naidu, "A Political Economy Take on W/Y," in *After Piketty,* eds. Heather Boushey et al.

3. Capitalism and Opportunity

1. Karl Marx felt that capitalism undermined and overwhelmed all existing social systems. Although some of today's institutionalist economists would agree, others would say it merely modifies them and grafts itself onto them. See Andreas Dimmelmeier and Frederick Heussner, "Institutionalist Economics," *Exploring Economics* (December 18, 2016), https://www.exploring-economics.org/en/orientation/institutionalist-economics/.

2. Data from the Federal Reserve and the *Wall Street Journal*; https://studentloanhero.com/student-loan-debt-statistics/.

3. And the unequal "wealth" referred to here may be understood to include prior endowments of human as well as financial capital.

4. Thomas Shapiro, Tatjana Meschede, and Sam Osoro, "The Roots of the Widening Racial Wealth Gap: Explaining the Black-White Economic Divide," *Institute on Assets and Social Policy,* February 2013, https://heller.brandeis.edu/iasp/pdfs/racial-wealth-equity/racial-wealth-gap/roots-widening-racial-wealth-gap.pdf; and Thomas Shapiro, *The Hidden Cost of Being African American: How Wealth Perpetuates Inequality* (NY: Oxford University Press, 2005).

5. Rakesh Kochhar, and Richard Fry, "Wealth inequality has widened along racial, ethnic lines since end of Great Recession," *Pew Research Center* (December 12, 2014), http://www.pewresearch.org/fact-tank/2014/12/12/racial-wealth-gaps-great-recession/; and Federal Reserve System, Survey

264 NOTES TO PAGES 71–80

of Consumer Finance, 2016, as reported by Kriston McIntosh, Emily Moss, Ryan Nunn and Jay Shambaugh, "Examining the Black-White Wealth Gap," *Brookings* (February 27, 2020), https://www.brookings.edu/blog/up-front/2020/02/27/examining-the-black-white-wealth-gap/.

6. Lisa J. Dettling, Joanne W. Hsu, Lindsey Jacobs, Kevin B. Moore, and Jeffrey P. Thompson, "Recent Trends in Wealth-Holding by Race and Ethnicity: Evidence from the Survey of Consumer Finances," *Fed Notes* (September 27, 2017), https://www.federalreserve.gov/econres/notes/feds-notes/recent-trends-in-wealth-holding-by-race-and-ethnicity-evidence-from-the-survey-of-consumer-finances-20170927.htm.

7. Thomas Shapiro, *The Hidden Cost of Being African American,* is an excellent account of this and other aspects of the economics of racial wealth disparity in the United States.

8. Tuition at a state college or university in the United States today runs from $5,400 a year in Wyoming to $16,600 in Vermont, the average for all states being $10,230 for in-state students. "Trends in Higher Education: 2018–19 Tuition and Fees at Public Four-Year Institutions by State and Five-Year Percentage Change in In-State Tuition and Fees," College Board (2019), https://trends.collegeboard.org/college-pricing/figures-tables/2018-19-state-tuition-and-fees-public-four-year-institutions-state-and-five-year-percentage.

9. Only about a quarter of adults have bachelor's or higher degrees in the United States. See U.S. Census Bureau, 2008b.

10. About half of full-time "traditional" college students worked while in school in 2010, around 10 percent in full-time jobs. About 80 percent of part-time students were employed, about half in full-time jobs. Laura W. Perna, "Understanding the Working College Student," AAUP, *Academe* (July–August, 2010), https://www.aaup.org/article/understanding-working-college-student#.W-Rn3-JOnb0.

11. Per student spending differentials across the fifty states vary by as much as three-to-one (U.S. Census Bureau, 2008d). Thus, the total of differential across school districts varies by a factor that is necessarily greater yet.

12. Samuel Bowles and Herbert Gintis, *Schooling in Capitalist America.* (New York: Basic Books, 1976), is the classic, groundbreaking empirical study on this point.

13. Pierre Bourdieu is probably the best-known theorist using these concepts, and for him they are significantly more complex than I render them here, referring directly to theoretical social power relationships and structures. On Bourdieu, see David Swartz, *Culture and Power: The Sociology of Pierre Bourdieu.* (University of Chicago Press, 1997).

14. In fact, however, there would be some major inconsistencies in such an imagined hypothetical. A need for public schooling, for example, suggests incomplete markets, specifically in this case, the lack of a market for a public good; and the existence and importance of social and cultural capital in people's lives suggests imperfect information. The supposition held by many economists that even in such a world "most markets are pretty well functioning" is therefore more than just a bit of a stretch, since according to general equilibrium theory in economics, if there are any market imperfections, optimality in equilibrium cannot be assumed of all other markets even if they "work well." (The latter is the so-called theory of the second best, originally stated in Richard G. Lipsey and Kelvin Lancaster, "The General Theory of Second Best," *Review of Economic Studies* 24 No. 1, 1956: 11–32. See also chap 2, fn 8 of this book.) And, of course, acknowledging that the world is never near equilibrium makes the whole story moot anyway.

15. Fernand Braudel, in his three-volume masterpiece *Civilization and Capitalism* (Berkeley, CA: University of California Press, 1992), even defined capitalism by reference to the concentration of capital. For him, the real capitalists were monopolists or nearly so. Concentration refers to a situation in which only a few firms dominate a particular market, and it is commonly measured by the concentration ratio (for example, the largest four firms' share of the market's total revenues). Very few real unregulated monopolies exist, in which a single firm has the entire market, but there are many oligopolies, that is, with only few firms. Within the latter, high concentration is common, especially when consideration is taken of the size and product scope of the market in question, as any decent textbook in the economics of industrial organization should attest. John Bellamy Foster, Robert W. McChesney, and R. Jamil Jonna in "Monopoly and Competition in Twenty-First Century Capitalism," *Monthly Review*, April 1, 2011, https://monthlyreview.org/2011/04/01/monopoly-and-competition-in-twenty-first-century-capitalism/ show vividly just how much concentration exists both in the United States and globally today. This issue is discussed further in later chapters.

16. I will be taking a dual or segmented labor market approach here. There are several different such theories extant in economics. The particular approach I take follows most directly from analyses of John Kenneth Galbraith, *The New Industrial State,* 3rd ed. (Boston: Houghton Mifflin, 1978); David M. Gordon, Michael Reich, Richard Edwards, *Segmented Work, Divided Workers: The Historical Transformation of Labor in the United States* (Cambridge University Press, 1982); and Barry Bluestone and Bennett Harrison, *The Deindustrialization*

of America: Plant Closings, Community Abandonment, and the Dismantling of Basic Industry (New York: Basic Books, 1982).

17.   Such firms, on the basis of their surplus profits and their size, also pursue and generally succeed in attaining congenial relations with government. Concerning their labor relations, just how congenial theirs are, if at all, in general depends importantly upon the quality of labor-management relations in the broader context within which such firms operate. In the United States in recent times, those external relations have deteriorated so dramatically, as indicated by the precipitously fallen union coverage rate, high unemployment, and antilabor legal atmosphere, that the necessity for congeniality within the firm has diminished for many firms, especially for those able to outsource significant portions of production. When solidarity or unionization among employees becomes impossible or fragile, the character of "congeniality" changes. Such a firm then may be "paternal," but it is a stern and demanding type of paternalism. Wages and benefits may be lowered, and privileges and job security lessened, relative to what they would be in a more congenial context. Thus, "congeniality" is a relative concept.

18.   Richard B. Freeman and James B. Medoff, *What Do Unions Do?* (New York: Basic Books, 1985).

19.   To put it differently, such artificial organizational hierarchies in firms are functional because (a) in the context of internal job markets, that is, promotion ladders, they provide *extrinsic* incentives for individual employees to strive for productivity improvement, incentives having nothing to do with productivity per se but with mere promotional advancement; and (b) by so doing, and by creating segments in the workforce, they divide and conquer groups of employees who might otherwise form solidarities with other groups in conflict with management, thus reducing managerial costs, a critical matter to be addressed in later chapters.

20.   The importance in U.S. culture of the "rags to riches" mythology first popularized by the Horatio Alger novels cannot be overemphasized, yet a critically important theme in the actual Horatio Alger stories is the nearly ever-present wealthy benefactor. An interesting critique of the myth is in Michael Moon, "'The Gentle Boy from the Dangerous Classes': Pederasty, Domesticity, and Capitalism," *Representations* No. 19 (Summer, 1987): 87–110, https://www.jstor. org/stable/2928532?mag=the-creepy-backstory-to-horatio-algers-bootstrap-capitalism.

21.   The volume of essays collected by Samuel Bowles, Herbert Gintis, and Melissa O. Groves, *Unequal Chances: Family Background and*

Economic Success (Princeton, N.J.: Princeton University Press, 2005), is an impressive exposition of both the theory and the empirics of the conclusions of this chapter. It also extends the arguments considerably into other aspects of the "intergenerational transmission of economic status," for example, internationally and even on personality and attitude resemblances between generations.

4. Power and Class in Capitalism

1. The so-called capabilities approach to human welfare is associated mostly with economist Amartya Sen (e.g., *Development as Freedom*, (Oxford University. Press, 2001)); and with philosopher Martha Nussbaum (for example, *Creating Capabilities: The Human Development Approach* (Cambridge, MA: Harvard University. Press, 2011)).

2. See Randall Bartlett, *Economics and Power;* Samuel Bowles and Herbert Gintis, "Contested Exchange"; and Eric Schutz, *Markets and Power*.

3. Leslie McCall, *Complex Inequality: Gender, Class and Race in the New Economy* (New York: Routledge, 2001), refers to their close association as "intersectionality." Here, simply focusing on each of the three will suffice for present purposes.

4. Karl Marx and Fredrick Engels were by no means the originators of the concept of class. In the West, it goes back at least to Socrates, Plato, and Aristotle, all of whom also referred to the kind of simple two-class model presented here. Needless to add, so too did the fathers of capitalist economic theory, such as Adam Smith, David Ricardo, and Thomas Malthus.

5. In contexts in which analysts are concerned with the behavior of whole classes, for example, as they are involved in political conflict, such considerations may be important. At this point there is no need for such concern, although later on they may become important.

6. If, in stock ownership, 50 percent of the outstanding stock plus one share gives one controlling interest, then we might alternatively suppose that employees all together do not own that much. In reality, only the very top of the employee hierarchy owns any of the typical firm's stock, and only rarely does even top management own anything near controlling interest. There is a minuscule sector of firms in the United States that are truly employee-owned in the sense of employees having controlling interest. The rest, including the vast majority of those in which employees do own some stock, are outside stockholder owned. See Marjorie Kelly, *The Divine Right of Capital: Dethroning the Corporate Aristocracy*, (San Francisco: Berrett-Koehler Publishers, 2003), on stock-holding, in general. There is an unfortunately little-known but lively literature on employee ownership and control. See

Agustin J. Ros, *Profits for All? The Costs and Benefits of Employee Ownership* (New York: Nova Science Publications Inc., 2001), and Gregory K. Dow, *Governing the Firm: Workers' Control in Theory and Practice* (Cambridge University Press, 2003).

7.   The largest 3,300 U.S. corporations reporting to the IRS in 2013, those with total assets of $2.5 billion or more each, collectively owned 81 percent of all the assets owned by U.S. corporations. "SOI Tax Stats – Table 2 – Returns of Active Corporations," IRS, https://www.irs.gov/statistics/soi-tax-stats-table-2-returns-of-active-corporations. It is extremely difficult to get asset data on noncorporate business in the United States. What data are available officially on business size are collected on sales receipts or employment, not assets.

8.   There may be rules in effect, that is, laws or social norms, that place limits upon capitalists' exploitation of their employees, but the compulsions of market competition incline capitalists against all such rules. Moreover, given that they have class power over employees, capitalists are themselves the ones who make the rules. They may indeed choose to make rules against overexploiting employees, since those capitalists among them who do so may actually harm the rest by hurting the quality of work that can be gotten from the labor force and even the size of the labor force available for work. But given their power over employees, that is a matter mainly for business owners to work out among themselves. As the history of such progressive laws as those on child labor and workplace safety and health shows, it may take some time indeed for the more thoughtful and farsighted capitalists to rule the day.

9.   Or as another example, while being the legal titular owner and entitled to the firm's assets and profits, the owner could be an equal with the rest of the workers in democratic processes that control the firm's operations, with one voice only alongside theirs, hence powerless to run things. As we will see, this is a question partly of legalities, that is, what particular arrangement has the imprimatur of the state's enforcement powers, and partly of other sources of the relative powers of owners and workers such as those to be discussed in what follows. However, it seems far-fetched to suppose that one individual with legal entitlements to all the assets and profits of the firms would not have an inordinate voice in an otherwise democratic setting, so such a situation would seem a bit hard to imagine.

10. The data on small business survival are somewhat sketchy, since so many small businesses are informal. The U.S. Small Business Administration keeps data only on those with employees, among which less than half survive past five years after startup. During the

Great Recession, of course, the failure rate was certainly much higher, and during the COVID-19 pandemic the failure rate has been very high indeed. Generally, the failure rate is higher the smaller and the newer is the business. See U.S. Small Business Administration, Office of Advocacy, "Small Business Facts," 2012, https://www.sba.gov/sites/default/files/Business-Survival.pdf.

11.   Typically, the workers' pooled funds are inadequate to buy out the firm even if they can supplement with borrowed funds. Equally importantly, having their savings tied up in a single investment, with no portfolio diversification of the kind capitalists normally have for themselves, implies an extremely high degree of risk to which to subject those savings. And clearly employees are less capable of bearing that kind of risk, given their small personal wealth accumulations. This subject will be further considered in chapter 10.

12.   Employers leverage the power they have over workers due to unemployment by using a number of organizational and operational strategies in the workplace as well as in the larger economic environment that, in effect, give them yet more power. As will be discussed in the next chapter, these include, for example, in the workplace, status stratification and bureaucratization, and in the larger economic environment, stingy unemployment insurance and minimum wage laws.

13.   See "Macrotrends," U.S. National Unemployment Rate, https://www.macrotrends.net/1316/us-national-unemployment-rate for an interactive graph.

14.   See "15 Indian Tribes Have Unemployment Rates over 80%," Native-Americans.com, August 30, 2013, https://native-americans.com/indian-tribes-unemployment-rates/.

15.   Why it should be nearly invariably so that technical changes improve labor productivity is something modern neoclassical economics cannot hope to fully appreciate. But the theoretical system of the classical economists—from Adam Smith through Karl Marx—based as it was in the labor theory of value, made it quite transparent. Since most new technologies are cost-reducing, and since all value is based in labor and ultimately therefore all costs are also, it follows that most new technologies reduce "labor content."

16.   A compelling argument may be made that capitalist technical change tends to be de-skilling overall, that is, when measured by, for example, the average amount of education and training per person required to reproduce a given labor force producing a given output level and mix. That even high tech technical change may have been overall de-skilling is indicated by considering how the high-tech capital resources, such

as computing and information processing equipment, digital sensors, numerical scanners, and so forth, that are now universally used simplify jobs from office and clerical work to surveying, from machining parts to designing machines that automatically machine parts, to designing machines that design machines that automatically machine parts. The classic case for such a view—since that of the classical economists and Karl Marx—was made by Harry Braverman, *Labor and Monopoly Capital: The Degradation of Work in the Twentieth Century* (New York: Monthly Review Press, 1974).

17. Note that if perennial unemployment may not have seemed clearly apparent throughout all of modern twentieth-century capitalist history, several trends have been effective throughout much of that period that either served to hide much of it or to stifle any major rise in the national unemployment rate. First, the expansion of Keynesian state-funded aggregate demand played a critical role: it provided for more or less continuous economic growth, thereby offsetting any relative stagnation in private consumption demand due to the continued pressure of technological unemployment. Second, a reduction of the workday and an expanding role of education and earlier retirement in place of jobs in people's lives absorbed some portion of the expanding unemployment. Third, the shifting of unemployment from the developed center to the less developed periphery of the world capitalist system removed much of it from visibility. As for the twenty-first century, things may be changing indeed, as many studies are now finding, including the *2016 Annual Economic Report to the President* as reported by Steve Goldstein, "The robots are coming for jobs that pay $20 an hour or less, White House," *MarketWatch*, Feb. 2016, https://www.marketwatch.com/story/the-robots-are-coming-for-jobs-that-pay-20-an-hour-or-less-white-house-finds-2016-02-22.

18. Keynes wrote this famous line in his *A Tract on Monetary Reform* (London: Macmillan, 1924) to urge less hesitancy regarding what today we would call monetary expansion, that is, less bank hoarding of money in the face of recession/depression when just the opposite was needed at that time in England and the Continent.

19. See William Mitchell, Randall Wray and Martin Watts, *Macroeconomics* (London: Springer Nature Ltd, London, 2019), chap. 17.

20. Typically, two-thirds to four-fifths of total private sector saving are corporate retained earnings as opposed to personal saving. Thus, in 2019, gross private sector saving in the U.S. was $4.75 trillion, *personal* saving was $1.29 trillion. See *Statista*, https://www.statista.com/statistics/246261/total-personal-savings-in-the-united-states/ and at https://www.statista.com/statistics/246241/gross-private-savings-in-

the-united-states/, both of which used U.S. Bureau of Economic Analysis data.

21. The portion attributable to their managing their business is easily estimated as whatever total compensation they would receive were they in an equivalent salaried management position elsewhere. Were they to spend that much of their total business proceeds on hiring some manager(s), the remainder, their actual profit, would still need to be explained.

22. And see n. 18 on just how much of total private savings is retained earnings versus personal savings. The owner-manager issue will be discussed later.

23. See see n. 18.

24. Readers should see David Schweickart, *Against Capitalism* (Boulder, CO: Westview Press, 1996), chap. 1, for a more complete rendering of the argument in much greater detail than has been given here.

25. This is most easily seen for the case of inherited or bequeathed property and the income coming from it. Adam Smith referred to landlords as virtually parasitical and rent as a monopoly price (*Wealth of Nations*, Book One, chaps. VI and XI (1776)). He had little better views on what we would now call interest. Even the U.S. Internal Revenue Service acknowledges property and similar incomes as "unearned"; see annual IRS 1040 tax forms.

5. Realities of Class Today

1. Chuck Collins and Josh Hoxie, "Billionaire Bonanza 2018: Inherited Wealth Dynasties in the 21st Century United States," Institute for Policy Studies, October 30, 2018, https://ips-dc.org/report-billionaire-bonanza-2018/. More up-to-date figures are in chap. 1.

2. Shannon Moriarty (editor), Mazher Ali, Brian Miller, Jessica Morneault, Tim Sullivan, and Michael Young, *Born on Third Base: What the Forbes 400 Really Says about Economic Equality and Opportunity in America* (Boston, MA: United for a Fair Economy, 2012), https://d3n8a8pro7vhmx.cloudfront.net/ufe/pages/4171/attachments/original/1564623834/BornOnThirdBase_2012.pdf. The authors found conservatively that for the 2011 *Forbes 400*, 65 percent received significant help of some sort getting there. This ranged from startup capital, a significant but less than $1 million inheritance, or upper-class background (for those "born on first base"), to sufficient wealth to be placed immediately on the list themselves (the 21 percent who were "born already on home plate").

3. In 2020, a net worth of $2.4 million would place a household at the 94.5 percentile, that is, 94.5 percent of households would have less than that;

see PK, "Net Worth Percentile Calculator for the United States in 2020," DQYDJ, https://dqydj.com/net-worth-percentile-calculator-united-states/ using information from the Federal Reserve Board's Survey of Consumer Finance. At a 5 percent rate of return, certainly decent by current middle-class standards as of this writing, that would yield on a portfolio of that value a gross income of about $120,000 a year, a quite comfortable "upper middle" class income, especially if "earned" without working.

4. As of 2016, the United States Census Bureau estimated about 25 million "nonemployer" businesses, and another 8 million with employees, according to Todd Kehoe, "What Counts as a 'Business'? It might not be what you think it is," *Albany Business Review*, April 11, 2019, https://www.bizjournals.com/albany/news/2019/04/11/number-of-businesses-in-the-united-states.html. The "off-the-books" numbers would probably inflate those estimates considerably. See G. Marks, "The US Census Bureau says there are 32m small businesses. They're wrong," *The Guardian*, September 23, 2018, online at https://www.theguardian.com/business/2018/sep/23/how-many-small-businesses-us-census-bureau-wrong.

5. Much of the "gig economy" of today adds a whole new dimension to this category. Many gig workers and similar "sub-contractors" may be thought of as something like kiosk capitalists.

6. Michael Zweig, *The Working Class Majority: America's Best Kept Secret* (Ithaca, NY: Cornell University Press, 2012).

7. Michael Zweig, *The Working Class Majority*, estimates using strictly occupational data, ignoring the additional criterion of accumulated wealth. The latter could significantly affect the estimate. Given how few have sufficient wealth or adequate liquidity to start a business of sufficient size or otherwise to live off of asset income, the size of the working class could well be much greater.

8. "A Profile of the Working Poor, 2018," Report 1087, *BLS Reports* (July, 2020), https://www.bls.gov/opub/reports/working-poor/2018/home.

9. There are other ways in which the existence of a poverty population matters critically for the social power structures of class, which will be discussed in later chapters. See Herbert Gans, "The Uses of Poverty: The Poor Pay All," *Social Policy*, July/August 1971: 20–24. This is a classic article and must reading on this subject.

10. Today, slavery (as forced labor) usually employs debt servitude in combination with fear of real violence by the "employer" and/or of deportation by the authorities back to harsh conditions at home. The ILO estimated that in 2016, 40.3 million people were in modern slavery worldwide, including five million in forced sexual exploitation and 25

million in forced labor; see International Labor Organization, "Forced labour, modern slavery and human trafficking," http://www.ilo.org/global/topics/forced-labour/lang-en/index.htm. The actual number is likely much larger, due to the difficulties of counting.

11. See Tim Knapp, "Hierarchies and Control: A New Interpretation and Reevaluation of Oliver Williamson's 'Markets and Hierarchies' Story," *The Sociological Quarterly*, 30 no. 3 (September, 1989): 425–440, on the distinction. See David M. Gordon, *Fat and Mean: The Corporate Squeeze of American Workers and the Myth of Managerial 'Downsizing'* (New York: Free Press, 1996), on the inflation of the managerial hierarchy.

12. The classic analysis here is Richard Edwards, *Contested Terrain* (New York: Basic Books, 1979).

13. Ibid. The expansion of management, stratification, specialization, and bureaucracy as means of increasing employers' power certainly underlies much of David Graeber's observations in his provocative *Bullshit Jobs: A Theory* (New York: Simon & Schuster, 2018).

14. Francis Green and Steven McIntosh, "Union Power, Cost of Job Loss and Workers' Effort," *Industrial and Labor Relations Review*, 51 no. 3 (April, 1998), 363–383.

15. This idea has credence, albeit not universally, within the mainstream of economics, where it is known as the "efficiency wage theory." As would be expected, in the mainstream it is not construed in terms of employers' power but simply profitability.

16. See Michael D. Yates, *Why Unions Matter* (New York: Monthly Review Press, 1998), for an excellent overview of how unions work, the laws affecting them, and their many benefits for working people in the United States.

17. Ibid.

18. The idea of "coordinatorism" as the archetype advanced twentieth century society has a varied following. John Kenneth Galbraith, *The New Industrial State*, 3rd ed. (Boston: Houghton Mifflin, 1978), referred to the "technocracy" in the United States. Michael Albert and Robin Hahnel, *Unorthodox Marxism: An Essay on Capitalism, Socialism and Revolution* (Boston: South End Press, 1978), argued similarly but from a different viewpoint regarding both the United States and the Soviet Union.

19. Strictly speaking, a true agency relationship is usually thought of as involving a contract with the principal. Employees' contracts are with the firm, however, not with their immediate manager. Still, the latter is often or even generally delegated virtual "hiring/firing" power and pay and promotion power over the employee by the owner(s), so the situation is essentially the same for our purposes.

20. Workplace congeniality implies less social friction or disagreement both among workers and between workers and managers. It may be improved not only by employing more affable managers who better acknowledge and respect workers as human beings, but also by providing workplace amenities such as childcare or organizing outside social activities among workers.

21. "Efficiency wages" (see also note 15 above) are wages that are deliberately paid by the firm to exceed what the going market wage would otherwise be, with the intention of eliciting more or better work from employees (that is, more productivity) through various effects on their attitudes toward the work. See, for example, Ronald G. Ehrenberg and Robert S. Smith, *Modern Labor Economics: Theory and Public Policy*, 13th ed. (New York: Routledge, 2018), chap. 11.

22. Once in a while, a stockholder uprising occurs, for example, the corporate scandals and uprisings that culminated in the Sarbanes-Oxley Act of 2002. The general trend seems not so much to have been to return real power in the firm to stockholders as merely to provide rules assuring that top managers guide their firms in close accordance with stockholders' economic interests, that is, maintain stock value and dividends. Thus "managerial entrenchment" is to be properly controlled, not eliminated.

23. In effect, economists leave out or gloss over an important aspect of the story in their account of managers as agents "ripping off" business owners as principals. Another way of describing what is happening is that managers are able to appropriate for themselves some of the loot available from the exploitation of their inferiors that is otherwise "supposed" to go to owners.

6. Business and Politics in the Real World

1. For example, the capitalist power structure of employer power both bolsters and is sustained by patriarchal power. Women's low status in the labor force disempowers them within the family and the larger community and society, while their low status within the family and other social sites is a bedrock of discrimination against women in the labor force. Assuring a labor force that is bifurcated by sex is part of the segmentation that is critical to employers' power, as discussed in the last chapter, and employers can generally be counted upon to lead the resistance against the expansion of women's empowerment both in politics and in business.

2. Robert R. Alford, *Powers of Theory: Capitalism, the State, and Democracy* (Cambridge, England: Cambridge University Press, 1985), provides a good overview of the variety of alternative such theories,

and a synthesis as well. G. William Domhoff, *The Power Elite and the State: How Policy Is Made in America* (New York: Routledge, 2017), is consistent with the view offered in this book. See for further comparison Clyde W. Barrow, *Critical Theories of the State: Marxist, Neomarxist, Postmarxist* (Madison, WI: University of Wisconsin Press, 1993).

3.   Most textbooks on comparative economic systems will have a section on the "guided capitalism" of especially Japan, or "Japan, Inc." More critically referred to by some as "crony capitalism," it is also called "corporatism" or "state corporatism." Space does not permit elaboration here, but I suggest that all modern capitalism is essentially that very system, with merely the particular details of the forms of state intervention varying from one case to another. At various geographic levels of development, leading firms or networks of the private sector—financial and industrial entities—initiate investments in coordination with the state, that is, ruling elements of federal, state and/or local government as appropriate. Those leading firms undertake the critical investments, the state providing various kinds of support, incentives, and sometimes leadership, and the rest of the business sector then follows the lead by providing necessary primary and secondary inputs, the latter including those necessary for labor markets (housing, infrastructure, consumer goods), and so forth. The leading financial firms, and possibly the state too if necessary, makes available whatever additional investment capital is then also required. J. K. Galbraith in his *The New Industrial State* (Boston: Houghton Mifflin, 1978) described a planning sector versus a competitive sector: the entire economy goes mostly where the planning sector takes it. The planning sector leads (with the biggest firms in it doing the leading) and the competitive sector follows it. For Galbraith this occurs mostly without overt or conscious planning but via public modes of communication. However, there is also a real planning sector, based on various formal and informal interfirm interlocks. See also Eric Schutz, *Markets and Power*.

4.   John Kenneth Galbraith's *The New Industrial State* is a classic statement of this. Examples abound. Consumers may choose from among many shapes and sizes of automobiles, but manufacturers know they can sell all of whatever style they choose to produce, and only with difficulty may consumers choose mass transit instead, even in these times of rising fuel costs. They may choose this style of home or that one, but seldom if ever are other forms of dwelling available than single, nuclear family residences for the average consumer.

5.   The important connections with matters of income distribution as higher profits get gobbled up by management and/or labor internally

if either has any power to do so were examined by Ralph Bradburd, Thomas Pugel, and Katrina Pugh, "Internal Rent Capture and the Profit-Concentration Relation," *The Review of Economics and Statistics* 73, no. 3 (1991): 432–440.

6. See John Bellamy Foster, Robert W. McChesney, and R. Jamil Jonna, "Monopoly and Competition in Twenty-First Century Capitalism," *Monthly Review* 63 no. 2 (April 1, 2011), for an excellent summary of the contemporary situation.

7. Thus, laxity of U.S. policy that has ruled since the 1980s has yielded major payoffs for the owners of such aspiring megafirms as Facebook, Amazon, and Google, and is a likely source of increasing inequality in its own right. See Tim Wu's excellent history, *The Curse of Bigness: Antitrust in the New Gilded Age* (New York: Columbia Global Reports, 2018), and Jonathan Tepper with Denise Hearn, *The Myth of Capitalism: Monopolies and the Death of Competition* (Hoboken, NJ: John Wiley and Sons, 2019). An excellent analysis of these matters is John Bellamy Foster, Robert W. McChesney, and R. Jamil Jonna, "Monopoly and Competition."

8. Amazon seems an example of an astonishingly broad and also unusually tight network of this type, its many participating independent retail sellers having precisely this kind of relationship with it. See Russell Brandom, "The Monopoly Busting Case Against Google, Amazon, Uber and Facebook: What Tech Companies Have to Fear from Antitrust Law," *The Verge* (September 5, 2018), www.theverge.com/2018/9/5/17805162/monopoly-antitrust-regulation-google-amazon-uber-facebook. The income transfer occurs partly by their receiving lower than competitive prices on their products or services or paying higher than competitive prices on their purchases; there may also be stockholding or credit interlocks that effect a direct transfer of dividend or interest income, as well as other means of transfer.

9. Standard measures of bank market concentration indicate market power in that industry as in others, correlating as expected with customer access to business loans (negatively) and loan costs (positively). See Nicolla Cetorelli and Phillip E. Strahan, "Finance as a Barrier to Entry: Bank Competition and Industry Structure in Local United States Markets," *The Journal of Finance* 61 no. 1 (February, 2006): 437–461.

10. I have referred to this elsewhere (Eric Schutz, *Markets and Power*) as *planners' power*, for other businesses that submit to it do so recognizing the general benefits to be gained among all in the affected regions or sectors. Beth Mintz and Michael Schwartz, "Corporate Interlocks, Financial Hegemony, and Intercorporate Coordination," in Michael Schwartz, ed., *The Structure of Power in America* (New York: Holmes

and Meier, 1978), and especially John R. Munkirs, *The Transformation of American Capitalism* (New York: M. E. Sharpe, 1984) theorized and documented extensively the kinds of interlocks involved here.

11. But Samuel Bowles and Herbert Gintis, in "Contested Exchange," theorize creditors' power. See also Corrado Benassi, "Asymmetric Information and Equilibrium Credit Rationing: A Survey," *Revista Internationale di Scienze Economiche e Commerciali* 35 (1988): 993–1020.

12. William K. Carroll, "Does Disorganized Capitalism Disorganize Corporate Networks?" *Canadian Journal of Sociology* 27 no. 3 (Summer, 2002): 339–371, shows how financial-corporate networks remain intact albeit looser in the age of globalized capitalism in Canada; Andrew Wood, "The Scalar Transformation of the United States Commercial Property Development Industry: A Cautionary Note on the Limits of Globalization," *Economic Geography* 80 no. 2 (2004): 119–140, shows grounds for similar skepticism regarding the effects of globalization in the United States, at least for one local market, that of commercial property development. On some of the advantages of a network-oriented approach to the analysis of firm and market behavior see Ranjay Gulati, Nitin Nohria, and Akbar Zaheer, "Strategic Networks," *Strategic Management Journal* 21 no. 3 (March, 2000): 203–215.

13. Debt restructuring of this sort for major cities is not unusual, among the most famous cases being perhaps those of the New York City and Cleveland defaults of the 1970s. The World Bank's "structural adjustment" programs are certainly the most notorious of this sort on the international stage.

14. The Keynesian analysis pertains here, even though what is referred to here is usually termed "monetarism," an approach that economists have posed as contrary to Keynesianism. According to the well-known textbook Keynesian analysis, higher interest rates due to monetary restraint reduce private investment spending, which causes higher unemployment due to the consequent fall in aggregate demand.

15. See Ben Bernanke, "Why Are Interest Rates So Low?" *Brookings*, March 30, 2015, https://www.brookings.edu/blog/ben-bernanke/2015/03/30/why-are-interest-rates-so-low/. This article also provides an interesting glimpse at how the Fed does indeed attempt, among its other goals, to maintain aggregate interest income. Of course, as a mainstreamer, he denies a role of the Fed in actually controlling interest rates: "The state of the economy, not the Fed, is the ultimate determinant. . . . "

16. Keynes's phrase is from the last chapter of his *General Theory of Employment, Interest and Money* (1936). Krugman's terse quote is in the *New York Times*, January 22, 2014, https://www.nytimes.com/searc h?query=krugman+euthanasia+of+the+rentier.

17. Pre-civilized societies are another matter. Considerable evidence suggests these were typically more democratic than anything even in modern times. The anthropology of "pre-state" societies is perhaps controversial, and certainly tribal life, even its "civic" aspects, was not generally idyllic. But it does appear that more or less universal participation in communal decision-making, with wide latitude given individual expression, was the general rule. Jerry Mander, *In the Absence of the Sacred: The Failure of Technology and the Survival of the Indian Nations* (San Francisco, CA: Sierra Club Books, 1991), has an interesting account of the Iroquois Compact, a very late written expression of one group's practices.

18. Robert A. Dahl, *On Democracy* (New Haven, CT: Yale University Press, 2000).

19. A definition of power might be such that someone who is subject to it must submit to decisions (in this case, political) to which they would not have consented in a truly democratic context (Eric Schutz, *Markets and Power*). It is true that the exact nature of consent may be debatable, an argument that obviously cannot be undertaken here. However, the relevant parts of this book taken as a whole, including later chapters, may be taken as at least supportive of the case.

20. Hence the importance of the movement these days in the United States toward such things as a voting holiday and extended early voting.

21. The high voter turnout for the 2020 U.S. election was particularly indicative of the strength of feeling of many lower-income voters on the presidential contenders. The correlation of political participation with income or wealth has been statistically verified in a number of studies, for example, Randall Akee, "Voting and Income," *Econofact*, February 2016, https://econofact.org/voting-and-income; Sidney Verba, Kay Lehman Schlozman, and Henry E. Brady, *Voice and Equality: Civic Voluntarism in American Politics* (Cambridge, MA: Harvard University Press, 1995).

22. Take two of the most notorious examples from opposite ends of the political spectrum. The Koch brothers (Charles and David, the latter now deceased) fund and directly run a considerable network of right-wing politically oriented organizations (see Jane Mayer, *Dark Money: The Hidden History of the Billionaires Behind the Radical Right* (New York: Penguin Random House, 2016). At the other end of the political spectrum is George Soros's well-known Open Society Foundations, a source of progressive funding worldwide, operated under his direction.

23. The notorious United States Supreme Court *Citizens United* case of 2010 made this a critically important aspect of America's currently precarious politics.

24. Today, Fox TV is certainly one of the most outstandingly nefarious examples. Political public relations, on the other hand, is much less well-known, yet perhaps equally critical in political electoral campaigns, in framing political parties' agendas, and in shaping the public's consciousness of what is "news." See Robert Wynne, "Five Things Everyone Should Know About Public Relations," *Forbes*, January 21, 2016, https://www.forbes.com/sites/robertwynne/2016/01/21/five-things-everyone-should-know-about-public-relations/.

25. Perhaps the best known of such policies are the "right to work" laws found mostly in the Southern states. These and other similar policies in these states set a kind of cheap labor tone to their economic development. See *Economic Policy Institute* (blog), January 27, 2014, "Life Is Worse in Right to Work States," 2014, online at https://www.epi.org/blog/life-worse-work-states/.

26. Yascha Mounk, "America Is Not a Democracy," *The Atlantic*, March 2018, https://www.theatlantic.com/magazine/archive/2018/03/america-is-not-a-democracy/550931/ outlines the now famous study (see Martin Gilens and Benjamin I. Page, "Testing Theories of American Politics: Elites, Interest Groups, and Average Citizens," *Perspectives on Politics* 12 no. 3 (September 18, 2014): 564–581, https://scholar.princeton.edu/sites/default/files/mgilens/files/gilens_and_page_2014_-testing_theories_of_american_politics.doc.pdf) in which it was found that "Economic elites and narrow interest groups . . . succeeded in getting their favored policies adopted about half of the time, and in stopping legislation to which they were opposed nearly all of the time. Mass-based interest groups, meanwhile, had little effect on public policy..." in some 1,800 different policy issues that were examined.

27. Thus, although there is not popular sovereignty, there is at least some important popular input.

7. Capitalist Culture

1. Briefly, value power works either by what amounts to simple deception (misleading or withheld information) such that people behave in accord with values they do not hold or by effectively altering their actual values. In the latter case, what might be called their "meta-preferences" may nonetheless remain unchanged even as their values or preferences are changed. This is a tricky one, there being perhaps some issue as to whether it is even possible to actually change people's preferences. That may be sidestepped here, since it is at the least possible to change people's expressed preferences and values along with their behavior and habits.

2. See Marshall McLuhan and Quentin Fiore, *The Medium is the Message*

(Berkeley, CA: Gingko Press, 2005). Of course, the distinction is only partly relevant. Their point was that the medium itself communicates a kind of content of its own in the form of the affective reactions it creates in audiences, for example, living room video versus film in theaters or digital recorded music versus live performances. Nonetheless, the film or music itself, or the news or commentary, is obviously distinct from that which conveys it.

3.   Ashley Lutz, "These 6 Corporations Control 90 percent Of the Media in America," *Business Insider*, June14, 2012.

4.   A number of scholarly works are available on the extent of media concentration, and the picture is unnerving. See, for example, Benjamin M. Compaine and Douglas Gomery, *Who Owns the Media? Competition and Concentration in the Mass Media*, 3rd ed. (New York: Routledge, 2000); Ben H. Bagdikian, *The New Media Monopoly* (Boston: Beacon Press, 2004); Eli M. Noam, *Media Ownership and Concentration in America* (Oxford University Press, 2009).

5.   It is likely that these are less discussed because most such discussions occur within the media themselves.

6.   One might venture that these biases are stronger and more visible the more advertising-driven the specific medium. TV and radio, for example, are perhaps most egregious, book publishing and films the least. But as the latter become themselves more ad-driven (commercials in movies are already ubiquitous, and electronic books are now beginning to use advertising), they will certainly move in the same direction.

7.   Thus, it is apparent that the new media, in conjunction with especially Fox News, OAN, and Newsmax, played a critical role in promoting Donald Trump's lies about the presidential election of 2020 and the insurrection that followed in Washington, D.C. The new media, by algorithmically inviting people to segregate themselves into their own preferred groupings, have served to fracture the citizenry into what often seem separate and mutually incomprehensible discourse universes, to the point of a nearly pathological factionalization of politics. As well, their undermining of professional journalism has been catastrophic for local news reporting, thus allowing the dominance of national monopolies there, of all places. In these and other ways, it appears the new media are doing at least as much harm as good in the United States.

8.   For the alternative perspective that instead many people are invariably involved in accumulating an individual's wealth, indeed all of society is involved, see the website of Chuck Collins, himself a wealthy heir: inequality.org.

9. "Margaret Thatcher: A Life in Quotes," *The Guardian*, April 8, 2013, https://www.theguardian.com/politics/2013/apr/08/margaret-thatcher-quotes.

10. An interesting apparent exception is the media reaction to the Black Lives Matter movement demonstrations. Focusing on race makes it somewhat difficult to avoid the issue of class. Indeed, conversations were even initiated on the subject of caste in the United States (see Isabel Wilkerson, *Caste: The Origins of Our Discontents* (New York: Random House, 2020)). The outrage and hand-wringing that occurred in the media during and since this episode may end up coming to nothing. However, given the pivotal usefulness of a poverty population in the American class system and the need to manage it discreetly and unobtrusively, and given the depth and breadth of racism in American culture. On American militarism in recent times, see Noam Chomsky, *Making the Future: Occupations, Interventions, Empire and Resistance* (San Francisco, CA: City Lights Publishers, 2012). On the mass media, Edward S. Herman and Noam Chomsky, *Manufacturing Consent: The Political Economy of the Mass* Media (New York: Pantheon, 1988), is a classic on this subject.

11. It is probably often forgotten that CNN's president, Jeff Zucker, effectively put Trump in the presidency—for ratings!—then continued its pursuit of ratings with a nonstop criticism of Trump's term in office, albeit much deserved. There is nothing like spectacle for "the news." See, for example, Pete Tucker, "CNN's Trump Problem," *HuffPost*, July 7, 2017, https://www.huffpost.com/entry/cnns-trump-problem_b_10833064.

12. The presidencies of Ronald Reagan and Donald Trump are merely the most obvious cases at the national level of the revolving door between the media and government.

13. In the United States, public higher education is now majority funded by student-paid tuition, about half of which comes from loans, grants, and scholarships. Only about 37 percent of higher education funding is from state and federal revenues. See Anne Stauffer and Justin Theal, "Federal and State Funding of Higher Education: A changing landscape," Pew Charitable Trusts, November 6, 2015, https://www.pewtrusts.org/~/media/assets/2015/06/federal_state_funding_higher_education_final.pdf; and American Council on Higher Education, "US Higher Education: A Brief Guide," 2007, https://www.acenet.edu/Documents/brief-guide-to-US-higher-ed.pdf.

14. The annual national scandal of the Texas Board of Education's textbook selection is a case in point. The board's notoriously conservative bias (for example, creationist biology texts, and history texts that downplay slavery in United States history) affects a much broader population of

students than just that of Texas insofar as book publishing companies craft their books for the largest buyers. Many other school boards more or less just go along to avoid controversy, especially in states with strong conservative politics. See American Civil Liberties Union of Texas, "The Texas State Board of Education: A Case of Abuse of Power," May 13, 2010, http://www.aclutx.org/files/aclureportfinal.pdf. Public school classroom teachers all over the country are constrained to follow their assigned textbooks and dictated content policies on pain of dismissal.

15. The teachers' accountability movement is based on the view that since poor quality in education must be due to poor quality teachers, rather than mismanagement, underfunding, poverty, or inequality, a businesslike quantitative testing and evaluation of teachers is necessary to maintain quality. For a more informed viewpoint, see Anna M. Wright, "Historical view of accountability and teacher labor," *Communication Education* 69:1 (2020), 105–118. The corporatist approach to administering education has a strong hold in higher education also, where 73 percent of all faculty in the United States in 2016 were off the tenure track. See "Data Snapshot: Contingent Faculty in US Higher Ed," American Association of University Professors, https://www.aaup.org/sites/default/files/10112018%20Data%20 Snapshot%20Tenure.pdf.

16. There is, in fact, such a tradition in education, but like all traditions, it requires living institutions to endure, in this case institutions that would counter a trend toward "classism" in education. Especially in these times, there seem few or no such institutions around. The most recent incarnation of federal education policy (the Trump administration) as of this writing may seem the logical conclusion of a trend. See Michael McGerr, *A Fierce Discontent: The Rise and Fall of the Progressive Movement in America, 1870–1920* (London: Oxford University Press, 2005).

17. Samuel Bowles and Herbert Gintis, *Schooling in Capitalist America*, showed how the primary and secondary education system not only accommodates to the specific needs of the class system but also helps in this specific positive sense to sustain it.

18. The importance of "pecuniary emulation" and "conspicuous consumption," even in the relatively simpler and pre-commercial society in which he lived in 1900, may be seen in Thorstein Veblen's *Theory of the Leisure Class* (Oxford University Press, 2008).

19. And of those "in the loop" who are totally taken in, it should not be forgotten just how difficult it is for the individual immersed in this cultural and social context to avoid being taken in.

8. More Inequality, Less Flourishing

1. Some commentators are focusing on top salary earners, as opposed to property income recipients, as the prime beneficiaries of the recent increase in inequality. Others have noted that both groups have benefited. Emmanuel Saez focuses on the former group, and his and Thomas Piketty's work have driven much of the mainstream commentary on the issue. See Emmanuel Saez, "Striking It Richer: The Evolution of Top Incomes in the United States (Updated with 2009 and 2010 Estimates)," September 13, 2012, https://eml.berkeley.edu/~saez/saez-UStopincomes-2010.pdf; and Thomas Piketty and Emmanuel Saez, "The Evolution of Top Incomes: A Historical and International Perspective," *American Economic Review Papers and Proceedings* 96 no. 2 (October, 2006): 200–205. Among the latter group are the heterodox Levy Institute scholars Edward N. Wolff and Ajit Zacharias, "Class Structure and Economic Inequality," Levy Economics Institute Working Paper No. 487 (Bard College, January, 2007).

2. See Edward N. Wolff, *Top Heavy: The Increasing Inequality of Wealth in America and What Can Be Done About It* (New York: New Press, 2002), chap. 6, for a good account of the effects of the stock and housing markets versus income inequality on the wealth distribution.

3. Suggestive of this hypothesis, statistics do seem to show a "blip" in the rise in wealth inequality in 2008, which halted with the stock and housing market crash, but since then has resumed (see Figure 1.4 in chapter1).

4. Compare this theory with Robert H. Frank and Phillip J. Cook, *The Winner Take All Society: Why the Few at the Top Get So Much More Than the Rest of Us* (New York: Penguin, 1996). In effect, it is argued here, it is huge economies of scale in a single aspect of a firm's operations, specifically, in networking and distribution, that have most importantly led to a lucky few getting the limelight.

5. There are some simplifications in this analysis. Professional athletes are often not salaried, and financial brokers are on commission. Readers should see, however, that the question posed here remains.

6. A review of this theory and its literature showing recent empirical work is Joanne Horton, Yuval Millo, and George Serafeim, "Paid for Connections? Social Network, Executive and Outside Director Compensation," Social Science Research Network, February 1, 2009, http://papers.ssrn.com/sol3/papers.cfm?abstract_id=1416935.

7. See Jonathan Tepper and Denise Hearn's careful study of concentration, *The Myth of Capitalism: Monopolies and the Death of Competition* (Hoboken, NJ: John Wiley and Sons, 2019). See also chapter 6 of this book, end notes 6, 7, and 8.

8. Some of these (most notably, amazon.com) are moreover especially able to exploit employees, by using gig workers and contingent workers. Among the best-known examples of gig workers are Uber, Lyft, Grubhub, and Amazon Flex drivers. Contingent workers include also part-time and seasonal workers and subcontractors of all sorts. Most of these get none of the standard benefits of employees—health and injury insurance, pensions, leaves—not to mention decent and secure wages.

9. Naturally, there is some debate over this. See Paul Gomme and Peter Ruppert, "Measuring Labor's Share of Income," *Policy Discussion Papers, Federal Reserve Bank of Cleveland*, no.04-07 (2004) http://www.clevelandfed.org/research/PolicyDis/No7Nov04.pdf?WT.oss=gomme percent20rupertandWT.oss_r=150.

10. Emmanuel Saez, "Striking It Richer: The Evolution of Top Incomes in the United States (Updated with 2008 Estimates)," *Journal of Economic Policy* 2 no. 3 (2010): 4, http://elsa.berkeley.edu/~saez/saez-UStopincomes-2008.pdf. All of Saez's and Piketty's work focuses almost exclusively on the top ten percent, one percent, or less of the distribution.

11. James K. Galbraith's careful work on this documented increasing wage inequality overall for the earlier portion of this period. See his *Created Unequal: The Crisis in American Pay* (University of Chicago Press, 1998), which focuses on both wages and other labor compensation. See also Lawrence Mishel et al., *State of Working America 2008/2009*: 134–139, which also focuses on the total of labor compensation.

12. Edward N. Wolff, *Poverty and Income Distribution*, 2nd ed., (Hoboken, NJ: Wiley-Blackwell, 2009): 387–389, gives a good summary of the work on both sides of the skill bias theory. Daron Acemoglu, "Technical Change, Inequality, and the Labor Market," *Journal of Economic Literature* 40 no. 1 (March 1972): 7–72, 2002, gives a nuanced version of the theory. Lawrence Mishel et al., *State of Working America 2008/2009*: 213–219, gives a good basic critique. David R. Howell, "Theory-Driven Facts and the Growth in Earnings Inequality," *Review of Radical Political Economics*, 31 no. 1 (March 1999): 54–86, gives an especially strong critique from the viewpoint of a power- or class-based theory of rising inequality.

13. As a long-run labor market equilibrium theory, the skill-bias technology theory is not concerned with excess labor supplies or demands. But in principle, much or all of the decline in wages closer to the bottom might occur due to a continual *disequilibrium* in the low-wage labor market—an excess of the labor supplied over that demanded—and the dis-employed seeking of new jobs not yet opening up but (presumably)

soon to be opening. Similarly, labor market disequilibria could account at least partly for the higher wages and salaries toward the top of the scale, with the higher-skill labor supplied lagging behind that being demanded. These disequilibrium effects are probably important in fact; see the section below on globalization.

14. See Special Report: "A mighty contest: Job destruction by robots could outweigh creation," *The Economist*, March 29, 2013; and Lawrence Summers, "The Inequality Puzzle," *Democracy: A Journal of Ideas*, 32 (Spring 2014). It has been well-known that in principle the economy's capacity to "absorb" or prevent the permanent unemployment of the technologically dis-employed in the longterm depends on many institutional factors, such as the length of the workday and year, the number of legal holidays, the legal retirement age and conditions, and the opportunities available in secondary, higher, and adult education— as well as the employment potential (that is, the labor-intensiveness) of rising new technologies. See also the discussion in chapter 4, end note 13.

15. The rise in employer power, it should also be noted, almost certainly explains the "puzzle" of very low unemployment alongside stagnant wages that occurred late in the decade just prior to the COVID-19 pandemic and that permitted President Trump to proclaim his economic policy prowess until the pandemic hit. In the past, when unemployment reached anything like that fifty-year low, wages would be rising significantly due to the consequent shift in the balance of power toward working people, as was discussed in an earlier chapter. That balance had got so out of kilter, however, because of the decline in labor unions and the rise of conservative/reactionary public policy (for example, states passing new "right-to-work" laws) that hardly any hints of wage increases had appeared when the pandemic hit.

16. James K. Galbraith, *Created Unequal: The Crisis in American Pay* (University of Chicago Press, 1998).

17. The change from the use of Gross National Product to Gross Domestic Product as the base measure of economic production perhaps marks the precise moment at which globalization was stamped as having been officially recognized. Regarding the policy convergence referred to, insofar as globalization has originated in the United States and other advanced capitalist nations, it is arguably an imperial phenomenon, a matter that will not be pursued here.

18. Bear in mind too that labor costs, for example, in a particular country, are a function not only of its wages (private and social) and other labor compensation components (benefits) but also of its labor-productivity.

19. Isabel Wilkerson's *Caste*, while an interpretation of things as they are

and have been, names what many might think of as the end point in this spiral: an inflexible system of virtually zero-mobility classes.

20. This is especially so in "right to work" states, where nonmembers in a firm with a union contract legally get a free ride with the same pay and work conditions as members in the union. But the point remains even in more progressive states, since the union/nonunion pay differential is reduced as union strength gradually wanes.

21. Robert Pollin, *Contours of Descent: United States Economic Fractures and the Landscape of Global Austerity* (London: Verso, 2005) shows the economic impact of the national politics of recent decades: the tight fiscal and monetary policies of recent times essentially worked to aggravate this erosion of labor's position vis-à-vis management.

22. As this was written, an important union certification election took place among workers at an amazon.com plant, the outcome of which could perhaps have helped turn the tide. Employing "union avoidance" consultants and lawyers who helped it apply all the usual tactics, Amazon crushed the unionization effort. Dave Jamieson, "How Amazon Crushed the Union Effort in Alabama: Inside the High-Stakes Campaign that Ended with a Lopsided Loss for the Union," *Huffpost* (April 13, 2021) https://www.huffpost.com/entry/amazon-crushed-union-threat-alabama_ n_60746e5ce4b01e304234929d.

23. See, for example, Joseph Minton Amann and Tom Breuer, *Fair and Balanced, My Ass! An Unbridled Look at the Bizarre Reality of Fox News* (New York: Nation Books, 2007) for an account of its rise in economics, an important part of the overall story. As for all of this being a kind of reaction to government corruption, if anything the corruption has arisen most notably from this trend itself, as is particularly clear in the events surrounding what may now perhaps be called the Trump Affair.

24. See James A. Aune, *Selling the Free Market: The Rhetoric of Economic Correctness* (New York: Guilford Press, 2002); and Naomi Klein, *The Shock Doctrine: The Rise of Disaster Capitalism* (New York: Henry Holt and Co, 2007).

9. Economy, Community, Biosphere

1. Economists use several different definitions of "efficiency," but neoclassical economic theory defines it as a situation where no one's well-being can be improved without damaging or hurting someone else. Alternatively, it holds when all goods and factors of production in an economy are distributed or allocated to their most valuable uses and waste is minimized. See Walter Nicolson and Christopher Snyder, *Microeconomic Theory: Basic Principles and Extensions*, 12th ed., (Boston: Cengage, 2016), chap. 13. As may be intuitive, economic

NOTES TO PAGES 197–201

growth, the increase in the economy's productive capacity over time, may be easier to achieve in conditions of economic efficiency. But although economic growth and efficiency are not equivalent, nor is the latter a necessary condition for growth to occur, economists and others often conflate the two as if they were equivalent goals of public policy. For the moment, suppose the two can be taken as equivalent policy goals for a society.

2. See Phillipe Aghion, Eve Caroli, and Cecilia Garcia-Panalosa, "Inequality and Economic Growth: The Perspective of the New Growth Theories," *Journal of Economic Literature* 37 no.4 (December 1999): 1615–1660, for a review of the theory and evidence. Louis Putterman, John E. Roemer, and Joaquim Silvestre, "Does Egalitarianism Have a Future?" *Journal of Economic Literature* 36 no.2 (June 1998): 861–902, review the theory from a broader perspective of comparative institutions.

3. Some might apply here a kind of majoritarian-utilitarian calculus: if the short-ended are a sufficiently small minority, then perhaps the majority may comfortably justify it to themselves.

4. For example, some of the writings of Karl Marx might be so interpreted—except for the fact of the *The Communist Manifesto* itself, which, along with other of his writings, was aimed precisely at immediately mitigating the situation of those on the short end. See Karl Marx, Friedrich Engels, and Robert C. Tucker. *The Marx-Engels Reader*, 2nd ed., (New York: Norton, 1978).

5. According to Donella H. Meadows, Jorgen Randers, and Dennis Meadows, *The Limits to Growth: The 30-Year Update* (White River Junction, VT: Chelsea Green Publishing, 2004), the world is right about at the point at which they predicted in 1972 that growth would begin to reverse into collapse because of resource and environmental overuse, as stated in several of the scenarios in those authors' *The Limits to Growth* (Falls Church, VA: Potomac Associates, 1972).

6. Presumably this pertains only for cases short of a completely rigid caste system.

7. It should be noted that although the Scandinavian countries are much more egalitarian in terms of their income distributions, their wealth distributions are about as inequitable as that of the United States, indeed those of Sweden and the Netherlands are even more so, as measured by the gini coefficient. See Credit Suisse Research Institute, *Global Wealth Data Book 2018*, October, 2018, https://archive.org/details/global-wealth-databook-2018. A sortable tabulation of gini coefficients of the world's countries, based on Credit Suisse data, is available at https://en.wikipedia.org/wiki/List_of_countries_by_wealth_inequality.

8.   It may be thought that this argument requires something like an assumption of "diminishing returns to investments in human capital accumulation" like that presumably usually made for capital goods accumulation, that a dollar spent on human capital investment for lower income people yields more human capital than one spent on the affluent, since the human capital of the wealthy is already well developed. But affluent people's spending on luxury goods that are of no consequence for their human capital one way or the other detracts from the resources available for lower income people's investments in desperately needed human capital, and that is wasteful regardless of assumptions of diminishing returns. See also the last paragraph of this subsection.

9.   See Bureau of Economic Analysis, "National Income and Product Accounts Table 5.1 Saving and Investment," 15 July 2010, http://www. bea.gov/national/nipaweb/SelectTable.asp?Selected=Y#S5. Business retained earnings as a fraction of total private sector savings ranges from around two-thirds to over four-fifths of the latter.

10. In other countries or in the less developed world, exports may also play a large role here.

11. Innovation in the private sector, and presumably also to some extent in the public sector, is increasingly organized using contingent labor and subcontracting, a fact that does not alter the point here. See Raúl Delgado Wise and Mateo Crossa Niell, "Capital, Science, Technology: The Development of Productive Forces in Contemporary Capitalism," *Monthly Review* 72 no. 2 (March 1, 2021), https://monthlyreview. org/2021/03/01/capital-science-technology/.

12. Harry Braverman, *Labor and Monopoly Capital: The Degradation of Work in the Twentieth Century* (New York: Monthly Review Press, 1974) is the classic work on this topic. A more recent work is Jason Resnikoff, *Labor's End: How the Promise of Automation Degraded Work* (Champaign, Illinois: University of Illinois Press, 2021). And on surveillance technology generally, see Shoshanna Zuboff, *The Age of Surveillance Capitalism: The Fight for a Human Future at the New Frontier of Power* (New York: Public Affairs, Hachette Group, 2018). The profit-oriented bias in capitalist technological development that is the basis of this conclusion has been of similar and momentous consequence in other contexts. Well-known examples are the historic belatedness in the development of alternative energy sources in the age of cheap fossil fuels, and the failure to devote funding for research on medical vaccinations for "Third World diseases," that is, those diseases not affecting the affluent populations of the developed capitalist nations.

13. For further discussion of this, see the subsection on the democratic worker-managed workplace in chap. 10. See also Samuel Bowles and Herbert Gintis, "Efficient Redistribution: New Rules for Markets, States and Communities," in Samuel Bowles, Herbert Gintis, and Erik Olin Wright, eds., *Recasting Egalitarianism: New Rules for Communities, States and Markets* (London: Verso, 1998), and the other contributors to that volume for in-depth discussion of these ideas.

14. Surplus productivity would be measured—with great difficulty, given the available data—by the ratio of the surplus to the total potential output. One such effort is Anwar Shaikh and E. Ahmet Tonak, *Measuring the Wealth of Nations: The Political Economy of National Accounts* (Cambridge: Cambridge University Press, 1996).

15. Well-known among anthropologists is Marshall Sahlins. His *Stone Age Economics* (Chicago: Aldine-Atherton, Inc., 1972) was an extended attack on capitalist values and the theoretical categories of neoclassical economics from the viewpoint of the alternative values and categories of what Sahlins called "the original affluent society" found in hunter-gatherer communities. See also John Gowdy, *Limited Wants, Unlimited Means: A Reader on Hunter-Gatherer Economics and the Environment* (Washington, D.C.: Island Press, 1997).

16. See Matt Ridley, *The Agile Gene: How Nature Turns on Nurture* (New York: Harper, 2004).

17. The classic *Habits of the Heart: Individualism and Commitment in American Life* by Robert N. Bellah, Richard Madsen, William S. Sullivan, Ann Swidler, and Steven M. Tipton (University of California Press, 1985) brilliantly shows how much Americans miss a sense of community. On the alienation extant in modern and postmodern communities, see Ronald A. Salerno, "Alienated Communities: Between Aloneness and Connectedness," in Lauren Langman and Devorah Kalekin-Fishman, eds., *The Evolution of Alienation: Trauma, Promise and the Millennium* (New York: Rowman and Littlefield, 2006). And in modern life generally, Johann Hari, *Lost Connections: Why You're Depressed and How to Find Hope* (London: Bloomsbury Publishing, 2019).

18. In times such as these in which there is great need for social adjustment to changing material circumstances, they are almost invariably conservative just when adaptation is most necessary. See the classic by Thorstein Veblen, *The Theory of the Leisure Class* (New York: Macmillan, 1899) on the roots of this conservatism.

19. David Matthews, "Capitalism and Mental Health," *Monthly Review* 70:8 (January, 2019), https://monthlyreview.org/2019/01/01/capitalism-and-mental-health/ is an excellent account of the roots of these

pathologies in today's capitalist system: ". . . capitalism is a major determinant of poor mental health."

20. The title says it all in Robert D. Putnam, *Bowling Alone: The Collapse and Revival of American Community* (New York: Simon and Schuster, 2001). J. Habermas, *The Structural Transformation of the Public Sphere: An Inquiry into a Category of Bourgeois Society* (Cambridge: Cambridge, MA, MIT Press,1991), first focused attention in the 1960s on a "public sphere" in democratic civic governance.

21. Robert H. Frank, *Falling Behind: How Rising Inequality Harms the Middle Class* (University of California Press, 2007), discusses the stresses on the "middle class" today due to pecuniary emulation and conspicuous consumption in a context of increasing inequality. Thorstein Veblen, who originated the terms pecuniary emulation and conspicuous consumption in his *The Theory of the Leisure Class*, had already noted these stresses in the much simpler times of America *circa* 1900.

22. This is somewhat well supported by the various cross-country "happiness studies" one may now find, all of which invariably report the apparent congeniality of life in the Scandinavian/Nordic countries, the egalitarian economics and politics of which are also well-known. Kate Pickett and Richard Wilkinson, *The Spirit Level: Why Equality Makes a Society Stronger* (London: Bloomsbury Press, 2010), is an excellent summary of much of this research.

23. As in William Damon, "The Death of Honesty," *Defining Ideas*, Hoover Institution, January 12, 2012, https://www.hoover.org/research/death-honesty.

24. Robert N. Bellah et al., *Habits of the Heart*.

25. The classic on this, but from the simpler age of mere television, is Neil Postman, *Amusing Ourselves to Death: Public Discourse in the Age of Show Business* (New York: Viking Penguin, 1985). An up-to-date view of the field Postman virtually created himself, media and communication theory, or "media ecology," is Lance Strate, *Amazing Ourselves to Death: Neil Postman's Brave New World Revisited* (New York: Peter Lang, 2014).

26. For example, Benjamin Y. Fong, "The climate crisis? It's capitalism, stupid," *New York Times*, November, 20, 2017, https://www.nytimes.com/2017/11/20/opinion/climate-capitalism-crisis.html.

27. See, for example, John Bellamy Foster, *The Robbery of Nature: Capitalism and the Ecological Rift* (New York: Monthly Review Press, 2020), and his *Ecology Against Capitalism* (New York: Monthly Review Press, 2002).

28. This year (2021) and last may mark a turning point in the progress of these developments, as major heat waves, wildfires, and floods

worldwide, including New York City's first-ever flash flood, vied with the COVID-19 pandemic for news headline space.

29. The present rate of species extinction is now so much greater than what is estimated to be the "background rate" that it is believed we are now in the midst of the sixth great species extinction, the last one being that of the dinosaurs sixty-five million years ago. See Richard Leakey and Robert Lewin, *The Sixth Extinction: Patterns of Life and the Future of Humankind* (New York: Anchor Books,1996) and Elizabeth Kolbert, *The Sixth Extinction: An Unnatural History* (New York: Henry Holt, 2014).

30. Externalities, the commons, and open access resources are discussed in detail in any good environmental economics textbook, for example, Jonathan M. Harris and Brian Roach, *Environmental and Natural Resource Economics: A Contemporary Approach* (New York: Routledge, 2018). See also John Bellamy Foster, *The Robbery of Nature*; and Eric A. Schutz, "Planetary Eco-Collapse and Capitalism: A Contemporary Marxist Perspective," *Forum for Social Economics* 49 no. 3 (2020): 257–280. In economics, the concept of externalities is usually attributed to the early neoclassical economist Arthur Cecil Pigou, and is a regular item in all introductory and advanced microeconomics, mainstream and otherwise. For example, see Walter Nicholson and Christopher M. Snyder, *Microeconomic Theory: Basic Principles and Extensions*, 12th ed. (Boston, MA: Cengage Learning, 2016). However, Karl Marx also noted the capitalist disregard for the environment in this same aspect of market competition (John Bellamy Foster, *The Robbery of Nature*). Garrett Hardin first raised for economists "The Tragedy of the Commons" (*Science*, December 13, 1968). Elinor Ostrom, the first female Nobel Prize winner, corrected him and began a literature on how "open access" resources typically arise historically from the destruction of the self-regulation of traditional societies' commons. See her *Governing the Commons: The Evolution of Institutions for Collective Action* (Cambridge: Cambridge University Press, 1990).

31. Herman Daly (see, for example, his *Beyond Growth: The Economics of Sustainable Development* (Boston: Beacon Press, 1997)) has certainly been one of the most effective environmentalists in the field of economics in these times. His work spans the whole spectrum of ecological economics, but falls short of recognizing these essential features of the capitalist market system and their critical relevance for an adequate environmentalist strategy.

32. William M. Dugger, *Corporate Hegemony* (New York: Greenwood Press, 1989), shows the ways in which corporate servitude to the values of the bottom line, cost containment, rationalization, objectification,

hierarchy, and so forth, has been extended to all realms of society, from government to labor unions, families, even churches.

33. Seeing the commonalities with the present national and global situation, such analyses of earlier social collapses are increasingly frequent these days. One of the best, Jared Diamond, *Collapse: How Societies Choose to Fail or Succeed* (New York: Penguin Group, 2005), argues that it is invariably ecological folly that brings societies down, and that the "disastrous decisions" that seal their fate are a matter of class, for example, elite unconcern or conservatism, the emulation of elite values, excessive inequality, or desperate elite shortsightedness. Diamond is acutely aware of the role of class in the present situation in the United States as well: see his chap. 14 and pp. 519–520.

34. Again, on conservatism too, see Thorstein Veblen, *Theory of the Leisure Class*.

35. It should be clear that in the view presented here a *green capitalism* is not even remotely possible. A green *business*, as described in, for example, Paul Hawken, Amory Lovins, and L. Hunter Lovins, *Natural Capitalism: Creating the Next Industrial Revolution* (New York: Little, Brown and Co., 1999), may be essential for sustainability, but it cannot be so in the context of a capitalist system.

36. How central these matters will be for dealing with the global ecological crisis is at least appreciated by one world leader. Pope Francis's *Encyclical on Climate Change and Inequality* was his first major declaration after assuming office.

10 What Could Be Done? What Can Be Done?

1. The inevitable energy crisis of modern civilization has been carefully documented by the Post Carbon Institute and its fellows and associates (https://www.postcarbon.org/). See, for example, Richard Heinberg, *Afterburn: Society Beyond Fossil Fuels* (British Columbia, Canada: New Society Publishers, 2015).

2. Thomas Piketty and Emmanuel Saez, "How Progressive Is the United States Federal Tax System? A Historical and International Perspective," *Journal of Economic Literature* 21 no.1 (Winter 2007): 3–24.

3. These determinations depend on assumptions about tax "incidences," such as who ultimately pays sales and corporate profit taxes (are they paid by business owners, or by employees?). Joseph Pechman's groundbreaking study, *Tax Reform: The Rich and the Poor* (Washington, D.C.: Brookings Institution,1989)) found the tax system overall, excluding Social Security taxes, "moderately progressive or slightly regressive" in 1985. The Institute on Taxation and Economic Policy, https://itep.org/category/tax-analyses/ finds that in 2020 "the share of all taxes paid

by the richest 1 percent of Americans (24.3 percent) will be just a bit higher than the share of all income going to this group (20.9 percent). The share of all taxes paid by the poorest fifth of Americans (2 percent) will be just a bit lower than the share of all income going to this group (2.8 percent)." Thus, the current system overall is barely progressive.

4. Famously, the top marginal rate was 94 percent back in the war year 1944, and it was 77 percent even in 1964. Presently, the top marginal rate is 37 percent. See James Fallows, "When the Top United States Tax Rate was 70 Percent—or Higher," *The Atlantic*, January 25, 2019, https://www.theatlantic.com/notes/2019/01/tax-rates-davos/581257/.

5. The record federal budget deficit right now is proximately due to tax cuts, especially those of the Bush era and the recent Trump-GOP tax cuts, military spending on a continuous war-footing, and unfunded old-age and health care benefits. It should be noted that the budget deficit and federal debt at this particular point in time are most likely not a problem but instead part of a solution to the current economic stagnation and recession. The modern monetary theory school of economics is notable in this regard for making such an argument from a heterodox viewpoint. Stephanie Kelton, an economic advisor to Bernie Sanders during his presidential campaign, makes that argument forcefully in her book *The Deficit Myth: Modern Monetary Theory and the People's Economy* (New York: Hachette Book Group, 2020).

6. See "The Estate Tax: Myths and Realities," Center on Budget and Policy Priorities, February 2009, http://www.cbpp.org/files/estatetaxmyths.pdf.

7. Edward N. Wolff, *Top Heavy: The Increasing Inequality of Wealth in America and What Can Be Done About It* (New York: New Press, 2002), gives a comparative account on a half-dozen countries' taxes on wealth, inheritances, and estates.

8. The worker productivity improvement effect should be clear enough. The improvement in aggregate consumer demand should follow from the income redistribution from people with lower propensities to consume (business owners) to people with higher propensities to consume (low-wage workers).

9. Preferential affirmative action could be a component of a commitment to a broader policy of "reparations" to African and Native Americans. Considering the state of these groups, this would have a major impact on the American class system as a whole. See William Darity, *From Here to Equality: Reparations for Black Americans in the Twenty-First Century* (Chapel Hill, NC: University of North Carolina Press, 2020).

10. To reiterate what was said in earlier chapters on this, not only was the average unemployment rate lower, but the average annual growth rate of GDP and of labor productivity was higher, and the benefits of that

growth were more fairly distributed, than was true before or has been true since those decades.

11.   James Simon's $1.8 billion in 2017 was the record single year income at that time; see Lucinda Shen, "Here's How Much the Top Hedge-Fund Manager Made Last Year," *Fortune*, May 16, 2017 https://fortune.com/2017/05/16/hedge-fund-james-simons-renaissance-technologies/. Such outlandish individual incomes are not at all unusual for the new millennium. See Stephen Taub, "A bad year for humanity was a wonderful year for the hedge fund elite," *Institutional Investor*, February 22, 2021, https://www.institutionalinvestor.com/article/b1qmsgpxhz0lpt/The-20th-Annual-Rich-List-the-Definitive-Ranking-of-What-Hedge-Fund-Managers-Earned-in-2020. Obviously hedge fund managers are way beyond ordinary corporate CEOs, but see also S. Anderson, J. Cavanagh, C. Collins, S. Pizzigati, and M. Lapham, *Executive Excess 2008: How Average Taxpayers Subsidize Runaway Pay—15th Annual CEO Compensation Survey*, Institute for Policy Studies and United for a Fair Economy, 2008, respectively, <http://www.faireconomy.org/files/executive_excess_2008.pdf. The Dodd-Frank regulation post–Great Recession required reporting CEO pay for the largest companies; in 2017, "Six C.E.O. Pay Packages That Explain Soaring Executive Compensation," *New York Times*, May 25, 2018, https://www.nytimes.com/2018/05/25/business/top-ceo-pay-packages.html noted that of the six that "stood out," their CEO-to-median worker pay ratios ranged from 5000/1 to 64/1.

12.   The so-called "individual mandate" requires penalties for the uninsured who are ineligible for exemptions in some states; originally it applied in all states. Louise Norris, "Is There Still a Penalty for Being Uninsured in 2021?" Verywell Health, November 22, 2020, https://www.verywellhealth.com/obamacare-penalty-for-being-uninsured-4132434.

13.   "Except in the case of minimum-wage workers most employer costs associated with health insurance are passed along to workers in the form of lower money wages. Because workers place high value on the insurance benefits they receive, there is good reason to expect the additional cost of health benefits will be borne mainly by workers rather than employers." Gary Burtless, "Employment impacts of the Affordable Care Act," USC Brookings Schaeffer on Health Policy, March 20, 2015, https://www.brookings.edu/blog/usc-brookings-schaeffer-on-health-policy/2015/03/20/employment-impacts-of-the-affordable-care-act/.

14.   The idea of a universal basic income could perhaps be listed here as a "new thinking" policy or perhaps in the next section of "more

radical ideas." It has not been listed here either way, on two grounds: (1) many of the items listed here would, when taken altogether, constitute a universal basic income *in-kind*; (2) the idea of a UBI is itself a fundamental principle of the egalitarianism represented in this book, so that listing it as a distinct policy would seem to that extent redundant.

15. See Michael D. Yates, *Why Unions Matter* (New York: Monthly Review Press, 1998), 140–143.

16. The United States House of Representatives passed the Protecting the Right to Organize Act in 2019. That would go a long way toward these goals, including eliminating states' so-called "right to work" laws, which egregiously undercut unions' viability in unionized workplaces by giving nonmembers there the uninfringed right to free-ride on union benefits. See AFL-CIO, "Letter Supporting the PRO Act," January 30, 2020, https://aflcio.org/about/advocacy/legislative-alerts/letter-supporting-pro-act.

17. Kathleen Romig, "Social Security Lifts More Americans Above Poverty Than Any Other Program," Center on Budget and Policy Priorities, February 2020, https://www.cbpp.org/research/social-security/social-security-lifts-more-americans-above-poverty-than-any-other-program.

18. Employment Benefits Research Institute, "Retirement Trends in the United States over the Past Quarter Century," *Facts from EBRI*, June, 2007, http://www.ebri.org/pdf/publications/facts/0607fact.pdf.

19. See Michael Sherraden, "Asset-Building Policy and Programs for the Poor," in Thomas M. Shapiro and Edward N. Wolff, eds., *Assets for the Poor: The Benefits of Spreading Asset Ownership* (New York: Russell Sage, 2001). The essays in this volume are together an excellent study of the need for and possibilities of assets-based approaches to redistribution for the poor.

20. *Citizens United vs. Federal Election Commission*, 558 U.S. 310, January 21, 2010.

21. This book was drafted just after the attack/insurrection on the United States Congress of January, 6, 2021, which was blamed on a "big lie" initiated in and spread in mainstream and social media about President Trump's supposed "win" of the 2020 election. A retrenchment in both streams of the media is already underway, as several social media have now restricted Trump and several far-right organizations from access. Fox News, having been sued for libel, has pulled several right-wing commentators from primetime news slots. To leave the necessary corrections to the private entities concerned, however, would be a huge mistake.

22. See Robert W. McChesney and John Nichols, *The Death and Life of*

American Journalism: The Media Revolution that Will Begin the World Again (New York: Nation Books, 2010), one of a number of outstanding works on this subject by these two authors. Others are less sanguine about the prospects for progressive change in the media. See Chris Hedges, *Empire of Illusion: The End of Literacy and the Triumph of Spectacle* (New York: Nation Books, 2009).

23. See Douglas J. Amy, *PR Library: Readings in Proportional Representation* (Mount Holyoke College, Massachusetts, 2006), http://www.mtholyoke.edu/acad/polit/damy/prlib.htm for a very helpful collection of materials on this subject.

24. Thus, as explained earlier, if the system cannot on its own generate adequate unemployement, monetary authorities may be expected to do the job. See Robert Pollin, *Contours of Descent: United States Economic Fractures and the Landscape of Global Austerity* (London: Verso, 2005), for an account of recent macroeconomic history that highlights the class orientation of both monetary and fiscal policy.

25. Edwin Palmer, "Popularity of Socialism Spiking in United States, with 43 Percent Now Saying It Would Be Good for the Country," *Newsweek*, May 21, 2019, https://www.newsweek.com/socialism-america-gallup-poll-1431266.

26. The literature on socialism is as vast as that on capitalism. Here is a provocative selection: Albert Einstein, "Why Socialism?" *Monthly Review* 1 no. 1, (1949); George Bernard Shaw, *The Intelligent Woman's Guide to Socialism, Capitalism, Societism and Fascism* (New York: Penguin Books, 1995); John E. Roemer, *A Future for Socialism* (Cambridge, MA: Harvard University Press, 1994); David Schweickart, *After Capitalism* (Washington, DC: Rowman and Littlefield, 2002). See also Andrew Zimbalist, *Comparative Economic Systems: An Assessment of Knowledge, Theory and Method* (New York: Springer, 1983) for a fair treatment of the subject, rare among economics textbooks on the subject.

27. Vladimir I. Lenin, *What Is to Be Done?* (Moscow: International Publishers, 1987), which explicitly urged imitating the capitalist corporation.

28. It is practically a ritual obligation to consider "what was wrong with all of this," and why it "did not work." Readers can easily find plenty of weighty tomes on that story, many, especially in the United States, still utterly deluded with McCarthy-like anti-communist bias. In a word, it did "work," at least well enough to scare the daylights out of the United States, the most powerful contending nation at the time, for several decades in the mid-twentieth century. A balanced and sympathetic American scholar on the USSR was the late Stephen F. Cohen, for

example, his *Soviet Fates and Lost Alternatives: From Stalinism to the New Cold War* (New York: Columbia University Press, 2009). See also Andrew Zimbalist, *Comparative Economic Systems.*

29. David Schweickart, *After Capitalism*, 49.

30. Ibid., 51–58.

31. The "impossibility theorem" referred to is most importantly due to Ludwig von Mises (see his "Economic Calculation in the Socialist Commonwealth," https.//mises.org/library/economic-calculation-socialist-commonwealth), and Friedrich Hayek, "The Use of Knowledge in Society," *American Economic Review* 35 no. 4 (1945).

32. For another well-known and impressive example, think of any of the automobile companies, with their globalized supply chains. Clearly, the planning that usually takes place in the context of a capitalist market economy, or a market socialist economy like Schweickart's, is only partial in scope, and thus apparently less problematic. However, in both World Wars, central planning of national scope was successfully used in the United States. Critics of market socialism argue that, given the goals of socialism, democratic central planning is a necessary element of a socialist system. Thus, in a cogent and forceful argument, Harry Magdoff, "A Note on 'Market Socialism,'" *Monthly Review* 47:1 (May 1995) contends that, in a socialist economy national planning would be necessary, among other reasons, for properly allocating capital investment funds inter-regionally in light of uneven development. However, "there is no necessary contradiction between central planning and the use of the market for the distribution of consumer goods and . . . intermediate production goods. Nor does central planning necessarily exclude . . . cooperatives, communities, family farms, or private small firms" (16). An extended account of the principles involved is Harry Magdoff and Fred Magdoff, "Approaching Socialism," *Monthly Review* 57:3 (July 1, 2005), https://monthlyreview.org/2005/07/01/approaching-socialism/#fn7. A further critique of market socialism is Matthijs Krul, "On Communism and Markets: A Reply to Seth Ackerman," The Charnel House: From Bauhaus to Beinhaus, https://thecharnelhouse.org/2013/01/30/on-communism-and-markets-a-reply-to-seth-ackerman-by-matthijs-krul/. See also Leigh Phillips and Michal Rozworski, *The People's Republic of Walmart: How the World's Biggest Corporations are Laying the Foundation for Socialism* (London: Verso, 2019).

33. A couple of sources on workplace democracy include David Schweichart, *After Capitalism*; Branko Horvat, *The Political Economy of Socialism* (Armonk, NY: M. E. Sharpe, 1983); and Gregory Dow, *Governing the Firm: Workers' Control in Theory and Practice* (Cambridge: Cambridge University Press, 2003). An important source

on worker self-management, and popular inclusion generally, in the context of Venezuela's struggle for socialism is Michael Lebowitz, *The Socialist Alternative: Real Human Development* (New York: Monthly Review Press, 2010).

34. See Gregory Dow, *Governing the Firm*; Jon D. Wisman, *Worker Empowerment: The Struggle for Workplace Democracy* (New York: Bootstrap Press, 1991); Michael Lebowitz, *The Socialist Alternative*; John L. Cotton, David A. Vollrath, Kirk L. Frogatt, Mark L. Lengnick-Hall, and Kenneth R. Jennings, "Employee Participation: Diverse Forms and Different Outcomes," *Academy of Management Review* 13 no. 1 (January 1, 1988); and Chris Doucouliagos, "Worker Participation and Productivity in Labor-Managed and Participatory Capitalist Firms: A Meta-Analysis," *Industrial and Labor Relations Review* 49 no. 1, (October 1, 1995).

35. Only co-determination (in which worker, usually union, representatives sit on boards of directors) and worker participation programs (in the United States at least, these are unfortunately mostly management-initiated pacification strategies) have gained much state support in capitalist countries thus far. Note that such partial strategies are subject to strong criticism from those who, in the socialist "reform versus revolution" debate, incline to the latter approach toward capitalism. This very compelling criticism is based on the expectation that an overwhelming reaction to gradualist reform strategies from the capitalist sector tends to doom such strategies to failure over the long term.

36. Again, see Robert A. Dahl, *On Democracy*.

37. It might also be helpful to read Barbara Ehrenreich, *Nickel and Dimed: On (Not) Getting by in America* (New York: Holt Paperbacks, 2008); or for a different perspective, read Isabel Wilkerson, *Caste: The Origins of Our Discontents* (New York: Random House, 2020).

Index